NEARLY NORMAL

NEARLY NORMAL

Surviving the Wilderness,
My Family and Myself

CEA SUNRISE PERSON

HarperCollins*PublishersLtd*

Nearly Normal
Copyright © 2017 by Cea Sunrise Person.
All rights reserved.

Published by HarperCollins Publishers Ltd

First edition

HarperCollins books may be purchased for educational, business,
or sales promotional use through our Special Markets Department.

HarperCollins Publishers Ltd
2 Bloor Street East, 20th Floor
Toronto, Ontario, Canada
M4W 1A8

www.harpercollins.ca

Library and Archives Canada Cataloguing in Publication
information is available upon request.

ISBN 978-1-44344-905-2 (trade paperback)
ISBN 978-1-44344-904-5 (hardcover)

Printed and bound in the United States of America
LSC/C 9 8 7 6 5 4 3 2 1

*To my amazing family—Remy, Avery, Emerson and Ayla—
who make me feel as close to normal as I ever could.*

NEARLY NORMAL

Prologue

1973
Kootenay Plains, Alberta

When folks came to visit us at our first wilderness home in central Alberta, they were provided with little more direction than to turn right immediately after a particular "curve" sign on the David Thompson Highway. They would then drive down a dirt road for a short distance and park near a footbridge at the North Saskatchewan River, where they would load their belongings on their backs and begin the five-mile hike in to our camp.

Here the beauty of the stark, yellow poplar leaves against the snow-topped mountains and massive open sky looked almost too picturesque to be real. Treading a log bridge across the Siffleur River, they would notice the hoodoos jutting along the bank like jagged stone fingers. Smaller wildlife abounded along the trail—rabbits, chipmunks, porcupines, eagles, woodpeckers and grouse—and on a good day, a bear or moose might wander into view. Farther inland, the variety and number of trees thickened into forest, where the smell of the air changed to include pine and moss. The silence was punctuated only by twittering birds, rushing water and leaves crunching underfoot.

By the time visitors walked into our camp, they could well appreciate why Dick Person had chosen this particular part of the world to move his family to. And by the time they tasted a wild game meal cooked by my grandma Jeanne, succumbed to the soothing rhythm of Papa Dick's rambling teachings and sampled some of my family's home-grown against a background of Jimi Hendrix, they'd feel like they never wanted to leave.

Perhaps the counterculture dream would have remained intact for Fred if it weren't for my uncle Dane. Then again, considering our complicated family dynamics, maybe Dane was just the biggest festering wound among many smaller ones.

I don't remember Fred. When he came to stay with us, I was three years old. He was one of many summer visitors who came to our tipis during that year and the year before and the year after, eager to meet my grandfather and learn our off-the-grid ways. I say "my grandfather" because even though my mother and two aunts and Grandma Jeanne and I were there, it was always Papa Dick they flocked to. Some suggested he might have missed his calling, that he had the rare brand of charisma found in a cult leader and could have been more than a wilderness guide who extolled the virtues of wild game meat and shit pits and life in the bush in minus-fifty-degree weather in canvas tipis. But my grandfather had none of the zeal required to assemble a cult following. The only religion he preached was nonconformity.

This was Fred's fourth visit to our tipis. He'd been introduced to my family by David, an experienced bush guide and regular around our camp. Fred didn't think there was a person in the world who loved the outdoors as much as David did, until he met my grandfather. Here was a man whose beliefs left no room for other people's opinions, and though Fred sometimes found this hard to take, he also admired it. With my grandfather, he always knew just what to expect—or so he thought.

This time when Papa Dick greeted Fred, David, and Fred's brother at the footbridge to accompany them into our camp, they were met not with blissful silence but by the grinding noise of a chainsaw. "My son's building a cabin," my grandfather said by way of explanation. "Just came up from Ponoka—arrived here last month, and he's been going at it ever since."

Fred nodded but didn't comment. My grandmother had mentioned to him once that they had a son with mental issues, but the son's presence wasn't as surprising as the fact that Dick was allowing a cabin to be built at all, much less with a chainsaw. Fred knew my grandfather's views on such things. Papa Dick had chosen to live in a tipi because he believed the thin walls brought one into closer alignment with nature and also because the circular structure encouraged the flow of energy, while square buildings blocked it with their man-made angles and thick walls. And other than the old VW bus my grandfather occasionally drove into town for supplies and the car battery he used to power his tape deck, he didn't believe in technology. Batteries, electricity and gas-powered motors changed the molecular charge of the environment, he explained, which was why he himself had built the structure for three tipis and all of our family's furniture using nothing more than a handsaw, an axe and a hammer.

As if reading Fred's mind, Papa Dick glanced in the direction of the noise. "I don't like it either. But at least he's not building at the camp. I wouldn't allow it. He's up Siffleur Valley a bit." He paused, scratching his head through his wool cap, then dropped his voice slightly. "And he's, well . . . off his meds."

"Ah. An unexpected visit, then," Fred responded through a plume of frozen breath.

Everything Grandma Jeanne had told him was coming back to him now—the paranoid schizophrenia, the years at Ponoka Mental Hospital, and the final straw that had sent him there: Dane snatching me from my mother when I was a baby and locking me in the cellar with him.

"You could say that. And there's not much talking to him. In fact it's best to not try at all. Here's the thing . . ." Papa Dick met the men's eyes in turn. "Dane's got a bow and arrow, and he's a good shot." Then he stepped closer and pressed his rifle into Fred's hands. "Don't be afraid to use this. If you feel threatened, don't hesitate to shoot first."

Fred stared at him as a jumble of questions whirled in his head. But Papa Dick had already turned to lead the way back to camp, leaving Fred and his companions exchanging uneasy glances in the fading daylight.

After they arrived at our camp, the first order of the evening was to organize accommodations. Since the frozen ground of late fall made tenting a rather miserable option, Mom and I decamped to the cooking tipi so Fred and his companions could sleep in ours. At that point, Mom and I were still a couple months away from having a real wood stove, so in the meantime our tipi was outfitted with the Guzzler, which wasn't really a stove at all but a rusty barrel with a hole cut out of it. The stove smoked incessantly and lent little warmth.

After shivering in his sleeping bag all night, Fred would come over and help Mom set up breakfast. The cooking tipi wasn't much better, because to make room for the stove's chimney, the flaps needed to be left wide open, allowing into the tipi a steady cascade of snow.

"Kids. They don't feel the cold, do they?" Fred commented to Mom, watching as I ran outside coatless.

"Probably just used to it. It's pretty much all she's ever known."

Fred tried being friendly to me, but I wasn't having it. Most men who visited our camp ended up doing the screwing with Mom, which meant Mom paid more attention to them than me, and attention was already hard to come by. But I needn't have worried about Fred. The real threat to my security was Randall, who came by regularly attempting to woo Mom back into his bearskin bed. Randall was the chief of the Cree Indian tribe across the river, and he and Mom had been going hot and cold practically since we'd moved here. Once, at the sight of Randall's face and while Fred looked on, I threw myself into Mom's lap and screamed as if I were being mauled by a bear. Fred was twenty-two years old and hadn't paid much attention to kids before, but I made myself pretty hard to miss. While I cried, he held my Suzie Doll out to me and tried to coax me to play. I ignored him, but the next day when everyone gathered for supper in the cooking tipi, I let him sit next to me.

For Fred, mealtimes were the best and worst part of his visit. Best because Grandma Jeanne was a fantastic cook, and food was abundant that time of year, so there were caribou tacos, bear meat with dried wild morels, grouse in soy sauce butter and pancakes served with strawberry preserves and homemade yogourt. But mealtime was also when Dane came around. As Fred walked over to the cooking tipi, my uncle would announce his presence by swaggering around outside with his bow and arrow, taking sudden aim at nothing in particular while muttering under his breath. Inside, Dane would stand near the stove, fingering the hunting knife at his hip while yammering on about fellow patients at the mental hospital. "Stanley, you know, he just can't keep it in his pants. We'll be sitting around at supper, and he'll whip it out and go for it right there. Even during group he'll do it. One time he did it and smeared it all over the walls before the nurses could catch him." He'd cackle wildly, but nobody else even broke a smile.

At least when supper was over, Dane would scurry away again, leaving the women to cleanup duty. With no electricity or plumbing, there was much to be done—water heated on the stove to wash the dishes, food put back in coolers and up onto the tree platform to keep it safe from animals, and preparations started for the next morning's breakfast. Papa Dick would clean his rifles or sharpen his hunting knives or read a book, but Fred didn't mind helping out. He'd dry the dishes with Grandma Jeanne while I put them away, then he'd grind the wheat to make flour for the next morning's pancakes. Other than me, Fred wasn't quite sure what to make of the Person females. My aunt Jessie was slow because of her mentally challenged state, but at least she was helpful—unlike my aunt Jan, who seemed like a different person each time she showed up. So far Fred had met screaming-and-throwing Jan, despondent Jan and maniacally productive Jan. My mother was the highest functioning of all of them, and even she lacked common sense and seemed way out of her element as a parent. But there were plenty of positives too. One thing Fred noticed was that no one ever complained about the work to be done—especially Grandma Jeanne, who seemed to carry the burden of it. She'd pass a joint around to Fred and her daughters, and as they tackled chores, they'd talk about food foraging and the uses of various plants and animal parts.

Fred and his companions' main reason for visiting us this time was to fell a big game animal with Papa Dick. They weren't sport hunters, of course, as such an ignoramus would never be tolerated by my grandfather. Whatever they hunted would be used completely—meat, bones, organs and hide. Day after day, as the four of them made their way through waist-high snow and across deep crevices along the Ram Ridge, the constant buzzing of the chainsaw faded into the background. That noise, which annoyed and likely scared off animals, actually became a comfort to Fred, because he knew that as long as he could hear it, the hunters were not being hunted. Still, as Dane continued to show up at the tipi with his tales of screaming paranoiacs and compulsive masturbators each night, Fred grew more uncomfortable. He tried to be sociable with Dane, but my uncle just growled in Fred's face and laughed at him like he were some sort of bad joke that only Dane was in on.

One night, everyone was eating curried elk ribs when I happened to toddle across the fir-bough floor in front of my uncle. He kicked his foot out and punted me across the tipi. Instinctively, Fred moved to comfort me as I screamed indignantly from my landing place in the woodpile, but Mom and Grandma Jeanne got to me first.

"You asshole!" Mom screamed at her brother. "What the hell is wrong with you?"

Dane shrugged and went back to his dinner. "Not everyone can like kids."

The next morning, Fred packed up, along with his brother, and left us with a heavy heart. His utopian ideal had been shattered. What's more, he was going home empty-handed; no big game had materialized during his visit. But as he got into his bus and began the drive south back to Calgary, there was one thing he couldn't get out of his mind: me. He thought about an only child in a world of questionable adults that included a deranged and potentially lethal uncle. He remembered Dane kicking me into the woodpile. But he also thought about the family members who had rushed to my aid. I may have been grubby, poorly dressed and at the mercy of the elements, but I was also well-fed and seemingly happy. At least I was loved—that much he could see. It gave him some comfort, because he knew he would never return to our tipi camp again.

I looked up from my notebook. "So, that's it?" I asked him across the table, and he nodded.

I tucked my pen and notebook into my handbag, once more becoming aware of the sounds and movements around me: orders for skinny half-caf extra-hot lattes being placed, BMWs and Land Rovers cruising by the windows. I was still here—the Bean, West Vancouver, 2015. My past was safely tucked away, only to be brought out if and when I felt like examining it. I leaned across the table.

"Thank you, Fred. You've given me the first chapter of my new book. But more than that, you've given me your honesty."

"I'm just happy I could help," he replied. "I guess I sort of always wondered—seeing that little girl like that, you know?"

I nodded. Sitting across from Fred, his hair still long and clothes still bush-ready, I felt closer to the spirit of my passed-on family than I had since I'd written about them in my first book. Fred was one of the many folks who'd known us in the wilderness and re-entered my life since my memoir was released eighteen months before. Initially I'd dreaded their responses, worrying they'd find my portrayal of my family too unvarnished, lacking the idealism of their own experiences. The reality had been the opposite—beautiful, heartfelt emails thanking me for revealing the complex facets of the Persons.

"You heard about David, right?" Fred said, sipping his herbal tea. "He died a few years later. After he left your camp and went off to live in the bush with his family."

"Yes. Rescuing his pot plants from a storm, is that right? Drowned in a river." I shook my head. This story seemed to sum up my feelings about my family's lifestyle—how opposite their values were to my own.

"Uh-huh. Crazy story."

I gave a little laugh. "Yeah, crazy. Seems to be the theme of my life. I mean, I didn't even know Dane was in the Kootenay Plains until you told me just now. I wrote my entire first book having no idea of that. Just goes to show how the past can change, even when it's immortalized on paper."

"Yeah. Well, Dane was the worst of them, but your grandparents didn't have it easy with any of those kids. At least in the wilderness, they didn't have to worry about them fitting into society. I guess you couldn't blame Dick for wanting to be free of his children's problems."

Maybe, I thought, except that my grandfather was at least partly responsible for them. Along with eschewing government and societal expectations, he and my grandmother had also shunned boundaries, discipline and formal education. Instead of spending their teen years at school, all four of the kids had spent them at home doing drugs and having sex with various partners. How much of an effect their lifestyle had had on their varying illnesses—from mental challenge to schizophrenia to bipolar and depression—was uncertain, but the result had been four uneducated adults with few life skills. One of them, of course, was a young parent destined to repeat her parents' patterns— my mother.

"Oh, well," I said lightly. "It gave me a great story to tell, right?"

Fred didn't crack a smile, and I felt my own wilt and vanish on my face. I recalled a conversation I'd had several months ago with another woman who'd known me as a child. *It's a miracle you survived your family at all*, Adrienne said to me. A lot like what Fred was saying to me right now. But until recently, I'd spent my life downgrading my experiences, choosing to view them as the carefree whims of a freedom-loving family, even seeing my past as comical at times.

Now I understood that what happened in my childhood had been more than abnormal—it hadn't been right. My family's insistence on living without fear and rejecting nearly everything deemed acceptable by society had made me constantly question my intuition about what felt wrong. In truth I'd been in real danger on more occasions than I could count. And I had my published memoir to thank for this revelation. Since its release, I'd fielded questions from hundreds of readers alarmed by my family's lackadaisical treatment of young Cea. Had I not written my book, would I ever have learned to trust my own gauge for "normal"? I couldn't be sure, and by virtue of that, my readers had given me a gift that I could never repay. If *North of Normal* had been a test of how my disclosures would be received, my second book would in part say thank you to readers for embracing them. Because now, finally, I was ready to tell the rest of my story.

Fred leaned forward in his chair. "So, I'm curious. Where does your new book pick up?"

I propped my hands beneath my chin, thinking of myself nearly two decades earlier at the age of twenty-eight. For years I'd managed to hold it together—succeeded at a career, formed reasonably functional relationships and kept the veneer of my past and present smooth and shiny-looking for outsiders and close friends. But I'd always suspected that the repercussions of my childhood would one day be my downfall. What I had never imagined was how far and hard that fall would be, or that it would take me almost a decade to make it through my dark tunnel of reckoning.

Chapter 1

1998
Munich

Vielen dank! Auf Wiedersehen!"
I blew a cheery kiss to the photo crew and exited the studio, closing the door quickly behind me. Standing on the sidewalk for a moment, I let my chin drop and my shoulders slump. The act was over for another day. I'd done my job, smiled for the camera and the client, cracked self-deprecating jokes with the photographer, learned the other model's life story in a day. In a month or so, I'd be rebooked for another job with this client and repeat the whole process, with no one ever suspecting that in the weeks between, I'd been desperately looking for a way to unmake this perfect-looking life I'd created.

I walked in the direction of the U-Bahn station, wishing I felt the same sense of urgency to get home that I imagined the drivers of passing cars to have. *Home*—it was a word I pondered all too often these days. I wondered what it must be like to take it for granted, to not question its definition nor yearn for something so basic. I'd lived in Europe for nine years, and still it didn't feel remotely like what I imagined home should feel like. In theory my home was Canada, a place where I'd rarely known a fixed address and yet whose memory still lent me comfort. It was strange to think of my country and not

11

be able to picture an actual shelter to return to. Back in Calgary, Mom lived in a rundown apartment with a boyfriend whose dislike of me was about as strong as mine was for him. My vision of home was a place that didn't exist yet—a cottage-style house with a front porch, furnished with white sofas and painted wood tables. I'd been collecting items for it for years, slowly building up an inventory of dishes and wineglasses and linens like a child with a hope chest. Lately I'd taken to opening my boxes of treasures and gazing at them longingly, furnishing my house room by room in my mind as I tried to ignore the whisper at the back of my mind: *You know it's not going to happen. Move to Canada and your career is over. Now put your pathetic little dreams away and get back to reality.*

This was true enough—Canada's small-scale fashion industry made it nearly impossible to support yourself as a model, especially in the western provinces. And for as long as I could remember, my career had been the one thing in my life I didn't have to question. I'd wanted to be a model as a child, I'd become one at thirteen, and I was enjoying a successful career. I'd always figured that when I was done with it, I would pursue writing, though I'd done shamefully little to prepare for such a career switch—since high school, I hadn't written much more than postcards to friends and a few tortured poems. I had every reason to stay in Europe, but at twenty-eight years old, I felt as lost now as I'd once been in the forest as a child. My past still haunted me. I drank and partied to forget it. Six months of therapy had done little more than pull the scabs off my wounds. The bottom line was that I wanted out, and these days, my choices seemed to have little to do with logic and everything to do with emotion.

I entered the U-Bahn and took the train to my neighbourhood of Schwabing—young, hip and full of trendy shops and restaurants that no longer held my interest. I let myself in to my apartment and picked up the mail from the floor. At the top of the stack was an envelope with a Vancouver return address. I smiled as I tore it open and pulled out a letter and photograph. James had been introduced to me through the mail by our mutual friend Suzana, and I'd taken the lead several weeks earlier by sending him the first letter. I gazed at his photo. He was handsome, in a Robert Redford sort of way, though not the type—tall, stubble-cheeked, ever camera-ready with a dazzling smile—that I usually went for. None of those men had worked out so far, so maybe it was time for a change. He was a man of substance, Suzana had assured me, brilliantly intelligent and ready for the right woman to come into his life. And he lived in Canada.

A switch turned on in my head. It was easy, too easy—but why shouldn't it be? I'd struggled for as long as I could remember: to survive my family's lifestyle, escape their values, establish my career, and move beyond my failed first marriage. Maybe it was finally my time for something to come to me painlessly. I placed James's photo on my bedside table and got out my writing paper.

A few days after I received the letter from James, I was robbed on a train. Though it was not evident to me until later, all my life I'd seen signs when I was making a mistake. But no, I thought. Not this time.

For as long as I can remember, impatience has been my greatest curse and blessing. My mother's nickname for me was Now-Now Girl, because I wanted everything right that minute. Mom was the opposite. Slow and leisurely, she often slept until well past noon and rarely got around to making decisions at all, instead letting life blow her where it would. As a result, I felt powerless over everyday activities. When I was a child, I just wanted her to wake up and make me some breakfast, or look for my coat because we'd just moved again and I wanted to go outside. When I could manage it, I'd help myself—find an apple in her purse, or unpack our bags one by one to find what I needed, leaving our belongings strewn about our latest tipi or tent. But when I was at her mercy—to find a school for me, buy us some groceries or walk me to a friend's house—I would sit waiting, ready to go, while she rolled out of bed, bathed, ate breakfast, smoked a joint, got dressed. Two, three hours I would wait. Near the beginning, the first prickles of impatience would crawl up from my legs into my stomach. An hour later, I'd feel like jumping out of my skin. The energy that built inside me felt like poison, so I'd try to expel it by pacing, commenting, looking pointedly at the clock if we happened to have one. This went on for years, until I became completely self-sufficient in my teens—and each time it happened, I reached my boiling point faster.

"You're so *impatient*, Cea," Mom used to say to me all the time. I saw it differently, that I was probably just *medium* impatient, but her lagging made it worse. Whatever the cause, the wait for any kind of gratification came to feel like a toxin crawling beneath my skin. My cure became a forward rush, arms stroking and legs kicking as if they could propel me ever faster through time, into newness and away from whatever situation was ailing me. Only when I became an adult did I realize that at some point, I had begun to equate patience with lack of productivity. And this was sometimes dangerously incorrect.

Right from the beginning, James made an effort to be in my life. I'd been in plenty of long-distance relationships over the years, and often I found that *I* was the one visiting; *I* was the one calling and writing and sending the mixed tapes in the mail. That was my pattern, of course—to take all responsibility off others so I could feel worthy of being loved. Once, I had a flash of insight—that my ex-husband Kevin, the one person who had clearly loved me more than I had him, had also been the man I'd cheated on with practically any guy who looked my way. I'd felt suffocated by and squeamish about the level of closeness he wanted from me, so after we split up, the easy answer was to seek out men who didn't desire such intimacy—men who cared less for me than I did for them. But that moment of recognition was fleeting and unwelcome, because I didn't like to think of myself as the same person who'd married at twenty-two for little more than a sense of normalcy. I wanted to think of myself as tough and independent, as someone who didn't need a man in her life but would welcome one into it if he was special enough.

My correspondence with James continued through the mail for two months. "I've always wanted to change the world," James said to me not long after we finally met in person. "But now I can't imagine trying to change it without you."

Yes. To me, James was special enough. Right away I sensed a loyal commitment in him that I could imagine stretching years into the future. His introversion balanced my extroversion. He had a brilliant mind, with no shortage of passionate ideas. When I imagined telling him the truth about my past, it didn't terrify me. I hadn't yet told much to anyone, and the one time I had, it ended badly. But now, for the first time in my life, I felt ready for someone to truly know me. Not long after we met, James flew to Germany so we could spend a week together. We visited the local lakeshores, drank beer at Oktoberfest and spent three days strolling the streets of Prague.

"Look," he said one day, pointing through the window of a café to an elderly couple walking hand in hand. "That'll be us someday."

My cheeks warmed pleasantly. "You think so?"

"Are you kidding? I never imagined I'd meet someone like you. I feel like the luckiest man alive."

"I feel the same way," I replied, and it was true. I'd fallen in love with him in a ridiculously short amount of time. That was my standard MO, of course, but I conveniently tucked that knowledge away. I'd already decided that James would be my home, the arms that welcomed me back to Canada, and any further insight into that decision would only present an inconvenience.

James smiled and took my hand. "Listen. I know it hasn't been very long, and you've got your career to think about—"

"My career? Well, I'm kind of at a crossroads right now . . ."

"Right. So. Would you ever consider moving in with me? In Canada, I mean."

"Yes. I mean, of course!" My stomach fluttered happily. This *was* going to be easy!

Six months after James and I first exchanged letters, I packed up my life in Munich and put it on a plane to Vancouver. I'd never been more hopeful that I was doing the right thing, because deep down I understood that if I couldn't bury myself in James's world, I had no idea how I was going to face mine alone.

Settling back into life in Canada was like renewing a relationship with an old boyfriend: comfortable and a little thrilling, but also a reminder of all the reasons I'd left. For me, the reason that stood out the most was my family—especially Mom. To say that she and I had grown apart during my twelve years away from Canada was a convenient way to satisfy those who enquired, but the truth was much more complex.

I knew my mother and I had been close when I was young; I could remember how I felt when she was near me, that I wanted happiness for her even more than for myself. But when I tried to think back to when that might have been, I kept coming up against barriers. I'd think it was when I was ten, after we moved to Calgary, but then I'd remember that she was taking me out to parties every weekend and bringing home strange men—so it must have been before that. When I was eight, maybe, the time she and I hitchhiked from Vancouver to the Yukon and nearly met our end when some psycho picked us up, but that's when she was pretending not to know her boyfriend had molested me—so it must have been even before that. When I was six, squatting in the summer cottage in Celista? Yes. Back then, I accepted her completely, because I had little understanding that our life should be any different. She was my entire world, and I believed I was an important part of hers. It wasn't until I was in my teens that I became certain I wasn't.

During my time in Europe, I'd tried to come to terms with my conflicted feelings for my mother. "She will never be the parent you want her to be," my therapist there said to me. "That doesn't mean she can't add value to your life. Find the good in your relationship, and release your expectations."

She was right, I had to concede, and from across the planet, it had all sounded doable. But her boyfriend complicated matters greatly. He'd entered our lives when I was eleven, quickly sweeping her out of my world and into his world, despite the fact that he was a married father. As Sam's presence in our home grew, mine seemed to disappear. Though my mother spent much of her time crying and I spent much of mine trying to talk sense into her, the affair continued. It was clear that Sam resented my disapproval and refusal to accept their relationship, so I learned that my best strategy was to avoid him as much as possible by staying in my room. But this also meant avoiding Mom, because every minute he was in our house, she was stuck to his side, and when he wasn't, she was pining for him in a faraway place that had nothing to do with me.

Five years into their affair, Sam returned to his wife, but not long after that he and my mother reunited. She swiftly moved in with him, putting me in the uncomfortable position of being forced to see him whenever I wanted to visit her. To mitigate the situation I tried to get her to come to Europe, but year after year she refused, insisting that she was needed at home. I did my best to choose justification over anger. *It's a long way to come. She always says how much she loves me and misses me. She tells me how happy she is that she had me.* I wanted to believe that we were not completely broken.

Now living in the same country as my mother, I came face to face with the full force of the expectations my therapist had tried to erase. "Come and visit me," I said to Mom again and again from James's place in Vancouver. "It's only a one-hour flight. I'll pay for it."

"I just can't," she'd say softly, and her unspoken words revealed to me again and again who was winning in the ongoing contest for her attention that I always seemed to wage against her lovers.

And then, just a few months after I moved to Vancouver, Mom called to tell me she had breast cancer.

Our conversation was terse, an exchange of information with little emotion. But after we spoke, I put the phone down and cried hysterically. Was this really how it was going to be? That her doctor had reported her tumour to be slow-moving and likely survivable offered me little comfort. With sudden force, all the layers of our relationship, all the trials we'd been through together and all the love she'd ever shown me gathered inside me in a complex bundle of pain, guilt and longing for what could never be. I'd been holding on to a secret hope that we could one day regain the close relationship we'd had when I was a child, with only each other to rely on.

Pushing my pride aside, I went to the house she shared with *him*, and I was sitting on the sofa drinking tea with her when he came in the door. He smiled at me as if we were old friends; I gritted my teeth and let him hug me. Mom beamed at us.

"It was so good to see you two getting along so well," she said later, and it occurred to me that she'd said these very words to me just a few months before her old boyfriend Barry started molesting me. "You see? You just had to give him a chance."

I kept my mouth shut. Was it really that simple for her? Did she think that decades of damage could be undone with one awkward hug? My mother's eagerness to bury painful memories was as strong as my own need to remember and privately process them. But if there was one thing we had in common, it seemed to be our shared inability to learn from the past.

A month later, Mom went in for a mastectomy. I was sitting in the hallway outside the recovery room with Grandma Jeanne and Sam when an orderly wheeled her by on a stretcher, and all three of us reached our hands out toward her. She squeezed her mother's hand briefly and then gripped Sam's, missing mine completely.

When I left modelling behind in Europe, I had a good idea of what I wanted my next career to be. Hadn't my high school English teacher always told me I had a talent for creative writing? I would write novels along the lines of Anita Shreve's, I imagined, full of multi-layered characters and family dramas resulting in tragedy. I figured I'd give myself some time to adjust to my new life, take a creative writing course or two and then get started. But not long after Mom's surgery, I was flipping through *Jane* magazine in my doctor's office when I noticed a section called "It Happened to Me." I stopped, read, scrutinized. *Readers—tell us your crazy story!* the banner at the bottom of the page urged me, and I mentally snapped my fingers. People had been telling me for years that I should tell my life story—people who barely knew the iceberg's tip of it. It wasn't fiction I was meant to write; it was my memoir.

Excitedly I rushed home and down the stairs to the basement. James was sitting at his workbench tinkering with his new invention, a contraption whose purpose I didn't have much hope of understanding. But that was one of the things that had attracted me to him—he seemed to contain mysterious, exotic depths of knowledge.

"Check this out," I said, jabbing a finger at the article. "You know how I've had this, like, really crazy childhood, and how I also want to write? I know I haven't told you much about my past, but—well, we can talk about that later—the point is, that's what I'm meant to write about! And I can start right now, with this magazine!" I thrust it in front of his face, and he laughed.

"You're so dedicated to finding your calling—I love that about you," he said. "Whatever you decide to do, you're going to be amazing at it."

He went back to his project, but I didn't mind. James was like that—calm, focused on his ideas, encouraging me to come up with my own. My writing, I was certain, would make him proud.

Over the next couple of days, I banged out three hundred words about my childhood in the tipis and slipped the pages into a mailing envelope. It was a crazy story, even I could see that—how could they *not* publish it? And that would be just the beginning—some editor would come across it, beg me to turn out my memoir, and *voilà*, my new career would be born! I got into my car and drove to the post office, buzzing with anticipation.

Two blocks later, I pulled over to the side of the road with my pulse jumping. *What the hell is wrong with me? Open this can of worms and I can never hide again. Everyone will know my past, my secrets, my shame.*

I drove home and dropped the envelope into the recycle bin. And as I did, something inside me closed. I realized that not only had I not gotten around to telling James much about my past, but he also hadn't asked about it. Maybe, I thought, the only way I could be with a man was to create and embody the person that both of us needed me to be.

I stood at the Banana Republic cash register trying to ignore my mounting anxiety as each beep of the scanner rang up my purchases. Part of who I was was a consumer. Shopping had been my weakness since I'd earned my first dollar. In my modelling heyday, I'd easily spent a few thousand dollars a month on clothes and shoes and household items, and even though I could afford it, I did sometimes question my deep need to acquire. Was it rebellion against my family's non-consumerist values, a reaction to growing up feeling ugly in my thrift-store finds, or an attempt to fill a deep well of emptiness by stuffing replacement love/acceptance/belonging into shopping bags like some stuffed food into their mouths? Or perhaps it had something to do with my growing up thinking "making money" was the change you got back from the cashier after you bought something at the store.

In any case, my dwindling bank account didn't keep me from indulging more than I should have, especially when my life felt directionless. Since giving up on my writing idea, I'd had little success in finding my life's purpose, and after working steadily since the age of thirteen with a clear intention, such aimless floundering was excruciating. I craved productivity, busyness, a place to focus the energy and drive that had propelled me for so many years.

"Keep at it. You'll figure it out," James would say. He believed in me, I knew he did—just as I believed in him. Unlike me, who could barely come up with a single creative career idea, James was full of them. Venture concepts bounced like rubber balls as he excitedly cast them out to me over dinner. Though I understood little of what he was saying—science, technology and business plans were not my forte—his enthusiasm was infectious.

The Banana Republic cashier read out my total with a smile, and I handed over my debit card. At least James wasn't here to see how much money I'd spent; though he'd come shopping with me, he was nowhere to be found. I did a quick round of the store and then walked into the mall, annoyed by his disappearance. I was about to dial his number on my cell phone, when I spied him in a jewellery store across the way. I rushed over and stood beside him, hand on hip.

"Hey, I've been looking all over for you. What are you doing?"

"Buying you an engagement ring."

"What?" I pulled back in surprise. This was typical of James, to deliver startling news with little emotion or preamble. I was sometimes struck by our absolute opposite characters—I was always rambling on to friends at parties while he stayed quiet; self-deprecating where he was serious; uncertain of my convictions where he seemed unwavering in his; grounded where he was busy dreaming up life-changing ideas. But so far, it seemed to be working.

"Sure. We've talked about it, right?" James said, shrugging. "Do you like this one?" He held out a modest solitaire set in white gold.

"Well, sure, I mean . . . okay." My thoughts were spinning.

We *had* talked about it, of course, and generally things were on track. We'd just bought a house in deep suburbia, the only area we could afford in this overpriced market, and I was hoping our new space on neutral ground would finally give me the sense of *home* that had continued to elude me.

I gazed down at the ring in James's hand. At least I had him. At least I wasn't going through the motions of a pretend-happy life alone.

"It's very pretty," I said.

"All right." James smiled, slipping it onto my finger. "We'll have to get it fitted, of course, but here you go."

I sat beside James in my window seat, staring glumly out at the whiteness shrouding the plane. I knew I should have been happy— after all, I was on my way to the beautiful island of St. Lucia to get married—but my head felt dark and heavy. Just before we left, Mom had called to inform me that although her oncologist had recommended a round of radiation to kill any remaining cancer cells, she'd decided against it in favour of alternative medicine. As far as I could gather, this would consist of Chinese herbs, acupuncture treatments, and her go-to homeopathic cure of Rescue Remedy drops. There was no talking to her about it, and I knew with absolute certainly that she was going to die. More than sadness, I felt helplessness and anger at her absolute refusal to face reality. It seemed this was destined to be the dynamic of our relationship—her making bad choices, me trying to make her see reason, each of us frustrated with the other. Sometimes I wondered if she ever saw the poor choices I'd made over the years— certainly she didn't comment if she did. I put it down to her unfailing determination to live in the present and remain positive, but sometimes it infuriated me—weren't mothers supposed to offer their unsolicited opinions? I would happily have labelled it guidance.

I sighed and turned to look at James's profile. The man I was four days away from marrying was right here, a potential captive audience to my musings for the next three hours, and I couldn't say a word to him about what was going on in my head. Since early in our relationship, it had been clear to me that James regarded my mother as little more than an annoyance, so what I shared about her had petered out to almost nothing. It occurred to me that my ambiguity over revealing my past had resulted in my subconscious choice in a man—someone who really wasn't interested in hearing about it. But maybe this was for the best, I thought. Maybe my childhood and complex family relationships needed to stay where they were, buried beneath layers of love and resentment and joy and pain. I could never hope to explain them to the man beside me, or to anyone else for that matter.

I sighed and opened my book, trying to redirect my foul mood. My cheeks felt too warm. I stripped off my cardigan and then my T-shirt. Even wearing just a tank top, I felt my face breaking out in sweat. I turned to James and put my hand on his arm.

"Hey. Are you okay?" he asked in surprise.

"No," I managed to say as I unbuckled my seat belt. "Bathroom—" I tried to step over his legs, and that's when I blacked out, tumbling into the aisle headfirst like a rag doll.

When I regained consciousness, James, two flight attendants and a passenger were looming over me.

"What happened?" I asked.

"You fainted," a flight attendant replied.

"That's weird. I've never fainted in my life."

"How do you feel now?"

"Fine. I think." I was helped up, put back into my seat, buckled in. "Thank you," I said to no one in particular, embarrassed by all the faces now turned my way. "We're, uh . . . on our way to get married. Just nerves, I guess," I added with a weak laugh.

The lady in front of James turned to peer at me between the seats. "Well, let's hope this isn't a bad sign, then."

Of *course* it wasn't a bad sign. If St. Lucia was lovely, our Sandals resort was magical, immediately putting me under its spell of breezy palm trees, bottomless piña coladas, and sugar-sand beach. This was the sort of place women in childbirth or people on the verge of painful death might transport their minds to, and being there did well to erase the tumult of my anxious thoughts.

A couple of days before our wedding, James and I went scuba diving. He'd recently introduced me to the sport, and though I'd quickly come to love it, I had only a few dives under my belt. As we swam side by side, I watched a school of fish go by in a synchrony of flashing yellow and blue. James pointed to a dark shape, a massive manta ray cruising the ocean floor above trailing sea plants. I swam after a baby sea turtle. Lobsters' antennae waved in the current. A moray eel darted out of its den, startling me. I stopped beside the reef wall. We were at 110 feet, my deepest dive yet, and I knew that between the depth and my nerves, I was sucking air too fast. I checked my dive computer. I was down to 400 PSI, just enough to get me to the surface again.

I spun in a slow circle, looking for James. I could see a few divers from our boat in the distance, but not my fiancé. James was an exceptionally safe and conscientious diver, and I knew I had a tendency to swim off. If I couldn't see him, he had to be just behind me, hidden by the reef. I started back that way, but anxiety was making me breathe fast, which was exactly what I shouldn't do. *Stay calm*, I thought. *You need to stay calm.* Ascending alone was a bad idea, but I would have to make a decision soon.

Suddenly James was beside me, holding my dive computer and signalling for me to remove my regulator. Relief rushed through me. I took the regulator from my mouth, trying not to think that all there was between life and death was a single, accidental inhalation of water. James pushed his spare regulator into my mouth and slammed the purge button.

Are you okay? he signalled with his hand, and I signalled back that I was.

We bobbed in place for a minute, while my heart rate returned to normal. James pulled out his underwater slate and started writing, then held it up for me to see. *I love you. Will you marry me?* he'd scrawled in messy black letters.

I nodded, filled with relief. Though I hadn't wanted to make him feel bad about his original proposal, it hadn't exactly bowled me over. But I hadn't given him enough credit—he *did* get it.

I put my hand in his, and we stayed like that, two people connected to a single life source. The moment felt symbolic. As we floated face to face, it occurred to me that maybe I'd been looking at James the wrong way—that his power in helping me heal lay not in his ability to listen and empathize but in the similarities I recognized between him and my family. In James I saw the protection of my grandfather, the hard work ethic of my grandmother, the optimism of my mother and the intelligence of the father I still yearned to connect with. Perhaps this was my second chance to experience their best qualities without their selfishness and dysfunction. Maybe I could actually *have* the happy life I'd always pretended to. Because for as long as I could remember, I'd been smiling through my pain.

1974
Kootenay Plains

If the porcupine caught up to me, it would jump on me and jab me with its quills. I counted as I ran: *one, two, three, four* . . . If I made it to the fallen log up ahead by the time I got to ten, I decided, the porcupine would climb a tree and leave me alone. I made it to the log by the count of eight, then I stopped for a moment to catch my breath. Not for long, though, because if my grandparents got too far ahead of me, I'd never find them again, and I'd be lost in the forest just like Hansel and Gretel in my Big Blue Book.

"Grandma Jeanne, wait up!" I called.

My grandmother stopped and glanced back at me. "Keep going, Cea. Try to keep up with us, okay?" She started walking again.

"But how much farther? How long?" I asked for the hundredth time.

"Soon. We're almost at the river. You're doing great."

I scrambled after them. Papa Dick walked just ahead of my grandmother, the quietest on his feet even though he had the heaviest load on his back. There had been a wet spot on my bum for the past hour or so, and I knew what it was without looking. My pack was filled with chunks of the caribou Papa Dick had shot this morning, and some of it had come free of its wrapping and was dripping blood. But there was no time to fix it. Papa Dick had said we had to get back to our tipi camp before sundown, so that we could get the meat into coolers before it spoiled. That and so we wouldn't get lost.

I was four, a year older than I had been when a man named Fred came to visit our tipi camp. I wasn't born in the wilderness, but I may as well have been, because it was all I remembered. Mom told me that she'd carried me all the way from California to Canada in her womb, that I was born right at sunrise and that we all lived in a drafty old house in a town called Hills. She had one picture of me in that house. I was sitting in a chair with a tray around my belly, and there was flowery paper on the wall behind me. I liked that paper. When I asked Mom why we didn't stay there, she told me that the house had never really been part of Papa Dick's grand plan. He'd moved his family to Canada so we could be in the wilderness, and we'd only stayed at that crappy house because Mom had been so sad about my dad leaving her, she'd almost gone crazy like my uncle Dane. At that part of the story, I stopped asking Mom questions, because I didn't even know my dad, so he was boring to talk about.

But hunting trips weren't boring. We'd been away from our camp for four days, and I'd loved every minute of it, even though Grandma Jeanne kept saying how she couldn't wait to get back to take a bath in our river and eat some real food. We'd taken just a few supplies along, so we could fill our packs with the meat from Papa Dick's kill. We wore the same clothes each day, ate dried meat and bread for every meal and slept in forts that Papa Dick built from tree branches and twine. Going hunting with my grandparents was like being on a treasure hunt. Papa

Dick would point out clues like broken tree branches, piles of poop, tracks, and marks on tree trunks, and when we found a few of those things in a row, we'd all stop talking and walk as quietly as we could to look for the animal. Papa Dick had even let me bring my bow and arrow along to practise. The only thing that made it *not* perfect was that Mom didn't like to come. She would stay at camp, because, she said, someone needed to look after it—but this time I knew it was because she wanted to be with Randall, the Indian chief from across the river. I knew they were back together because they were doing the screwing again.

My tummy was grumbling. "I'm hungry," I said as we walked. "Can I have a snack?"

Without stopping, Papa Dick reached into his pocket and passed a leather pouch back to me. I opened it, already knowing that it held pemmican, my favourite. I ate the dried, powdered moose meat as fast as I could so I wouldn't have to slow down. At least the taste of the food distracted me from the pain in my feet.

I tucked the pouch away and tried to come up with my next game. I'd already done a bear and a cougar chasing me, and I was getting bored of pretending to be their next dinner. I watched the ground as I walked, trying not to step on rocks, because if I did, the earth would open up and swallow me whole. When I got tired of that, I just started chanting in my head to the beat of my footsteps. *One more step . . . almost there . . . one more step . . . almost there . . .* And finally, there it was, the best sight in the world—sun-dappled water sparkling through the trees.

"The river!" I shouted, darting toward it. Thirsty from the pemmican, I dropped down, stuck my whole face into the water and drank until I was full.

My grandparents filled and drank from their enamel cups, and when they were done, Grandma Jeanne knelt down beside me.

"Let's take a look at your feet. How are they doing?"

"Okay." I smiled gamely, glancing down at them. I knew my

grandparents were proud of me because I hadn't complained about my feet once. And anyway, they *were* in pretty good shape, seeing as I'd been walking barefoot for three hours. My soles were tough enough to protect me from most pokey things, but my toes were covered in scratches and thorn pricks, and there was a long cut on the inside of my foot from stepping on a sharp rock.

It was all my stupid moccasins' fault. Grandma Jeanne had already fixed them a few times, and yesterday they'd fallen right off my feet. "Talk about timing," she'd grumbled as she threaded sinew into her needle, but no amount of thread could put them together again. After that she'd tried strapping the leather pieces to my soles with twine, but they hadn't held on longer than a few minutes.

"It's okay, I can do it," I'd said to her bravely, and I had.

Looking down the riverbank now, I couldn't see our canoe, but that was probably just because Papa Dick had covered it with tree boughs before we left it. No one ever came down the river this far into the bush, but Papa Dick was extra careful about our canoe. "It's our primary source of transportation," I'd heard him say more than once, and whatever that meant, it sounded important.

Papa Dick took one more drink of water and pointed at the sky. "The light's fading. We have to keep moving."

"Where's the canoe?" I asked.

Instead of answering, he just pointed and started walking along the shore. I followed behind Grandma Jeanne. The rocks here were sharper than the twigs and fallen logs in the forest. *I won't say anything won't say anything won't say anything*, I repeated in my head. But time passed, and there was still no canoe in sight. My sore foot was hot and red now, and my grandparents were getting smaller and smaller as I fell behind.

Suddenly I'd had enough. I stopped and stood as solid as a tree. "*Ow!*" I yelled. "My feet hurt!"

"Not much longer, sweetie. Just around the next bend," Grandma Jeanne called back, turning and giving me a smile.

I rubbed my eyes and kept walking. But there was no canoe around that bend or the next one either. I was getting tired and hungry and mad, and the rocks were hurting with every step. I stopped again, but this time I dropped my bow and arrow and let my pack slide to the ground. Then I wiped my hand across my butt, looked at the blood and let out a howl.

My grandfather turned to me impatiently. He was so far ahead he had to shout for me to hear. "Cea! You know we don't have time for this!"

I howled harder. "I can't walk anymore! Carry me! *Carry meeee!*"

"We can't, Cea. You know that. Now come on, we're almost there. You're being such a big help—don't give up now."

I crossed my arms over my chest. "No! I don't want to be a big help. I want you to *carry me!*"

My grandparents looked at each other with squinty eyes, the way they always did when they weren't happy about something. But I didn't care. I was staying right there until someone picked me up.

Suddenly Papa Dick's gaze swung toward the trees above the riverbank. He was still, and then he shot his hand out to let Grandma Jeanne and me know to be quiet. The only reason would be for an animal, but we already had our caribou. My tears forgotten, I walked on tippytoes toward my grandfather.

"What is it?" I whispered.

"Shh . . ." He knelt down beside me. "Look."

I followed his pointing finger and saw a large brown rabbit with a twitchy nose. I slumped over, disappointed. Bunny rabbits were nothing to get excited about. Actually I sort of hated seeing them, because sometimes Papa Dick would kill one for dinner, and they were icky and tough. I was just about to say so, when a shot rang out beside me. The rabbit fell onto its side with a little bloody hole over its eye. Papa Dick threw his rifle over his shoulder and picked up the animal by its back legs.

"Is that for supper?" I asked with a scowl.

"No. This is your new shoes. Winter's on its way, and I bet your grandmother will be able to make some nice warm moccasins out of this fur."

"Wow. Really?" I reached out and touched the rabbit's fur, thinking how my feet would feel wrapped in that softness.

"Really," Grandma Jeanne said with a smile. "All you have to do is make it home, and you'll have some nice new shoes to look forward to."

Papa Dick nodded. "Now let's get going. We don't have time to fool around."

I did a little dance on the spot and started walking again. New rabbit moccasins, Mom waiting for me at home and caribou for dinner! I was pretty sure I was the happiest kid in the whole world.

Chapter 2

2003
Vancouver

When James and I got married, a baby was not in the plan. James already had a teenaged daughter from an early relationship, and though when I was little I'd dreamed of having a baby girl, that dream had faded completely in adulthood. It took time for me to realize that this change was likely the result of years of the mother–daughter role reversal I'd experienced with Mom, but my desire for a baby had not returned. But at the age of thirty-four, biology spoke to me in a voice louder than anything I'd ever experienced, drowning out logic and reason. Between one day and the next, the thought was there, as sudden and insistent as if a microchip had been inserted into my brain.

I want a baby, I thought as I swung my legs out of bed one morning.

What?

I gave it time. Refusing to let my usual impatience run the show, I convinced myself it must be a phase. Not that it mattered much—whatever the case, I was pretty certain I knew what James's answer would be. Not only did I know his feelings on the topic, but also in our five years together, I'd come to believe that his drive to find professional success came above all else.

Two months later, when the microchip was still giving off its signal approximately every three minutes of my waking life, I knew I needed to talk to someone about it. Since Mom was the only person in my life who'd known me when I was younger and wanted a baby, I decided on her. She and I didn't chat much, partly because my relationship with her always made me feel like a failure. I seemed to be the lowest rung on her ladder of priorities, like everything she was doing despite her vows of love to me—forgetting my birthday, only visiting me when it was convenient for her boyfriend (like when they were driving through town, for example), even trying to cure her spreading cancer with herbs—was an insult to me. And yet I didn't seem to possess enough courage or bitterness or principled conviction to cut her from my life. So instead we existed in a place of absolute inauthenticity, chatting every few months about this or that without sharing anything meaningful. Maybe one day, I thought, something would matter enough to bring us together again.

"A baby? Darling, that's wonderful! You'd be an amazing mother," she said, her voice airy with pot smoke when I delivered my eventless news. "And about time. I've been waiting for you to have one since you were a teenager."

I rolled my eyes in annoyance. "No, it's not wonderful. James will never agree to it. And it's not like . . ."

"What?"

"Well, it's not like we're doing really great or anything."

It was the first time I'd admitted this truth out loud. Our little house in suburbia had not cured my homesickness, nor had it done anything to further unite James and me. His company seemed to be taking off, which was positive, but it meant our dinner conversations now revolved mostly around how I was going to get *my* business off the ground. We both knew he was bound for huge success, but the same wasn't obvious of me. I knew his insistence on my prosperity should have motivated me—after all, he was older, wiser and more experienced in entrepreneurship than me, and there was nothing I craved more than his approval. And I recognized that no one in my life had ever had expectations of how I should behave or what I should achieve—certainly not my mother or other family members—so it stood to reason that I had much to learn from my husband. All the same, I found myself wishing for a more defined separation of career and marriage.

The saving grace was that at least I'd finally decided on my second career. Inspiration had struck one day when I was putting on a bikini to go to the pool. I had a collection of swimsuits from around the globe acquired during my modelling days, and it hit me just how ridiculously happy those two pieces of pretty fabric made me. What I'd seen in Vancouver stores had left me wanting, so I had signed up for a pattern-making course and started sewing samples on my home machine. My life had purpose now, though it often seemed I was feeling my way through a dark room full of obstacles; I had no idea how to start a business, especially one as complex as clothing design. More than that, I sometimes felt like I'd plucked my career from a tree of desperation just to prove to James that I was moving forward. Shortly after I made the decision to start that business, I'd fallen asleep at the wheel and totalled my car. I'd broken my hand and had to spend the next two months cutting, pinning, sewing and doing graphic design and computer tasks one-handed. But if I saw it as a sign of anything, it was that as with modelling, I'd have to work extra hard to attain my goal.

Over the phone, I could hear Mom clanging pots around, emptying the dishwasher.

"Really?" she said to me. "You're not happy?"

I sighed. "Just . . . we're very different. We seem to want different things."

"Most men do. I've never met one who wanted what I did."

I snorted, regretting the words I said even as they tumbled out. "Mom, you've never chosen a man in your life. You just let yourself get picked, no matter how incompatible you might be. Just look at who you're with right now."

"Cea—"

"What? This is a little different, okay?"

"Is it?" she asked with uncharacteristic sharpness. "Look at you. You could have any man in the world, and you're telling me you're unhappy. So why did you pick James?"

I didn't have an answer for her, at least not one that made sense to me, and that unsettled me more than anything. I finally hung up the phone, pissed off, because I still felt like my mother was to blame for many of my bad choices. How was I supposed to choose a suitable life partner after what she'd modelled to me as a child? My anger at her was always just below my calm surface, and I didn't *want* to feel like that anymore. I *wanted* to be healed of my past, to feel responsible for my own happiness, but I didn't. I'd read every self-help book on the market, gone through therapy twice, medicated for years with antidepressants. It wasn't that I felt like a victim; it was just that I was so tired of being a survivor.

Each day, my microchip beeped a little louder. As I went about my work, I imagined a baby playing at my feet, eating in a high chair, reaching tiny arms up to be held. Suddenly it seemed like every other woman I saw was pregnant. Finally I could take it no more. This was not a phase; four months had passed since the morning I'd woken up with a baby on my brain. I'd already tried the obvious with James— casually bringing up baby tidbits, pointing out cute pictures—but he wasn't biting. So I would talk to him. He was my husband, after all— surely I could share such a natural female urge with him.

"So it looks like more and more of my friends are hopping on the baby train," I said to him one night at dinner, trying to look casual as I twirled spaghetti around my fork. "Even some of my modelling friends now. I heard from Heather this morning."

"Mm."

I worded the request in my head and plowed on. "Yeah. And, I mean, I never thought I'd say this, but I guess . . . well . . . I kind of feel like maybe I want one too. I mean, not kind of, but actually kind of a lot. Want a baby a lot, I mean." I cringed. It had come out all wrong—inarticulate, messy, a little desperate.

James shrugged. "Nicole just had a baby," he said, referring to one of my close friends. "And you've never really been around one before, right? It's probably just got your hormones going a bit."

I nodded. "That would make sense, except it's been a few months now, and the feeling's not going away. In fact it's getting worse." I brought my fingers to my temples and continued before he could respond. "Listen, I don't like this either, you know? I feel a little betrayed by own body. It's like my head would happily say no, but my body won't let me. Like it's taken my brain prisoner or something."

He grinned then took a long drink from his water glass and set it down. "I think we need to keep our long-term goals in mind."

"We will! This doesn't change our career plans."

"I think you can say that, but you don't really understand what the reality will be. Babies are a ton of work."

My shoulders slumped. It was a point I couldn't argue—after all, he'd already had one.

My urge to reproduce turned me into a woman I barely recognized—weepy, rash, willing to bargain anything to get what I wanted. I returned to my swimsuits with new determination, thinking that my business would eventually either replace my desperate need or become successful enough that James would have to give me what I wanted. My will to succeed became relentless, often driving me to sit at my sewing machine or computer through the night. Sometimes in the middle of a task, I'd start crying uncontrollably. I didn't doubt that my microchip was the cause of it, but I also felt besieged by an acute loneliness, because I knew I couldn't talk to my husband about the most pressing matter in my life.

That I finally got my way nearly a year later is a testament to the power of biology, persistence and James's willingness to try to make me happy. When he relented I threw my arms around him, filled with a love I hadn't felt for him since our earliest days. But strangely, this did not give me renewed hope for our marriage. Rather I questioned, if only briefly, the ethics of bringing a child into the world with him when I knew that our relationship was most likely doomed to slide downhill from this moment on. But my ethics were no contest for my hormones.

Should a baby actually materialize, the work of caring for it would be mostly on me, James warned me fairly, and I happily agreed. I'd heard countless times that raising a child was the hardest job in the world, but I didn't believe it. I'd survived a childhood in the wilderness, my mother's version of parenting, her crazy and lecherous boyfriends, the fashion industry, a failed marriage and my own start-up company. I would be a protective and attentive mother, nothing like my own had been, and it would be easy compared to everything I'd already been through.

"Halifax?" I repeated incredulously, bouncing Avery on my hip. He rubbed at his eyes and started to whimper. He was over a year old and as fussy as the day was long. He was also still up several times each night, so between my work, caring for Avery, and my exhaustion, time passed in a foggy blur. Not that I cared much, because at least I *had* him. My son had filled my heart, and I could see that he'd filled James's too. "Why there, of all places?"

James shrugged and sank farther into the couch. "I don't know. Why *not*? We need a new beginning."

My tummy fluttered anxiously. Though the idea of moving across the country to a city I'd never been to was daunting, it was also tempting. In this situation, I saw an uncomfortable truth about myself. I tended to take extreme measures to solve problems, action that was often disconnected from the problem itself. During a childhood marked by frequent moves and instability, I'd been taught to drop everything and run when things became too difficult. I'd done this often as an adult, and though it hadn't always worked, at least it had made me feel like I was doing something. At least I hadn't accepted stagnation or let failure sweep me into an open pit of depression—and right now, my life was definitely failing.

I placed Avery on the floor amid a scatter of toys, and he immediately started to howl. James flinched. I picked up our son again and started bouncing him on my other hip. The look on my husband's face scared me. Things weren't going as planned at his company. CeaSwim was taking too long to get off the ground and costing us way too much money; after struggling through yet another batch of failed samples from a Canadian manufacturer, I'd had to take my business to China. And as it turned out, being a mother *was* the hardest thing I'd ever done. I would support my husband—of course I would—just as he had supported me in my need to have Avery. And really, what was the difference between living here or somewhere else? Because as much as I hated to admit it, even after seven years, Vancouver still didn't feel like home.

I sat down beside James and nursed Avery. James put his hand on my leg.

"We'll get through this," he said. "I need you with me, I really do."

I put my hand on top of his. Being needed wasn't the same as having my own needs met, but maybe that could change. And really, if I put my own needs first, how was I any different from my mother?

"Okay," I said quietly. "Let's do it."

A month after we decided to move, I boarded an overnight flight to Halifax on a singular mission: to find us a house there in twenty-four hours. On the plane, I kept my mind occupied with celebrity gossip magazines, because the moment I thought about what I was doing, the insanity of it all began to ping around in my head. Moving across the entire country. A place neither my husband nor I had ever been to. A city that contained not a single friend or acquaintance or even business contact—besides Eileen the Realtor, of course, who had promised to meet me at the airport.

Eileen turned out to be a delight, and she seemed to know better than to ask direct questions. She bought me breakfast, took me on a tour of the city and shared her deep connection to the place where she was born and raised. She assured me that my family would love it here too. After showing me five houses that didn't work for one reason or another, she took me through a cute 1920s heritage place with three upstairs bedrooms. It was cottage-like, reminiscent of a home I'd once squatted in for several months with my mother and her boyfriend. I emailed James some photos and then went to find Eileen in the kitchen. She was standing at the sink, turning the tap on and off.

"Water pressure's not great." She glanced up at me. "Might want to get a plumber in to check—"

"Do you have the paperwork?" I asked.

She looked surprised. "Well . . . yes. You're sure about this? I mean . . . James wouldn't want to see the house first?"

I shook my head. "That's not really an option. Anyway, this is just to get the ball rolling, right? Nothing will be final until he signs too. And the offer has to be accepted, of course." I smiled extra hard, realizing how rash I must look to this woman. But what I couldn't explain to Eileen, who'd never left the security of her hometown, was that this was all-too-familiar ground to me. At thirty-six years old, I had moved more than sixty times in my life. Of course, many of those moves had involved little more commitment than relocating camp when I was a child or unpacking my suitcase at another modelling apartment in my teens, but I'd also known the pressure of signing rental leases and, on three occasions, taking on a mortgage. I was making a decision the only way I knew how: by trying something out to see if it worked.

Many would have called my process reckless, but if there was another way to go about finding answers, I didn't know what it was. Weighing consequences for my actions had never been one of my strong points. I'd married two husbands with doubt in my heart, left a successful career behind in Europe on little more than a whim and had a baby knowing I'd need to simultaneously raise him and run my business from home. The Persons were famously bad at planning for the future—and was it any wonder? *Live in the present. The past and future don't exist*, Papa Dick used to preach when I was a child, and it seemed that his words had had their desired effect on me.

1975
Kootenay Plains

Apache's tongue was as big as my face and as wet as a dishrag. I always let him lick my hand before I climbed way up on his giant back for a ride. Randall would lace his hands together to give my foot a boost, and then I would be on top of the world. There were six horses at the Indian camp, but Apache was everyone's favourite, because he was the biggest and gentlest. His hide was black and white, kind of like a cow's. I'd never seen a cow in real life before, but I'd seen a picture of one in a book.

Randall led Apache by the reins with one hand, his other arm around Mom's waist. I could see Mom smile when she turned toward him. Apache rocked underneath me and shook his mane in the summer breeze. I was Cea Person, I was four years old, and I could ride a horse all by myself without a saddle. There was nothing in the world I loved more than horses, except maybe Suzie Doll and my family. Across the river at my tipi camp, I had my very own corral of stick horses. I rode them and played with them and made them pretty reins out of leather and feathers, and I'd even named one of them Apache. But he wasn't as good as the real thing.

Randall stopped and looked at me. "Do you want to hold the reins?"

I nodded happily. He handed me the reins, and Apache put his head down to nip at the grass. Mom and Randall walked ahead a bit. Randall's hair was even longer than Mom's, hanging down his back in two black braids. Mom said he only let it out when he was being a medicine man, and I knew that was true, because he'd been a medicine man for me once when I couldn't stop coughing. Randall had told me it was called whooping cough, and he'd made it go away by burning sweetgrass and telling the evil spirits to scat.

Snowy mountains surrounded our meadow. Birds tweeted and called. The river rushed in the distance. Indian paintbrush and tiger lilies bloomed bright orange. I lay forward across Apache's back, breathing in his straw-like smell. The sun shining down on my head made me feel sleepy.

And then I was falling. Slipping to one side, and—*wham*! Flat on my back. My head hit the ground hard. I tried to yell, but my lungs were stuck. I stared up the sky and waved my arms and legs back and forth like a flipped-over beetle.

Mom! I called in my mind, but nothing came out. I turned my head to look for her, but she was nowhere. Apache's huge black nostrils swung above me. He lowered his head and touched my shoulder, then he blew on my face and whinnied. Suddenly Mom and Randall were charging out of the trees toward me. My lungs unstuck, and I heaved a giant breath.

"Cea!" Mom looked scared as she knelt beside me. "Are you all right?"

"Yeah," I said. I stood up, and Apache pushed his head into my belly.

"You see? You're fine. Apache wouldn't let anything happen to you."

"I know." I brushed off the seat of my pants. "Can I get on again?" I asked Randall.

"Sure thing. But you better stay awake this time," he said, and we all laughed.

When the first scream came, everyone in our camp turned toward it—me, Mom, Papa Dick, Grandma Jeanne and a few summer visitors. A second later, Papa Dick grabbed his rifle and ran in the direction of the log bridge that connected our camp with the Indians'. There was another scream. One of the guy visitors took off after Papa Dick, and before anyone could stop me, I ran after him too. My moccasins gripped the log bridge as I raced over it. Ahead of me, I could see my grandfather disappearing into the trees, and I ran even faster so I wouldn't lose sight of him. Branches grabbed at me, but I didn't even feel them scrape my skin.

The screams had turned into crying. Two of the Indian women were kneeling on the ground and rocking back and forth. I could hear voices—Papa Dick, the summer visitor, Randall, and someone I didn't know. I ducked behind a tree to hide and peeked out.

The first thing I saw was three strangers with green-and-brown hats. They all had rifles slung over their shoulders, and one of them was waving his hands in the air while he talked. "Wandering in the trees . . . fired a shot . . . Who would expect a horse around here . . . ?"

Papa Dick stepped forward. He was shorter than the man he was talking to, but that didn't stop him from jabbing a finger into the man's orange vest. "A *deer*? You thought he was a *deer*? Are you fucking *blind*?" Papa Dick was yelling really loud.

Randall stood quietly behind him with his arms crossed.

My grandfather waved a hand at the people who were crying. "Do you even realize the grief you've brought upon these good people? You should be disgusted with yourselves and your sick city ways." He swung his arm out and pointed through the trees. "Now, I suggest you get your goddamn asses out of here. *Now!*"

The men looked at each other and then hurried off in the direction Papa Dick was pointing. My grandfather dropped his rifle and sat down against a tree trunk. I looked around for the deer they'd been talking about, but I couldn't see anything except trees and Indians hugging each other, almost the whole camp by now. Papa Dick put his head in his hands, and I realized he was crying.

I didn't care about hiding anymore. I came out from behind my tree and ran toward him. "Papa Dick! Papa Dick!"

He looked up at me, and his face wasn't mad or even surprised; it was just sad. I slammed into his arms, and that's when I saw it over his shoulder.

Surrounded by crying Indians, an animal lay on its side. A really big animal, black and white . . .

"*Noooo!*" I screamed, struggling to escape Papa Dick's arms. "*No no noooo!*"

He let me go. I ran to Apache's body. Blood was leaking from a hole in his head and making a sticky red pool in the dirt. I threw my arms around him. He was still warm.

"Will he ever come back again? Will he? *Will he?*" I cried.

No one answered me, but I felt a hand on my shoulder. I looked up and saw Randall. His long braids were swinging, because he was shaking his head. There were tears on his cheeks.

"It's only his body," Randall said to me. "His spirit will never die. It's only his body."

It seemed like I stayed there for hours, but finally Mom pulled me off Apache and curled me into a ball in her arms. I buried my face in her neck, thinking there could never, ever again be anything as sad as the day Apache died.

"Mommy. When will Apache come back?" I asked for the twentieth time. If I'd once understood that Apache wasn't coming back, all I felt now was confusion. Where had he gone, and how could he really never be coming back?

"Never, darling. I'm sorry." Mom was lying across our bed, smoking a joint and looking at her astrology calendar. Since Papa Dick thought anything that told time was for folks living in fear, she always kept it hidden under our bed. "Here," she said, tearing out a page from the front of her calendar. "Why don't you draw a picture of him?"

I took the page from her and stared at it. It was covered in squares, numbers and a weird wavy symbol. "But there's no space."

"Sure there is. Just use the margins."

The margins were barely big enough for me to draw a heart or flower. I thought about going over to my grandparents' tipi to ask for some paper, but I wasn't sure they'd have any either. It had been a few months since Papa Dick made a trip to town for supplies.

I got out the cutting board that I used as a lap table, then I dug around in my backpack for my crayons. All the prettiest colours like pink and purple and orange were worn down to papery stubs. I pulled out black, which was still so new its tip was sharp. Pressing hard, I turned the two wavy lines on the paper into Apache's flowing mane. Then, drawing right over the numbers, I traced out his body. Still using my black crayon, I circled dark patches on his body and coloured them in. Then I gave him a big red smile.

"Mommy, look," I said, holding my drawing up.

"Oh, honey, it's beautiful!"

For the next couple of weeks, I did almost nothing but make drawings of Apache. Some were just of his foot or his ear or his tail. Others were filled in blue or purple with huge yellow suns above him and green grass under his feet. I drew on book pages, shopping lists, my grandfather's rifle manual, and an old *Rolling Stone* magazine. I gave my pictures away to Mom and Randall and the Indians and the summer visitors and my grandparents.

Papa Dick smiled and ruffled my hair when I gave him his. "Remember, Peanut, Apache was wonderful, but he's gone. Don't waste your beautiful energy on living in the past."

I nodded, even though I wasn't exactly sure what he meant. But I did notice that he didn't tape the picture of Apache to his bookshelf the way he did some of my others—the ones of bears and flowers and tipis, and him and Grandma Jeanne with huge smiles and legs that ran all the way up to their necks.

A couple of days later, instead of reaching for my crayons when I woke up, I went outside and rode my stick horses. "Apache, Apache, Apache," I sang softly as I galloped around the meadow. The words matched the rhythm of my feet. "Apache's gone, Apache's gone . . ."

A little while later, Mom found me crying beside a log. She dropped down beside me and took me in her arms. "Shh . . . it's going to be okay," she whispered.

And, of course, it was.

Chapter 3

April 2014
Vancouver

*T*oday *I'm a published author,* I thought when I woke up. I reached for the iPad on my bedside table and typed *North of Normal* into the Amazon search engine. There it was, number one-million-something in the sales ranking. I smiled as my belly pinged nervously. I'd been counting down to this day for a year and a half, ever since my book was bought by HarperCollins.

I rolled toward Remy and kissed his shoulder, woke the kids, showered, and wound my way through the forest of stacked boxes into the kitchen. A drizzly rain mixed with fog pressed against the windows as my family gathered around the island for breakfast. I poured cereal into plastic bowls, packed lunches, refereed chaos at the door as we searched for misplaced coats and socks and shoes. We were moving in two days, and as usual I'd been overly efficient in my packing, as if getting everything in boxes would make the big day come that much sooner.

"Do you want me to drive them?" Remy asked as I herded the boys out the door, Ayla in my arms.

"No, just keep Ayla," I said, passing our youngest over. "I'll be right back."

I drove the mile to school, parked and got out, tossed Avery his backpack as he burst out of the minivan. Then I grabbed Emerson's hand and pulled him toward his preschool classroom. I'd run out of the house without my raincoat, and a fine mist settled on my hair and clothes. I felt weirdly jumpy. I'd dreamed of this day ever since I started writing my memoir seven years earlier, and many times, as I faced rejection from publishers or agents, I'd wondered if it would ever come. Now that it was here, all I could think of was the question I'd been asked countless times since my book was bought: *Won't it feel weird for the whole world to know about your life?*

Yes. It would. I knew how most people likely saw me now: stay-at-home mom, upper middle-class, happily married, friendly to everyone, easy-going. Normal, maybe even a little boring. As familiar parents waved and smiled, I couldn't help thinking how their opinion of me might change if any of them read my story.

"Nice weather, huh?"

I snapped my head up. As if reading my mind, there was Christina, the mother of one of Avery's schoolmates. She smiled at me, and I laughed lightly and kept moving. Our friendship circles overlapped, and I'd seen her occasionally at parties, but we'd never really talked. I was certain she would be horrified by my unsavoury past. The thought of the expression on her face as she read about the shit pit and Mom's habit of giving blowjobs in moving cars almost made me giggle.

Mom. As I dodged a flying tetherball on the way back to my car, I thought about what this day would have meant to her. I knew she would have celebrated it with me, though I also knew that my book, in all its honesty, would have been difficult for her to read. I hoped that my portrayal of her would convey the complexities of our relationship—how despite having sometimes disregarded my best interests, she had always loved me.

A memory had been circling in my head for several weeks. It was a day I'd spent with Mom well over a decade ago, shortly after she received her cancer diagnosis. I'd been visiting her in Calgary, and on our last afternoon together, we'd gone for a hike. "I brought something with me," she said when we stopped to rest, and she drew an old spiral notebook from her backpack. As I looked at the cover, a flood of memories washed over me. *Shretson and the Great Castle:* a thirty-page story complete with illustrations that I'd written during the year I'd lived in the Yukon with my grandparents. I would have been eight, I realized, the age that had held more shadows for me than any other. Sitting beside a glittering waterfall on that summer afternoon, Mom and I had spent an hour reading, laughing and reminiscing, and then she'd turned to me. "You always wanted to be a writer, even when you were little. Don't give up on your dream, okay?" It was the best day I could remember having with her.

Among other stories, this was one I wished I'd included in *North of Normal.* I wished I'd written about how the escape of reading had saved me over the years—how I'd read my only childhood book a hundred times, how I'd cried my eyes out over *Call of the Wild,* how I'd begged Mom to buy me used books at the thrift store for a quarter each, how I'd started riding the bus on my own to the library just weeks after I moved to the city for the first time, how I'd discovered Judy Blume books at a friend's house when I was nine and borrowed every single one, how I'd read *Fear of Flying* at age ten after finding it at Mom's bedside, and how I'd weighted my suitcase with English books when I was living in Europe and traded everything from Wayne Dyer to Danielle Steel with my modelling friends.

Unexpectedly, tears sprang to my eyes as I buckled my seat belt. I was incredibly lucky—a publisher had deemed my story interesting enough to release to the world. But had I blown my one chance to say everything I needed to, everything that was in my heart? The book I'd crafted for my readers was the most honest account I could muster during the time I wrote it, but I had not included everything that mattered to me. I knew very well that a permanent recording of a life story on paper would always leave room for shifting remorses, opinions and conclusions, but I couldn't help wishing for a perfection that could never be. It hadn't occurred to me while I was writing my memoir that as much as I might worry about what I'd included, I would also regret what I'd left out.

"So, how does it feel?" Remy asked when I got home.

"I'm not sure yet," I responded honestly.

Remy was the only person in the world who knew my entire story before I put it into a book. I'd told him about it when we were dating and given him an early draft to read, and his wholehearted acceptance had encouraged me to continue writing it over the next five years.

"Bring on the Twitter haters," I said with an uneasy laugh. "Assuming a few people even read it."

Remy wound his arms around my waist. "Lots of people will read it. It's a wonderful book. And no one is going to hate you."

"Except for anyone who knew my family, maybe. It's not exactly a love letter to them."

"It's the truth—the truth well told." He kissed the top of my head and glanced at his watch. "Now let's get over to the Realtor's office. We've got a house to buy."

I smiled at him. It seemed fitting that on the same day the story of my life growing up in tipis, tents, empty summer cottages and unfinished houses was released, I should be signing papers to take possession of my dream house. In three days, I was due to fly to Toronto to begin publicity for my book. I was living my dream, through and through, and I was happier than I'd ever been.

So why did some memories still refuse to release their grip on me?

1975
Central Alberta

When Papa Dick found the lady on the mountain, she was in pretty bad shape. She'd been living on her own in a big canvas tent for a few months, he told me and Mom and Grandma Jeanne when he got back to our tipi camp, and it hadn't been going well. The lady had gotten really sick from eating meat that went bad, and then she'd run out of firewood and had to burn the bed she'd built. After that, she'd fallen out of a tree when she was climbing it to store her food and broken her leg in two places. One of the breaks made the bone poke through her skin, and she'd bled a whole lot. So it was a stroke of crazy luck that my grandfather came across her while teaching one of his courses.

Papa Dick loved teaching his Wild and Woolly Wilderness Thrival courses, because he said the more people who learned how to hunt and climb and canoe and build shelters out of branches and twine, the more people could live just like we did—which he thought should be just about everyone in the whole world. This time he'd been taking a student up a mountain for an overnight trip when they'd walked right past the lady's tent. Papa Dick thought he'd just stop in to say hi— after all, it wasn't every day he came across a bush camp—but he found her lying there on the ground, and she asked him for some water. He wrapped his wool shirt around her leg along with a splint of wood, and then he and the student brought her home to our camp. Along the way she told them all about her problems, but Papa Dick said we couldn't believe her for sure because she was probably delirious. Mom explained that meant that a lot of stuff she said didn't make sense, kind of like my uncle Dane but not that bad.

When Grandma Jeanne saw Papa Dick carrying the lady, she rushed over to make a bed for her. I peered through the door flap as my grandmother cleaned the lady's leg, wrapped a big bandage around it and made her swallow some herbs. Mom sat beside her, dabbing the lady's forehead with a washcloth and looking worried.

"How is she?" Papa Dick asked when he came to check on her, but Grandma Jeanne shook her head.

"Not so hot."

Papa Dick nodded. "Best get her to town quick."

"What happens if we don't?" I had to ask.

"She might die."

"Wow. Really?"

As soon as Papa Dick announced a trip to town, our camp began buzzing. It was a good hour's walk through the forest and then a two-hour drive to the nearest hospital, so plans had to be made. It was decided that Papa Dick and the student would carry the lady through the woods to our VW bus, and that Grandma Jeanne would go along to help her not die during the ride to town.

Papa Dick said they would need a better way to carry the lady. I watched as my grandmother, using her treadle sewing machine, quickly sewed a large piece of canvas into a tube. Then Papa Dick stripped two thick tree branches with his axe and slipped one into either side of the tube. They carefully laid the lady on the stretcher. Her eyes were closed, her face was puffy and red, and she was moaning. Papa Dick and the student hoisted the lady into the air, and then everyone disappeared through the trees.

I was glad Mom and I were staying behind, because that lady had kind of freaked me out. I'd never met someone who might die before.

The ball was huge and shiny and red and had a handle for me to hold on to when I sat on it. I pushed off with my feet over and over again, feeling the plastic squish under my thighs as I bounced. Papa Dick had bought it for me in town, and it was the neatest thing I owned besides Suzie Doll and my Big Blue Book. *Bounce bounce bounce.* I bounded past our VW bus toward the big cabin at the end of the road. Papa Dick had come here to help his friends cut up a moose they'd hunted, and I'd begged him to bring me with him. I loved it when it was just me and Papa Dick. The whole drive here, he'd told me stories about when he was a kid, and the night before, he'd made up songs for me on his guitar.

I parked my ball at the door of the cabin and went inside. The flimsy metal door closed behind me with a bang. There was nobody in the main room, but I could hear my grandfather's voice down the hall.

"Papa Dick, I'm hungry," I said, but he didn't answer. I was just about to turn down the hall to get him when I saw something on a table. I walked over to it and stared. It was a telephone. I'd never seen a real telephone before. I picked it up and put it to my ear. To my surprise, I heard a man's voice. *Hello?* I almost said but stopped myself. The voice was familiar. It was Papa Dick, I realized—but how could it be if he was in another room? As I turned to look down the hall, I heard a woman's voice. I jumped a little.

"When can I see you again?" she asked.

"Soon. Pretty soon."

"I got the cast off last week."

"Good. Don't forget to take the arnica I gave you. It'll help speed healing."

"I will."

"Hey," he said, and his voice went lower, like he was telling her a secret. "I can't wait to lick your pussy again."

I almost dropped the phone. I knew exactly what he meant, because Mom's boyfriends did that to her, sometimes right in the bed beside me. She had told me that's what you do when you and a guy like each other. But I was pretty sure Papa Dick was only supposed to lick Grandma Jeanne's pussy, not some other lady's. I wondered if I should tell her—

"Just what the hell do you think you're doing?"

I spun around. Papa Dick was standing in the doorway, and his face looked madder than I'd ever seen it before. I dropped the phone onto the table with a clatter. He pointed at it.

"That is not a toy, young lady. How long have you been listening?"

"I—I just picked it up. I'm sorry . . ." I started to cry.

After a moment, Papa Dick walked over and put his arm around me. "It's okay, Peanut. But don't ever do that again, all right? Sometimes grown-ups have private things they need to talk about."

I hugged him back, even though I didn't really feel like it. I was confused. Papa Dick had always told me that private things weren't allowed in our family and that trying to hide stuff was a sign of fear. I pulled away and looked at him. "Papa Dick. Won't Grandma Jeanne be mad if you lick that lady's pussy?"

He was silent for a moment. "I don't think so," he finally said, and then he gave me a little smile. "Your grandmother and I, we don't have those kinds of expectations in our relationship."

"What do you mean?"

"It means . . . that we're not bound by society's definition of marriage."

I stared at him blankly.

"I have sex with other people if I want to," he finally said.

"Oh. Grandma Jeanne too?"

He glanced away. "You'd have to ask her that."

Grown-ups were sure weird, I thought. I'd never have sex with anyone when I grew up, because everyone knew that sex was the reason people got all screwed up. Maybe, I thought, that was why they called it *screwing*.

Chapter 4

2006
Halifax

If impatience was my weakness, resilience was my strength. Though Halifax may not have been my first choice of cities to call home, I began our life there with a fierce determination to make it work. Our new house, filled with character and bought ridiculously cheaply compared to anything in Vancouver's overpriced market, made me feel both displaced and hopeful. In a burst of optimistic energy, I painted all the rooms in my favourite colours and watched them come to life as I placed my collected objects throughout the house. Wineglasses from Germany, serving dishes from Spain, tea towels from France. These items had survived countless moves, and I would too.

When I could no longer put it off, I got back to business. James and I shared a small office at the back of the house, where I sat on the floor printing shipping labels and laying out orders. I kept my eyes and my mind focused on my work rather than on my husband, knowing he resented the financial hole CeaSwim had sunk us into. When I finally decided to move my work into the living room, both of us seemed relieved.

And then there was Avery. All the time there was Avery, my beautiful, cherubic child with his pale ringlets, endlessly needing me. The

53

pendulum of my day swung between caring for him and trying to work. Give him breakfast, pack some orders. Read him a few books, bill some clients. Get him interested in a toy, sew a sample. Take him to the playground, hit the post office on the way home to ship orders. Asking for help was almost more trouble than doing without, but sometimes I'd break down and do it anyway. "James," I would call, my arms filled with orders while my phone rang and Avery cried. "Could you please take Avery?"

He would, and afterward, when I watched him return to his office and close the door between us, I wouldn't scream. Instead I'd remind myself of what I had—Avery. The baby I'd so desperately wanted was mine, and that simply had to be enough.

I glanced at my watch as I typed, knowing my time to work was coming to an end. The text for my new brochure was due at the printers' in a few days, but I'd find a way to finish it—just as I always did.

I heard Avery's plastic bowl hit the kitchen floor with a clatter. I sighed, rose from my armchair in the living room and found him in his high chair with an oatmeal-smeared face.

"Ah? Ah?" he said, thrusting his sippy-cup at me.

"Hi, angel. Do you need a drink?"

"Ah!" He nodded, his blond curls bouncing. I lifted him from his seat, and he followed me as I headed for the fridge. Half water, half apple juice. I handed the cup back to him, and he crumpled onto the floor in a heap of tears.

"What is it, honey?" I asked, though I already knew. He hurled the cup across the room and thrashed his feet on the floor. "You wanted to help pour the juice. Mommy's sorry. Here, can we do it again?" I retrieved the cup, unscrewed the lid and dumped the contents back into the juice bottle.

"No!" he screamed, flailing his arms and legs. *"No no no!"*

My cell phone was ringing. I grabbed it off the counter and glanced down at the number. A 416 area code—one of the stores that carried my swimwear line in Ontario. Shit. We had arranged this phone call yesterday. I thought of trying to stick Avery on my boob, which usually worked to calm him down, but one look at his furious face told me all bets were off. I ducked into the bathroom and closed the door, knowing he would be on me in seconds.

"Cea speaking," I said quickly.

"Cea? It's Jennifer at Oasis Swimwear."

"Hi, Jennifer. Like I said in my email yesterday, I'm so sorry your shipment hasn't arrived yet. I've had a few challenges with my factory—" Avery was pounding on the door now, screaming at the top of his lungs. I raised my voice. "Sorry about the noise, I'm just—anyway, I can promise your shipment will be at your store within two weeks. Will that suffice?" There was a beat of silence, quickly filled in by a loud wail from Avery. "I'll give you a ten-percent discount," I added hastily.

"All right," I thought she said, though I could barely hear her over the noise. ". . . tell you the truth . . . only because your line sold so well last season . . . cancelling the order . . . over a month late now."

"Yes, and again, I truly appreciate your understanding. I'll send you an email the minute your order leaves my supply warehouse." I hung up quickly, took a deep breath and opened the door to tend to my son. His red face was streaked with snot and tears, and his matted hair stood out from his head. I picked up his sobbing body and wrapped my arms around him, then looked down at my watch and sighed: ten fifteen. I had a whole day of this ahead of me.

Though it was painful to admit, CeaSwim had become a monster I could barely manage. I'd made the mistake of thinking I could start small and grow slowly, but after a year of receiving poor quality samples from Canadian factories, I realized I was in the wrong country for manufacturing swimwear. James and I decided to buy the equipment, at a much bigger investment than we had anticipated, so that I could sew the samples myself. My first collection had received a boost when

I was offered a spot at a Golden Globes swag party. At this celebrity goody-grab, emerging companies were invited to give their products away at their own expense in the hopes that celebrities would wear and get photographed in them. After two stars were snapped in my suits, I hired an L.A. publicist to keep up the momentum. She indeed had, landing my bikinis in every magazine from *In Touch* to *InStyle* and on nearly every starlet's body in Hollywood, but at a great price. Though orders were being placed and customers were happy, the amount of money coming in wasn't nearly a match for the amount going out. Trying to run a business together while keeping our marriage healthy had proven an impossibility, and though I was willing to take the blame for it, doing so did nothing to mend the current situation. I felt like a lone person at the bottom of a deep well with no ladder, no tools and a time bomb ticking away on the ground beside me.

And all the time, there was Avery. "Shh," I said to him as his small, heaving back began to settle. "Shh, my sweetheart. It's okay. Everything's going to be okay."

My eyes filled with tears. More than anything in the world, I wished someone would say those same words to me.

On Avery's first night home from the hospital after he was born, he'd screamed his lungs out for seven hours straight. I spent the night pacing, rocking, patting and trying to feed him, interspersed with trying to sit down with him in my arms so I could rest for a few minutes. Everything I'd read about newborns told me they slept for a huge portion of each day, so I kept looking down at him and thinking that this couldn't be happening, that a newborn couldn't possibly stay awake this long, but stay awake he did.

Miraculously James slept through the whole episode. When he popped his head into the nursery the next morning to check on us, a feeling of panic like none I'd ever experienced welled up inside my chest. What had I done? How could I possibly have thought this was going to be easy? And if this was to be my son's temperament—much like mine had been as a baby—how would I ever survive? I thought about a story my mother had once told me. By the time I was about six months old, she'd figured out that she could manage my constant crying by smoking copious amounts of pot, but on one occasion even that hadn't helped. While I was screaming and writhing on the floor, she happened to look in the mirror. A green serpent emerged from the top of her head, looked her in the eye and invited her to lose her mind. Thankfully she'd declined, but after my first night as a mother, I could well understand what had driven her to such a vision.

After I told James about my night, he'd smiled at me. "See? You're a great mother already," he said, and that was it. Though I hadn't addressed it consciously, I realized that I'd been harbouring doubts about my ability to parent because of my mother's failings, and that my husband's validation was exactly what I'd been looking for. He thought I was a good mother, and now I would work even harder and sacrifice whatever was necessary to make sure he maintained that opinion.

As it turned out, Avery wasn't as difficult as I'd been—if the legend was to be believed—but he was nowhere near easy. My son's constant want and need of me filled me with new emotions—overflowing joy, resentful exhaustion, and guilt that I couldn't devote my every moment to his well-being. Running a business with a toddler in my lap was close to impossible, but, as so many times before in my life, my missing gauge for what constituted acceptable and manageable levels of stress caused me to question my own judgment. *At least you have a mother who loves you. So many people have it worse than you,* Mom used to say to me when I was little. This statement had done more to form my opinion about my rights to my own feelings than anything else from my childhood. As long as I had love, I shouldn't expect anything more. And James loved me, right? He told me he did, and I knew he loved his son.

But my ability to cope was slipping. I'd actually gotten so desperate that I'd hired an assistant to come in a couple of times a week, but as wonderful as she was, her help just scratched the surface of the many tasks that needed to be done. I still ended my days feeling overwhelmed and dreading whatever the next morning held for me. I'd once convinced myself that I could be everything—full-time mother, dynamic career woman, efficient housewife who brought home the groceries and cooked the meals and kept the house clean—and now I was paying the price for it. I thought about my revelation from years before—that the only way I could be with a man was to create and embody the person that both of us needed me to be—and I realized that once more I had painted myself into a corner.

One evening at dinner, I opened my mouth to begin our usual careful exchange of pleasantries—*how was your day, did I tell you about the cute thing Avery did*—and found I simply couldn't do it. I closed my mouth again and returned to my lasagna. I'd ended the afternoon in tears with a sea of unfilled orders and unpaid bills scattered around me, watching as the clock ticked my deadlines down while Avery screamed to be picked up. As always I'd managed to pull myself together, get Avery calmed down and dinner on the table by the time my husband got home, because he never seemed to be around for the moments that truly tested my sanity. I knew I couldn't continue like this, but the words I needed to say stuck in my throat. And when I noticed the sun streaming through the dining room's stained glass window, filling the room with beautifully coloured light, I almost swallowed them completely. I had a pretty house to live in, food on the table and a husband who hadn't abandoned me. What right did I have to anything more? I cleared my throat.

"James, listen. I know you've been helping with the photography for the new brochure, and that's been so great. And Lisa taking care of the billing and sales calls is giving me more time to focus on the new collection. But . . . I think I need more help. With Avery, I mean, or with CeaSwim. I just don't think I can do both anymore."

"Really?" He looked genuinely surprised. Maybe he was, I thought. Maybe I'd become so adept at concealing my overwhelmed state that even my own husband was unaware of it. "But you're doing such a great job!"

I shook my head. "No, I'm not. Not at all, actually. I've got so much work to do, and Avery . . ."

James set his glass on the table. "Avery . . . yes. Well, I guess we can see about getting someone in. We could probably manage once or twice a week."

I nodded. This was the best I could have hoped for. "Thank you," I said, and immediately regretted it, because this was another thing. It seemed that throughout my life, I was always the one saying *thank you* or *I'm sorry*, which further enforced that I was the one failing.

Doris, my son's new caregiver, was an angel with a face like the Wicked Witch of the West. The few teeth she had left were sharp and pointy, her hair was patchy and thin and Avery immediately adored her. While the two of them hit the playground or read stories, I'd set Lisa up with a few tasks and then spend the day putting out fires. Supply warehouse? *Ha!* If only Jennifer at Oasis Swimwear knew the truth. My supply warehouse was my basement floor, strewn with boxes of product labelled by number. My order centre was my laptop and printer. My packing company was my own two hands, stuffing suits into boxes stuck with ink-jet labels. My shipper was my local post office or UPS store. My pattern maker, fabric and trim sourcer, sample sewer, label creator, bookkeeper, graphic designer, catalogue and website copywriter, market researcher, trade show organizer and set decorator, sales rep, even model—yep, all me. And very occasionally, I got to do the actual thing that had attracted me to the whole idea of starting a swimwear line in the first place: design swimsuits.

One day I was sorting through a pile of suits when I had an epiphany. *I started a swimwear company because I wasn't allowed to wear a swimsuit as a child.* Of course—it made so much sense. The life I'd chosen was as polarized from my family's as could be, and I'd always considered that to be one of my greatest successes. So what else was I subconsciously doing to sabotage myself in the name of proving something to my family?

I flipped over an order form and started writing. *I was taught that city life is evil / I've lived in Paris, New York, L.A., etc. The Persons hated consumerism / I've got credit card debt from too much stuff. Papa Dick believed that houses own people / I have a mortgage. My grandparents rejected relationship expectations / I'm basically staying married for my son. My family hid nothing from each other or me / I haven't told a single person the truth about my past.*

I sat back on my heels and stared at the list. The facts were right there: the one thing I had in common with my family was that we had all tried to escape what we felt trapped us—for them, society's values, and for me, *their* values. But what had started out as a positive, ambitious drive to break away from their ways had turned into a settled life of mediocrity. All I'd wanted to do after modelling was write my memoir, and I'd been too afraid—of people's reactions, of my shame, of my rusty writing skills. And now I was going through life without knowing what drove me, where I'd gone wrong, or how my family had influenced me. But it occurred to me now that maybe, by honouring my long-held dream, I could finally figure out what I was all about.

A few days before my thirty-seventh birthday, I got a call from Mom. Papa Dick was gone, she told me tearfully, dead one year after his cancer diagnosis. Since childhood my perception of my grandfather had changed—he'd gone from hero to opinionated narcissist—but that didn't mean I'd stopped loving him in my own distant way. As I gripped the phone, I reflected on how wrong his death was on so many levels. With his daily practice of yoga and absolute avoidance of pollutants, preservatives and sugar, his cancer diagnosis seemed like the ultimate injustice. At age seventy-eight, he hadn't even made it to the national average male life expectancy. But considering he'd chosen to fight his disease with herbs and hope—the same method my mother was currently using—it probably wasn't surprising.

"He was so wonderful," Mom kept saying to me. "The most wonderful man I've ever met."

I sat in an uncomfortable silence, fighting my usual involuntary urge to fill it with words of agreement. I wouldn't give my mother the peace of thinking that the man who had practically washed his hands of me after I left his wilderness utopia had bewitched me into holding a high opinion of him. After I put the phone down, I willed myself to feel something other than the numbness that had overcome me. I thought about the last time I'd talked to him, about a month ago. In his final years, he'd moved out of the tipis into a remote cabin and had even allowed his partner to put in a telephone line. When I called him that day, I knew it was probably the last time we'd talk. I wanted it to be a memorable exchange, but we didn't really have much to say to each other. He talked about the view from his window, and I told him about our move to Halifax and Avery's new words. Nothing very interesting or revealing was exchanged, yet it occurred to me that I'd probably remember this conversation for much longer than some of importance.

After our call ended, I opened my laptop on a whim and typed out our conversation. Looking at it in black and white, I realized something: I'd always assumed that it was only the big, dramatic stories that had formed who I was and my beliefs about myself, but it was also the smaller things—the firsts and lasts, the passing moments of recognition, the modest triumphs I didn't bother celebrating, and the little failures I couldn't forgive myself for. *Especially* the failures, and the guilt I still carried for them even when I wasn't to blame. Moments that seemed to render all my adult perspective and intelligence and analysis useless, as if I were stuck inside my child-mind with my childish definition of reality still running like one of my mother's old cassette tapes on an endless loop.

1975
Central British Columbia

The boy was about six or seven, a year or two older than me.
Our eyes met as he passed our truck on the highway somewhere in central British Columbia. He was riding on the back of a motorcycle, leaning into the driver as the wind whipped the hair away from his face. I stared at them, wondering if the driver was the boy's father. Then I noticed something else.

"Mom," I said, shaking her awake. She'd been dozing between Karl and me while he drove.

"What is it?" she asked, snapping her head up.

I pointed. The motorcycle was right beside us now, and in between the two bodies I could see a puppy's head peeking out.

"Cute." Mom smiled, rubbing her neck. Reaching between her feet, she found her stash pouch and started rolling a joint. She and Karl passed it back and forth as he drove.

"Another hour or so," Karl said, waving at a passing sign. "Better stop for gas."

Karl always looked like a man with a purpose, but never more so than when he was driving. Even when we weren't sure exactly where we were going, he would lean forward in his seat as if he couldn't wait to be there. His dark hair was raked back from his face as the sun reflected off his blue eyes. Mom rested against his side. She never wore makeup, but today she had on her favourite fringed top, a macramé belt and, as always, a Swiss Army knife through one belt loop and two long leather cords hanging from another. Mom always told me how important it was to look good for your man, but we were also still spending a lot of time in the wilderness, and Papa Dick had taught her to always be prepared.

Exactly where we were driving to or from on that day, I don't recall. Mom had met Karl when he came to my grandparents' tipi camp as a visitor and quickly decided it would be a great idea if we went to live with him. Until then I hadn't realized that you could live with someone without actually having somewhere to live. Karl was a man with ideas as big as his dazzling white smile, and most of them depended on us keeping moving. The torn vinyl bench seat that I occupied between Mom and the passenger window that framed my world felt as familiar to me as another child's bedroom might to them. And whether we were running from the cops to escape a drug bust, stealing from or spending the night in empty summer cottages or moving from one canvas shelter in the forest to another, Mom never had much to say about it. She sometimes cried when the two of us were alone, but she always wiped her tears away before Karl could see them.

Karl put the joint out, exited the highway and pulled into a gas station. After filling up the tank, he lit up a cigarette and then disappeared into the small building.

"Do you need to pee?" Mom asked me.

I shook my head.

"Okay. Be right back."

After Mom slid from the truck, I rolled my window down and hung Suzie Doll outside by the arm, swinging her back and forth. When I leaned out far enough, her feet traced a trail in the dust.

"My dad's buying me a box of Mike and Ike," said a voice, and I snapped Suzie Doll back into the cab. Standing in front of me was the boy from the motorcycle, still holding the puppy in his arms.

"What's Mike and Ike?" I asked, sitting Suzie Doll beside me on the seat.

"Candy," the boy answered. "It's green and red and blue and purple and tastes like fruity stuff, and it's my favourite. Dad promised me, since we have to get rid of Shyla."

"Shyla? Who's that?"

Instead of answering, the boy held the puppy out to me. I slowly reached my hand out to her. She tilted her head to the side and licked my fingers, so I pulled away and wiped my hand on my pants. I hated dog slobber.

"Why do you have to get rid of her?"

"Dad says she's slowin' us down. Too many poop and pee breaks."

"Oh. Do you have to go somewhere fast?"

"I dunno." The boy shrugged. "That's just what Dad says. Plus we found her at a garbage can, so Dad says she's probably got bugs and stuff."

"Oh." I didn't know what else to say. I saw Karl in the distance, heading back toward the truck. Shyla whined and gazed up at the boy, landing a lick on his chin. "My mom's in the bathroom," I said finally, waving at the building. "She takes a super long time."

"That's okay. I don't have a mom anymore."

"You don't?" I looked at the boy a little harder. I'd never met someone who didn't have a mom before, except Karl, whose mom died when he was fifteen. He didn't really count, though, because he was a grown-up. "What happened to her? Did she die?"

"No. She liked another guy better than my dad, so she went to live with him in Regina."

"Wow. Really?"

"Yeah."

"Oh. Regina rhymes with vagina, you know."

The boy didn't say anything. He was staring at the ground, pounding his heel into the dirt. I suddenly felt like giving him a hug, like I did when Mom was feeling blue. But there was a truck door between us, and besides, his puppy would probably try to lick me again.

"Well, I don't have a dad," I said instead. "I mean, I do, but he lives in California and everything. Mom says I met him when I was two, but I can't remember." I dropped my eyes. Whenever I thought about my father, I saw in my mind the exact same thing: the only photo I'd ever seen of us, him holding me and looking sad while I looked mad. Mom told me that when she met Greg, she thought they would be together forever, but that forever had turned out to be just over a year. He hadn't even stuck around long enough for me to be born. But Mom said my dad was a good man who sent her a hundred dollars every month even though he couldn't afford it, and the reason he hadn't stayed was that it would have hurt him too much to see me. As much as I tried, I couldn't figure out why looking at some baby would hurt anyone's feelings.

The boy grunted something and pointed past me. "What about *him*, then?"

I turned to see Karl back in the driver's seat, shuffling through our eight-tracks with an unlit cigarette dangling from his lips.

"That's Karl," I said, as if it explained everything. And maybe it did, because suddenly the boy smiled and held the puppy out to me again.

"Do you want her? 'Cause Dad says if someone don't take her, we're gonna have to leave her by the road. Let someone else pick her up."

"Oh, I don't think—"

"Sure she does," Karl said. "We could use us a guard dog, couldn't we, Small Fry? Hand her over, partner."

I turned to Karl in surprise.

The boy smiled at him. "Really?"

"I wouldn't kid ya, kid," Karl replied, lighting his cigarette.

"Okay." The boy looked down at Shyla, then he closed his eyes and pulled her hard against his face. They stayed like that for a minute, and then he passed Shyla to me through my window. "'Kay. Bye, then."

"Bye," I said softly.

And with that, he turned and ran back to the motorcycle. His father was just coming out of the gas station. The sun glinted off his black leather jacket. He caught the boy in his arms and bent down to say something in his ear. The boy laughed and threw his arms around his dad, and I wondered just what he had said to make him so happy.

"Hey. She's pretty cute, eh?" Karl said behind me.

"Yeah. I guess so," I said, still staring out the window.

"Did you catch her name?"

"Her name? Um . . . Shyla," I replied.

"Shyla. Nice."

I finally turned to look at Karl. Shyla was on the seat between us, flipped on her back to show us her tummy. She sighed happily as Karl scratched her side.

"I wonder what's taking Mom so long?" I asked, glancing back at the gas station.

"Lady things . . . who knows?" Karl lifted Shyla onto his lap. For some reason, my eyes filled with tears. Karl took a drag on his cigarette. "Hey there. Small Fry?"

"Yeah?"

"Nobody has to know for sure you don't have a dad. You dig? I mean, I know I'm not the real deal and all, but . . . you know?"

I blinked at him. If anyone had asked me how long Karl had been with us, I wouldn't have been able to say, but it was long enough that my memories of life before him were a little fuzzy. The times when it was me and Mom and Papa Dick and Grandma Jeanne and my aunts seemed kind of like a dream. And my uncle Dane. More than anything, Uncle Dane felt like a dream. Karl's hand landed on my shoulder and patted it, kind of like he had patted Shyla.

"Yeah." I nodded. "Okay."

Pressing my chin against the door frame, I looked at the boy and his dad. They were back at the motorcycle, and the boy was giggling while his father chased him around and around. What was that boy's secret? I wondered. After all, he didn't even have a mom. I did, plus someone who said he would be my pretend dad. Mom always said I should be grateful just to have a mother to love me, and I was. But I knew that no matter what, I'd never be as happy as that boy looked right now.

Our home after we got Shyla was a log cabin on a creek, somewhere in time between the stealing sprees on Shuswap Lake and our year in Lake Minnewanka in the stolen wall tent. The cabin was tiny, just a square room with a wood stove and a few cupboards built into one corner. There was a path that led down to the creek, and every morning I would walk there to fetch the water before Mom and Karl got up. A bucket in each hand kept me balanced as I climbed the slope back up to the cabin, trying not to let the water slop over the sides. Then it was time for breakfast. Mom had taught me how to slice her homemade bread with a knife, so I'd hack off a piece and spread it with butter and molasses. While I ate, Shyla would sit at my feet without even begging, because she knew she was next. Karl bought Shyla's food in town—a huge shiny bag that I used Mom's measuring cup to scoop little brown pebbles out of. One time I'd tried eating a few of them, just for the heck of it, but they tasted like I thought sawdust must taste. I thought it would be pretty boring to be a dog, eating the same old sawdusty food every day, but Shyla didn't seem to mind.

Shyla was the second dog Karl had owned since Mom and I had been with him. The first one had been a big orange thing with a black tongue named Bear. He'd bitten me on the chin a few weeks after Mom and Karl met. When we left my grandparents' tipi camp in Morley to go live with Karl, Karl had dropped Bear off at the Indian reservation and told them they could just go ahead and shoot him if he got too out of hand. When he said that, I could feel a little worm crawling around in my stomach. The worm felt hot and mean and like it wanted Bear to get shot, because he had bitten me and I still had a scar on my chin and it would serve him right. But Shyla was different. I knew she'd never bite me. She played in the creek with me and sprayed me when she shook the water from her fur. She ran beside me as I bounced on my big red ball in front of our cabin. She slept in my bed, keeping my mind off the noises Mom and Karl made at night that I hated. Shyla was almost bigger than me now, and her fur was grey and black and white. She even knew better than to lick me, because I told her I didn't like dog slobber. And she was good at keeping strangers away. One day a man walked through the woods and right up to our cabin, and Shyla ran up and bit him on the leg. After that, Karl got really mad. He kept telling Mom it was the third time, and they were going to get in trouble.

I didn't know the name of the creek we lived on or how long we would stay there. I didn't know if the cabin belonged to us or some other people who might show up and be mad and kick us out. What I did know was that I loved Mom and Karl, and especially Shyla, because she made everything seem okay even when it wasn't.

I sat on a chair, squeezing my eyes shut while Mom brushed the knots from my hair.

"Almost done, almost done," Mom said soothingly.

"Can't you just cut it off?" I asked, but she laughed as if that were the most ridiculous thing she'd ever heard.

"Darling. You know men don't like short hair. They like it long, and yours is beautiful."

"But I don't care about any men."

"You'll understand when you're older. It's very important for men to like how you look."

"But I don't even know any men besides Karl, and anyway, he already likes me, right?" I glanced around our cabin. "Hey. Where is Karl, anyway?"

"He went into town early to get supplies."

"With Shyla?"

"Yes."

"Oh." I hated it when Shyla was out of my sight. When she was, I couldn't help but imagine all the horrible things that might happen to her. She could get lost, or run over by a car, or stolen by someone who thought they loved her more than we did. She could even get shot by accident like Apache. "When will they be back?"

"I don't know, sweetie. Soon, I guess." Mom pulled the brush through my hair one last time, picked up her mirror and rubbed it with some spit. "There, see? My gorgeous girl. There isn't a person in the world who wouldn't think so."

I looked away, bored. I looked the same as I did on any other old day. "Can I go play now?"

"Of course."

I grabbed Suzie Doll and went down to the creek. She needed a bath and a change of clothes. I was halfway through sewing a new dress for her out of one of Mom's old dish towels, and Shyla always snoozed by my feet as I sewed by candlelight.

After a while, I started to wonder where Karl was. I ran up to the cabin a couple times to ask Mom, but she just shrugged and kept on puttering. Finally, when the sun was starting to drop in the sky, I heard Karl's voice, and then Shyla's bark. I snatched up Suzie Doll and made a dash for home.

As soon as I walked into the cabin, I could tell something was wrong. Karl was pacing back and forth and talking too fast. Shyla sat in a corner, following him with her eyes.

"What's wrong? What happened?" I asked.

"Shyla. She bit someone again," Mom said. "The man threatened to come after Karl."

My stomach dropped. "Come after him how? Does he know where we live?"

No one answered me. Suddenly Karl walked over to the gun rack and took down his rifle.

"You stay here with your mother, Small Fry. I'll be right back."

"But where are you—?" My voice stuck in my throat as he clipped Shyla's leash onto her collar and pulled her outside. "What are you doing? No! *No!*"

But Karl had already shut the door behind him, and Mom was wrapping her arms tightly around me.

"It's for the best," she said to me. "She's going to get us into trouble. We just can't afford any more trouble than we already have."

"But we can train her to stop! We can—"

"No, honey. I'm sorry. You'll . . . you'll understand when you're older."

I hated it when Mom said that to me, because I knew that no matter how much older I got, I would never do some of the dumb things grown-ups did. I squirmed and kicked and jabbed my elbows at her until I finally broke free. Then I ran out the door, not even caring that she was screaming at me to stop.

Down the path, over the fallen log, falling flat on my face, getting up again, down to the creek, branches tearing at my sweater. *"Shyla! Karl! Shyla!"* No answer. Had I heard a shot yet? Stumbling along the creek, water splashing, Mom still screaming for me. I turned and headed into the forest, ran toward the sound of barking.

Blasting through the trees, I saw Karl first. He was standing with his back to me, loading his rifle. And there was Shyla beside him. Tied to a tree trunk, barking and tugging against her short leash. She stopped barking when she saw me, and her tail wagged, just once. Then she whined a little, her eyes never leaving mine. I wiped my cheeks with the back of my hand and tried to send her a secret message: *Don't worry. I'll save you.*

"Karl!" I shouted, running up to him and grabbing his arm. "Please. Please don't."

He finished loading his rifle and snapped it back together with a horrible metallic click. "It's for the best, Small Fry."

"No. It's—I can train her, I promise."

He shook his head. "I'm sorry. Now go on home." He raised the gun to his eye. Shyla started jumping wildly with her tongue hanging out, and I was sure she knew what was coming.

I needed to think fast. I searched my brain for something, anything, that I could say to stop him. And then I had it. Taking a deep breath, I yelled as loud as I could, "Dad! Please don't do it! *Don't do it, Dad!"*

Karl lowered the gun and looked at me, and his eyes were sad.

Then he gave his head another little shake. "Turn away, Small Fry," he said quietly. "Turn away."

I covered my ears and did as I was told. After the shot rang out, I ran as fast as I could back to the cabin and slammed into Mom's arms. She held me tightly, stroking my hair as she murmured into my ear.

"It's okay," she whispered. "Everything will be okay."

"No, it won't!" I shook my head hard, shook it so many times that after a while I wondered if I could even stop shaking it if I tried. I saw Apache, lying on his side in a pool of blood. When he died, everyone had been sad, not just me. Papa Dick had even gotten mad at the hunters and sent them away. But this was different. I'd trusted Karl, even let him try to be my dad, but he hadn't loved me enough to stop. Would I have mattered enough to him if I'd been his real daughter? I could still see Shyla looking at me, begging me with her eyes to save her. I'd failed the one being who'd never failed me. And as my head finally came to a rest and my hysteria turned to hitching sobs, I realized the truth. Shyla had died because of the mean worm in my belly. I'd wanted Bear to get shot, so it had happened to Shyla instead. I should have listened to Papa Dick, I thought. After all, he'd always told me that the things we think about come true even more than the things we try to make happen.

Chapter 5

2007
Halifax

Though the decision to write my memoir seemed to have been made in a moment, it actually developed over decades. When I finally began it, lines and stories I'd held in my mind for years reminded me of their presence, flying from my fingertips as fast as I could type them. I worked in tiny pockets of time stolen between tasks for CeaSwim and caring for Avery, and very quickly writing became a drug I needed each day.

"What are you up to?" James asked once, catching a glimpse of my monitor.

"Just getting a few childhood stories down," I replied, snapping my laptop closed more forcefully than I'd meant to. "I want to do it before Mom, well, you know . . . dies."

He nodded. "Good idea. As long as it doesn't take away from your other focuses."

I gave him a mollifying smile, but as I looked down at my laptop again, my eyes filled with tears. How had I messed things up so badly? I'd come back to Canada with the intention of healing my relationship with my mother, and it seemed that all I'd succeeded in doing was turning my husband against her. Now that she was deteriorating rapidly, I'd tried switching the gears of communication about her to a more positive note. I kept the right stories ready in my head, just in case I had an opportunity to tell them: the cake she'd made for my sixth birthday when we were squatting in the cottage and not allowed to use the oven. The apple she'd given me, going hungry herself, when we were hitchhiking. The stuffed Garfield cat I'd coveted for months when I was ten that had shown up on Easter morning. The time my mom gave me her last twenty to replace the babysitting money I'd accidentally overpaid the cab driver who drove me home. But James and my relationship was so devoid of intimacy that saying any of this to him at this point would have felt forced. It was simply too late— too late for Mom and James to bond, and too late for it to make any difference to our limping marriage.

James's reaction to my writing made it clear to me that, as per the terms of our relationship, CeaSwim and caring for my son would continue to be my primary pursuits. I started writing only at night, and a few weeks later, when James saw that I was still serious, he started showing some interest in my book. At first this made me happy, but then I realized something: his questions mostly revolved around the publishing and marketing of the book, not the life I was writing about.

A few weeks into writing my first draft, I received a package in the mail from a friend. I ripped it open and stared at an unfamiliar book. *The Secret* by Rhonda Byrne. I flipped it over and read the back cover, then scanned the first chapter curiously. By the time I closed the book, I felt like I'd stepped through a portal that reflected my entire life back to me at a new angle. Manifestation: this wasn't a foreign concept to me. When I was little, my grandfather had preached living in the moment, allowing in thoughts only of the positive reality you wished to create. *Never underestimate how quickly your negative thoughts can send you into ruin*, he'd say to me and others. He'd also lectured on the evils of television, white sugar and preservatives—truths now accepted as mainstream—far ahead of his time. So was he right about this as well, and was I only ready to accept it because it was now the subject of a book that had sold millions of copies? With my big-box, middle-of-the-road thinking, I truly was the opposite of my family. But maybe it was time for me to admit there had been some value to their teachings, however much I'd tried to shun them.

Excitedly I read the book cover to cover, and the next day, I went out and bought the DVDs. I marvelled at my new awakening, as if overnight I'd gone from blind to sighted. All this time, worry and anxiety had been ruling my life, when success, happiness and wealth had been mine for the taking. And it was so easy—according to *The Secret*, I could even bring myself money simply by envisioning receiving random cheques in the mail! This was just what I needed, I thought, not only to attract wealth and success but also to mend my marriage. I left the book on James's desk and was pleased the next night to see him reading it. I felt certain that everything was going to turn around.

Shortly after I discovered *The Secret*, my father and his wife, Lara, came to visit. Over the past decade, my relationship with my father had been radically transformed. Until then our history would have filled only a few pages of a book—meeting him for the first time when I was two, when I'd apparently sworn at him and screamed whenever he touched me; flying to San Francisco to see him at age eight, when I'd hidden behind his wife, terrified to be alone with him; a few visits during my teens, when I was introduced to his other daughters and tried hard not to be resentful; and several short visits in my twenties, when our attempts to communicate always seemed badly timed. When he wanted to clear the air about the past, I wasn't receptive, and later, when I was, he seemed closed off. But after a difficult conversation that finally brought our respective walls down, he had become someone I identified with far more than the mother who'd raised me. Our similarities in taste, mindset and mannerisms never ceased to amaze both of us.

I spent the weekend showing Dad and Lara around the city, Dad and me often swinging a laughing Avery by the arms. They offered polite comments about Halifax, and I pretended not to see the question in their eyes: *Why here?*

On their last evening in town, I snapped photos of Dad and Avery as they worked on a puzzle. When it was finished, Avery snuggled into my lap, tugging lightly at my hair as his eyes grew heavy.

"You're a great mother," Dad said suddenly. "And I have nothing to do with it."

I smiled, caught between gratitude and a resentment that had nothing to do with my father. They were words I needed to hear, but I wished they could have come from my husband. I searched my brain for something I could say that would prove Dad's second statement wrong.

"That's not true. You're still my father, right? And I'm still learning how to be a mom."

He grinned. Down the hall, I heard James's office door open, footsteps, water running in the kitchen. He entered the living room.

"Hey," I said. "All done for the night?"

"Not quite."

I nodded, wishing desperately—as I did each day—for my husband's happiness. I could still see the goodness in the person I'd fallen in love with, even if he was completely incompatible with me. The reasons he'd chosen me were as baffling to me as why I'd chosen him, but since we had done so, it seemed tantalizingly possible that we could rediscover what had brought us together in the first place.

James crossed the floor and bent to smile at Avery. "Well. Good night," he said to us. A few seconds later, we heard the door to his office close again.

Dad caught my eye, and I shrugged. If there was one thing *The Secret* was teaching me, it was awareness of how my mindset affected everything. I had made my choices in life, and no one but me was responsible for whatever consequences those decisions might bring upon me.

According to the law of attraction touted by *The Secret*, both positive thinking and creating good karma should become daily practice. The timing seemed perfect for my new attitude, as spring finally broke through Halifax's winter deep freeze. Buds were forming on the trees, and I put Avery's snowsuit away and started taking him to the playground again. I avoided talking to James about anything that didn't involve sunshine and rainbows. I weaned myself off the antidepressants I'd been taking for seven years. Though it seemed difficult to remember a time in my life I *hadn't* felt depressed, it wasn't lost on me that I'd finally resorted to drugs not long after I'd moved in with James. I'd always been a woman of action, except when it came to leaving men that I knew were wrong for me; it seemed I preferred to numb the effects of my resulting misery with alcohol and Celexa. But no more. The new Cea would be ruled by light, manifestation and unsurpassed positive karma.

At least the positive karma part was easy. I cleaned out my closet and donated the clothes to a women's shelter, helped a man jump his car when his battery died and, though I truly couldn't afford it, paid for a woman's groceries when her credit card was declined. And a few times a week when I passed by him on the same street corner, I handed a homeless man some change through my car window. My resoluteness to stay positive was like a stiff march; I was soldiering forward to an unknown place of salvation.

"How are you doing?" asked my mother, father and back-home friends when they called.

"Really *great!*" I'd say with a huge smile they couldn't see, and I'd quickly change the topic because I had nothing else to add. My being really *great* didn't come from a feeling within or from changed circumstances; it was my state of being because I'd decided that it was. If people started poking around for details of my *great*ness, they'd find nothing there. So week after week, I buried myself in my work, wrote down my memories until the screen blurred in front of my eyes, smiled at James when I felt a fight brewing, and held Avery lovingly when he screamed. When I went to bed each night, I would mindlessly recite times tables or try to remember which countries made up the United Arab Emirates. My positive state of being allowed no space for daily reflection.

One day I was shopping at Old Navy with Avery when my phone rang. It was my credit card company, asking when they might be able to expect my missed payment. I hung up, flustered, and tried to banish the anxiety that flooded my body. Given the circumstances, the last place I should have been at that moment was shopping, but I wasn't actually buying clothes for myself. I was buying them for Avery. *Avery.* I looked around for him, but he was nowhere to be seen.

"Avery," I said loudly, sprinting up the aisles, calling his name. Shoppers stared. An employee approached me and asked if she could help.

"Yes," I replied urgently. "He's two. Yellow jacket, wavy blond hair."

"Don't worry. We'll lock the store down and find him."

I nodded, my eyes no doubt wild with fear. Two new employees joined me, and we all spread out in different directions. Even a couple of shoppers moved in to join the cause.

"Check under the racks," I shouted, moving from one rack of clothing to the next in search of a small pair of legs. Avery loved hiding in the racks, but this time, he was nowhere. My mind was running crazy, writing headlines and imagining the worst. "Please, please, please," I muttered under my breath as I rushed around, ignoring people's thank-god-it's-her-and-not-me pitying glances. *What will I do?* I thought wildly. *What will I do if I never find him? What will I have to live for?*

Just then I heard crying, and I turned to see an employee rushing toward me with Avery in her arms. I grabbed him from her and hugged him hard.

"I found him in the parking lot," she said, a little apologetically. "Just happened to see him wandering around out there. The doors. They're automatic, so they slide right open. Kind of dangerous for a little guy."

"Yeah," I said. "It's okay. Thank you, thank you so much." I stood there holding my son for a long time, waiting for the adrenalin to stop pumping through my limbs. When we were both feeling a little steadier, I carried him to the car and strapped him into his seat. I was immensely relieved, but my nerves were still jangled. I tried to think of something that would calm me down. I would drive home, I decided, and do something I rarely had time for, like drink a cup of tea in the bath or some damn thing. Isn't that what all those magazine articles about managing stress told you to do?

I was on my way home when I saw the homeless guy. It was the one I gave change to every week, and he was pulling up to an apartment building on his Harley. His *Harley*. It took me a moment to compute what was wrong with this picture. I hit the brakes hard, pulled up behind him and leaned out my window.

"Hey! Hey, you!" I shrieked indignantly.

He turned toward my voice, his face shocked.

"Yeah, you! What the fuck, dude? You drive a *Harley* and hang out on street corners begging for change? And I guess this is your cozy little apartment?" Through my fury, I could hear Avery talking to me in a small voice. "Why you scream him, Mommy?"

"Every week I've been giving you money, and you know what? I can't even pay my credit card bill! Get a job! Fuck you, you stupid *shithead*!" His mouth was still hanging open when I hit the gas and entered traffic again, shaking.

"Mommy? *Mommy!* Why you scream him?"

"It's nothing, sweetie, okay? That man just made Mommy really mad. I'm sorry I scared you." I took a deep breath and tried to relax. My breath was coming out in jagged whooshes. I knew I was cracking, and hard.

When I got home, I bypassed the tea completely and reached for a bottle of wine. Then, instead of taking a bath, I put Avery in front of *Cars* and sat down to write.

Being positive all the time is just another form of denial, I typed. *An edge of negativity is part of my natural personality, and I happen to like it that way.*

I sat back and read the words I'd written, already feeling a little better. Fuck this shit. I would not pretend anymore. My history dictated that I would rather face the truth about a situation, no matter how scary it might be, and I would continue to do so. And fuck *The Secret* too, which was obviously nothing more than a money-grabbing ploy aimed at desperate suckers who wanted to believe they could change their luck with something easier than hard work or talent. How different was that, really, than my mother's attempts to cure her cancer with herbs and water? For just a second, I hated both myself for being so gullible and my family for setting me up to fall for such garbage. But at least now I was myself again. And just to prove it, I went into the bathroom and popped a Celexa. Yes, I was prone to depression and fear, and who the fuck could blame me? One day—when I had a supportive husband, for example, or a break from trying to raise a child in tandem with running a business, or some friends who lived in the same city as me, or a past that no longer had the power to remind me of how worthless I was— yes, maybe then I would have the strength to kick my happy sidekick to the curb. But right now, I just needed to get through each day, locked and loaded for whatever life might throw at me next. Papa Dick had been wrong about fear being useless; sometimes, it could save your life.

1976
Lake Minnewanka

"I'm scared," I whispered. **Through the mesh window of our** tent, I could see the bumpy moon. It spread its shallow white light across my sleeping bag.

"Shh . . . it's okay. Just stay quiet," Mom whispered back, brushing my tears away. "Whatever it is, I'm sure it'll go away soon."

I held my breath. I was so still that I could hear the beating of my heart, *thumpa-thumpa-thumpa* in my ears. I felt the butt of Mom's .22 rifle against my feet, but it wasn't much comfort. I knew that if there was a big animal out there, this gun didn't have the power to take it down. For the first time since Mom and I had run away into the forest, I wished we were back at camp with Karl.

The way I saw it, we were here all because of Karl's limp dick. Until a few weeks ago, the three of us had been living in a wall tent on Lake Minnewanka near another family. But then Mom and Karl had the big fight about the fuzz busting them for pot and Mom's shrivelling twat and Karl's limp dick, and Mom had decided to leave. But since she didn't have any money or way of getting us from the dirt road to the highway, our only option had been to go deeper into the wilderness. For the past month, she and I had been living in a tent, bathing in a creek, and foraging for wild berries and mushrooms and other plants, like dandelion greens, which tasted horrible and bitter. We had brought a few supplies with us, but they were running out fast.

I heard thrashing and twigs snapping again. "Mommy—"

"Shhhh . . ."

I ducked my head into her chest, trying not to think about how hungry I was. Lately I almost never *didn't* feel hungry. My tummy let out a loud rumble. I wrapped my arms around it to muffle the sound. Mom reached quietly into her knapsack and took out a plastic bag. Not long ago it had been filled with granola, but now there was only a small handful left in one corner.

"Open your mouth," Mom whispered, and she poured the cereal onto my tongue.

I crunched it slowly, trying not to make noise.

"We'll go hunting for a grouse tomorrow, okay? We'll have plenty of food," she said softly, and I believed her.

Each time our food supplies were nearly gone, Mom would pull something out of her sleeve—a handful of wild berries or a grouse or a porcupine shot with her .22. I knew she'd never let us starve.

The noise came again, closer this time. "It sounds big. Maybe you should use your gun to scare it," I whispered.

She shook her head. "Can't afford the bullets. Only a few left."

I pressed my body even closer to hers. There was a new noise now, along with the snapping of twigs, and it took me a moment to realize it sounded like breathing. Yes. Whatever was out there was sniffing at our tent. I felt a stab of fear, and Mom must have too, because she placed her hand on her rifle. She leaned toward the mesh opening, trying to catch a glimpse of the animal.

"Stay here," she whispered. "I'll be right back."

"Where are you—?"

"*Shh!* I said I'd be right back." She stood up as far as she could inside the tent. "Roll onto your tummy," she said, pushing me with her foot. "And stay that way. Whatever happens, don't come outside. Be as still as you can. Even if it comes after you, play dead. Remember what we talked about. Okay?" Even though she was whispering, her voice sounded panicked.

"Okay."

I knew the drill, or at least I was supposed to. Mom wasn't usually big on preparing for the future, but a few days after we'd moved into the forest, she'd stood in front of me and placed her hands on my shoulders. She only did that if she was going to tell me something I didn't want to hear, and with my mother, it was never "I'm very disappointed in you for such-and-such, so you won't be getting any dessert tonight," it was more along the lines of "The cops have found our pot plants again, so we need to get out of here pronto."

I braced for the worst. But instead, she just asked me a question. "So, sweetheart, tell me. Which way is the lake from here?"

I pointed down the creek. It was easy, because when Mom and I had left Karl's camp, we'd headed for the lake and then followed a creek into the woods, so we wouldn't get lost.

"Good. So let's say, for example, that something happened to me. What would you do?"

"Wait for you to come back."

"Right. Except imagine I couldn't. Let's say you waited a few hours, and I didn't show up."

"You mean, like, because you were dead?"

She stared at me for a few seconds. "Yes. That's the only reason I wouldn't return. You know that, right?"

I nodded. This was just survival talk, and I'd heard it my whole life, especially from Papa Dick. "Then I'd go back to Karl's camp."

"Yes. Along the creek to the waterfall, over the boulders and through the thick wall of brush, the same way we came. Right?"

"Right."

"And if you see a bear or a cougar when I'm not around—what do you do?"

"Don't look in its eyes. Walk away backwards but not fast. Play dead if he comes after me."

"And? How do you play dead?"

"On my tummy. Arms covering my head. And don't move, don't even breathe, and don't make a sound."

"Right. Okay, good."

Yes. We had had that chat just a few weeks ago. But now that it was real, I didn't have a clue what I was supposed to do. How long should I wait for her to get back? And then should I run back to Karl's camp? Or walk back? And anyway, it was dark outside, so how was I supposed to find my way?

"Arms over your head," Mom whisper-shouted, and then I remembered: *play dead.*

I did as she said, and I could have sworn there was a growl right beside my head. I heard Mom unzipping the door, and I peeked under my arm at her. She had her rifle in one hand and our frying pan in the other. Suddenly she ran out the door, banging them together.

"Go away! Get out of here! Scram!" she yelled at the top of her lungs.

I heard a grunt, and then I knew it was a bear for sure. I squeezed my eyes shut. Mom's footsteps were running away from me. She was still shouting, and there was some serious thrashing going on. I pulled my shoulders up even closer to my ears, burying my head in my sleeping bag. Papa Dick had told me once that in all his years in the wilderness, he had never been attacked by a wild animal. They were much more afraid of us than we were of them, he always said, but in that moment, I found his words hard to believe. A bullet rang out, and then everything went quiet.

I couldn't take it anymore. I popped my head up and scrambled out of the tent. Mom was standing about two canoe-lengths away from me, looking into the trees. I rushed toward her.

"Is he gone? Is he gone?"

Mom nodded, still breathing hard. "Yes," she said. "He's gone."

"Will he come back?"

She put her arm around my shoulders. "I don't think so. I think it worked. I think I made him believe I was the boss."

"What do you mean?"

"Well, you know. The boss of this territory. He needs to believe that, or he'll try to push me out."

"Push you out how?"

"By killing me, of course."

I nodded. "But he didn't. He's gone now."

Mom took my hand. Over to the east, I could see the first rays of sunrise. She pulled me back toward the tent.

"Come on, let's get some rest. Then we'll go hunting in the morning, okay?"

"Okay. How many bullets do you have left?"

"Two."

"That's not very much."

"I know. But we're lucky I didn't have to use them. That bear was big."

"How big?" I asked, lying down beside her in my sleeping bag.

"Huge." She smiled, wrapping her arms around me. "But not nearly as huge as my love for you."

I smiled in the dark. I knew Mom loved me, of course, but tonight there was another feeling I hadn't had very often. I felt protected by her.

Chapter 6

2007
Halifax

I **glanced at my watch; it was almost time. Stupidly I** actually felt nervous, as if I were hosting some grand dinner party rather than Monday morning playgroup. I walked into the living room to survey my set-up. Chairs lined up in a semicircle, toys at the ready, juice boxes and snacks on the table. Coffee, tea and muffins set out for the adults. As a final touch, I slipped in a CD of nursery rhymes.

We'd been in Halifax for seven months, and I'd decided it was time to make some friends. Ever since I had been able to make my own life choices, I'd given friends a much bigger role in my life than family, and many of those relationships I'd maintained since early adulthood. I was still close to women I'd modelled with in Europe, despite our having dispersed all over the world. And in leaving Vancouver, I'd also left behind several close friendships I'd formed over my seven years there. Given my manic work and parenting schedule, I hadn't had much time to miss them, but whenever one of them called to check in, I appreciated their carefully worded support of my decision to move here—always enquiring, yet never questioning. Of course it was no mystery why I placed so much value on friendships: during my nomadic childhood I'd had so few. Despite my longing to fit in, I was always too tall, too weird-smelling, too poorly dressed, too eager to please. And now here I was again, six years old at my first day of school. *Just like everyone else feels sometimes*, I reminded myself. I wasn't the only person in the world who felt like an outsider.

I pulled the door open with a smile, and they streamed in with their charges: mother of one, nanny of three, mother of two, nanny of two. I'd only met these women once or twice before, but I already envied every single one of them—the nannies for their sense of purpose, the mothers for their contented choice to stay at home with their children. I was neither and both—a mother who worked from home with a toddler at her feet. As if on cue, Avery let out a shriek and threw himself on the floor in protest of sharing his Fisher-Price workbench. A plastic socket wrench skidded across the floor and landed at my feet.

"Everything's in the living room, if you can get past the demon who just possessed my child," I said to the ladies, inwardly cringing at my tone. With this first social attempt on new ground, I recognized that my standard MO was fully back in motion: art-direct my life to make it look perfect, and then, knowing full well how intimidating it appeared from the outside, make up for it by being the self-deprecating friend who was always more interested in talking about them than herself. It was a survival mechanism, but it was also very handy, because it kept people from knowing the truth about me, both present and past. *I just need to get through this*, I thought. *If I can just appear happy and capable until I actually am, then I can afford to let my real self show.*

"My goodness, your house is gorgeous," one of the moms said as she stirred sugar into her tea. "So, you moved here from . . ."

"Vancouver."

"Right. What brought you out east?"

I pushed aside the memory of James and me sitting on our sofa back in Vancouver, making a decision that I'd forgotten how to rationalize. "Oh, we just . . . you know, needed a change of pace," I replied with a breezy smile.

She nodded as if such a thing were perfectly understandable and scanned the food table. "And you're at home with your son, then?"

"Yes. I mean, I work, too, but I do it from home."

"How convenient! What is it that you do?"

"I have . . . a design company," I said vaguely, not wanting to get into the details of the business that was currently sucking the life out of me. "But what about *you*?"

I smiled and nodded while she talked, switching my attention between her and Avery. I could see him in the living room, gleefully *vroom*ing a HotWheels car up and down one of the nanny's legs. Clearly he didn't give a crap about whom he impressed. It occurred to me that there was a lot I could learn from my young son.

Just as playgroup was ending, James came out of his office. He greeted the women awkwardly, a lone father in a sea of females.

Eventually the moms and nannies straggled out the door, and I started cleaning up. "Coffee?" I asked James, and he nodded.

As I handed him the mug, I imagined for just a moment that we were a normal couple, one that squabbled about things like who took the last cup of coffee or whose in-laws to spend Christmas with, and then laughed at how petty their arguments were in the big, wonderful picture of their life. *We could have had that*, I thought. *At one time, we really could have.*

As I watched my husband wander back down the hall and close the door between us, I thought about a day several years before. James and I had taken the ferry over to the Gulf Island I'd lived on as a child. Part of my reason for going there had been curiosity—would returning to the scene of some of my darkest moments help cure the nearly constant depression that plagued me?—but I also had an ulterior motive. I was thirty-four and in the midst of my baby yearning, and I thought that maybe showing James a bit of who I was as a child would make him more receptive to the idea of having one himself.

After giving James the tour of my old school, the leech-infested lake I used to swim in and the beach I spent hours playing on below our first cottage, I took him to see one last place—the house I'd been living in when I was molested by Mom's boyfriend Barry. As we pulled into the driveway, the first thing I saw was his old El Ranchero, rusted out and propped up on wooden blocks. But when I saw the house, I was certain we had the wrong place.

"There's moss on the roof," I said in shock, though my observation wouldn't mean anything to my husband. When I lived there, the roof had been bare plywood. Then I realized: of course it had moss on it—that was almost thirty years ago.

"Aren't you going to see if he's there?" James asked, and I shook my head.

Instead I stared at the front door, daring it to open. Was Barry in there looking out at our car? What would I say if he came outside? Would he recognize me? I tried to tell myself I didn't care one way or another. Everything was different now—I was an adult, my life had turned out pretty well, I had a loving husband. Yes. A husband who deserved to know a thing or two about my past.

I took a deep breath and turned toward James, and I told him what had happened in that house between Barry and me. He listened, said some sympathetic words, and then he told me about a friend of his whose story was more horrific than mine. I sat perfectly still and quiet beside him, almost jealous that his friend's story was flashier. It occured to me how twisted it was for me to feel that way—that if abuse was worse than dysfunction, then being raped was worse than being molested and being beaten was worse than being neglected. I was once again registering on the low end of the scale in my own mind.

As we drove down the hill again, I thought of the other husband I'd told my story to a decade earlier. From him I'd had a completely different response, one that had caused me to push him away and ultimately leave him. *Two husbands, two strikes,* I thought, and I vowed to never tell any partner, present or future, anything about my childhood again. I had finally come to understand something: those who knew the truth about me hurt me the most, because they made me feel like my pain was insignificant.

1977
Gulf Islands, British Columbia

The wind tugged wildly at my hair as I rode down the hill. Left bend, right bend, straight, another left bend and I was at the pond. I shot past it, pedalling furiously toward the little silver trailer at the edge of the woods. I prayed he would be home. I had run out of the house to escape Mom and Barry having sex, and if Art wasn't around, I wouldn't have anything to do except catch minnows in the pond. And I was really craving a Fluff sandwich.

It was a warm August morning, and I was seven years old. Nearly two years had passed since Shyla was shot, and I never thought about her anymore. I hardly ever thought about Karl either. He and Mom had broken up not long after we moved here. There were plenty of other things for me to think about now—like school, my friends and Mom's new boyfriend, Barry, whom we'd moved in with a couple of months ago. Living with Barry wasn't so bad. Even if he and Mom were always screwing, at least Mom was happy. And Barry hardly even glanced my way, except to tell me to clean up my corner sometimes. The house was a single room with their bed in the middle and mine in one corner, though Barry liked to remind Mom that he had big plans for walls and a toilet and a refrigerator and shingles on the roof some-day. For now I called it the "half-finished house," because that's what it was—just a plywood frame with some electric wires running through it and pink insulation stuffed in the walls. But at least I knew the cops couldn't come and roll this house up and take it away, the way they took our tent in Lake Minnewanka when they busted Karl for stealing it.

"Ding dong!" I said loudly at Art's front door. It was the way I always greeted him, because he didn't have a doorbell. Art had told me that fancy houses had doorbells. I didn't tell him that not only had I never had one, but I'd only just recently experienced walls.

"Doll!" he said as he opened the door, his wrinkly face crinkling into a smile.

Art was ancient. At least ninety, I was pretty sure, and barely any taller than me. I'd been visiting him ever since I moved into the half-finished house, and he was always happy to drive me to the lake so I could go swimming, or give me a snack of the most heavenly junk food I'd ever eaten. Actually, the *only* junk food I'd ever eaten. Mom would have killed me if she knew.

I walked into Art's tiny trailer and took a seat at his kitchen table. I loved how Art's home was full of little secrets, like the living room wall that slid open to reveal shelves and the second bed that pulled out from under his mattress. For when his granddaughter came to visit, he told me, though she never seemed to.

I smiled as Art opened a cupboard and took out a loaf of Wonder Bread. He spread a slice with Fluff in a perfect white cloud and pushed the plate across to me along with my napkin. This was the only thing I *didn't* like about visiting Art: he always gave me the exact same cloth napkin, and he never seemed to wash it. I could see smears of food on it from my last visit. I put my hands under the table and sneakily wiped them off on my shorts instead.

"So how's my beautiful doll doing today?"

I beamed. Art always had a compliment for me that made me feel all warm inside. "Pretty good. I was going to go to the lake today, but I . . . uh, left the house too fast to remember my swimsuit."

"Is that so? Well, maybe Art should just buy you a new one. Then you'll always have one here, just in case. Hmm?"

"Really? You mean—you'd *buy* me a swimsuit?"

"Of course! I'm going to Victoria tomorrow, to see my grand-daughter. I'll pick one up for you then."

"Wow. Thank you!"

I slid off my chair. For some reason, the thought of Art buying me a swimsuit made me feel shy. I excused myself and walked to the bathroom, locking the door behind me. I loved that Art had a real bathroom. At home we did our business in a porta-potty out back behind the house. As I sat on the toilet, my eyes fell on a book lying on a pile of magazines. The cover was kind of strange. A girl about my age was running away from the camera wearing nothing but a hat. I picked up the book and opened it. Page after page showed pictures of naked children. I leafed through it, wondering why anyone would want to look at kids' bodies, which were boring and all looked pretty much the same compared to grown-ups'. Personally I couldn't wait to get boobs like Mom. I put the book back and flushed the toilet.

"Um, I should get going," I said when I returned to the kitchen, stuffing the rest of the sandwich into my mouth. I headed for the door, still chewing.

Art hurried after me, limping on the bum leg that he'd told me a hundred times had gotten pulverized in some war.

"So soon? I thought we could play Yahtzee."

"Yeah, just . . ." I stopped at the door and shrugged, wondering what to say. I didn't want to hurt Art's feelings, but that book had weirded me out a bit. "I'll come back tomorrow," I said, turning away.

"You mean the day after. I'm not here—"

"Oh, yeah, I forgot." I ran down the steps, got on my bike and sped away. "Bye!" I pedalled furiously, knowing I could make it about a quarter of the way up the hill to home if I got enough speed up.

After I turned into our driveway, I propped my bike against a tree trunk and walked toward the house cautiously, listening for screwing sounds. All was silent, so I opened the front door. Barry was nowhere to be seen, and Mom was sitting naked on her bed eating scrambled eggs. Her long boobs swayed above the plate. I sat down beside her. Not only had the half-finished house not made it past the framing stage yet, we also didn't have much furniture.

"Hey, sweetheart," Mom said between bites. "Did you go for a bike ride?"

"Yeah. I went to see Art-from-down-the-hill." I always called him that, because if I just said "Art," she never remembered who he was.

"That's nice, honey."

"Yeah." I hesitated, and then I blurted it out before I could stop myself. "He's got a book of naked kids in his bathroom."

"Wow. Really?" She chewed thoughtfully. "What kind of naked kids?"

"I don't know. Just, you know, a bunch of kids running around at the beach and climbing trees and stuff. But they don't have any clothes on."

"Ah. Well, that sounds pretty harmless to me. I think it's great that your friend has an appreciation for the human body. You know when we lived in the tipis, we hardly ever wore clothes." She smiled at me and ruffled my hair.

"Yeah, I know. It's just . . ."

"What, honey?"

"I don't know. I just wonder why anyone would want to look at naked kids."

"Honey, your body is a beautiful thing. You shouldn't be ashamed to show it off," she replied through a mouthful of food.

"But—"

"What?"

"Nothing."

She patted my arm. "You don't need to be uptight about it, okay?" she said lightly, standing up to carry her plate to the basin.

I crossed my arms over my chest. Mom's words didn't make me feel any better, and I couldn't help wondering if Art would want to look at my body like he wanted to look at the pictures in that book. My tummy felt like it had a big rock in it, and I decided right then and there that I wouldn't go and visit Art anymore.

Two days later, I screeched to a halt in front of Art's trailer. Despite my promise to myself to stay away, the lure of a new swimsuit and a bag of potato chips was just too much for me to resist. I knocked quietly on his screen door.

"Doll!" he said, opening up. "You didn't ring the doorbell!"

"Oops, I forgot. Um . . ."

"Come in, come in."

I followed him into the living room, where he was eating his lunch. Art always ate food that came packaged on its own plate with little compartments to keep everything separate. He said they were called "TV dinners," because you could eat them in front of the TV without making a mess. I asked Mom to buy me one once, even though we didn't have a television, and she'd nearly had a heart attack. I didn't tell Art, though; I figured if he'd made it into his nineties by eating TV dinners, he wouldn't be too interested in Mom's ideas about food.

"I've got a little something for you," Art said, holding up a shopping bag. "You know Art always keeps his word, right?" He reached inside and pulled out a swimsuit. "What do you think?"

I grinned happily. It was dark blue with little white swans swimming across the waist. I took it and held it up in front of me. "I love it. Thank you."

"Aw, shucks. My pleasure, doll."

"So did you, um, see your granddaughter?"

"Sure did!" he said, smiling extra hard. "But can I tell you a little secret?"

"Sure."

He gave the tip of my nose a light tap. "I like you even better," he said in a loud whisper. "And I wish *you* were my granddaughter."

I was smiling as hard as he was.

"Now," Art said, "what say you try that swimsuit on, and we go to the lake to give it a whirl? You can change in there." He pointed to his bedroom.

I walked into the room and shut the door behind me. There was a mirror behind his door, and I'd never seen my body in a mirror before. I stripped my clothes off and stared. I looked like a stick person, everything too long and skinny. I picked up the swimsuit and stepped into it.

"Doll, I forgot to tell you—" Art barged into the room, and I jumped back with the swimsuit still around my knees. He stopped, staring exactly at the spot I didn't want him to. Then, with a speed I didn't know he had, he shot his hand out and touched it. "Oh . . ." His voice sounded funny. "That sure looks good, doll . . ."

A memory flashed through my mind, electric-fast. I was four years old, living in the Kootenay Plains. As I was peeing in the forest, one of my favourite Indian men stumbled on me and stuck his hand on my crotch. I pushed him away and ran.

Now I shoved Art's hand away, pulled the straps up over my shoulders, *snap snap*, and pushed past him out of the room. As I dashed for my bike, I heard him yelling.

"It's a compliment, stupid! You wanted it! You're no better than that daughter of mine—"

I pedalled until the wind whistled in my ears, drowning out the sound of his voice. *Damn it damn it damn it*, I swore to myself all the way up the hill, *it's my own fault. I knew he was a creep, and I should have stayed away*—up and up and up until I got home, exploding breathless into the empty house, stripping off the suit and stuffing it into the bottom of the trash can. Then I pulled on some clothes and lay down on my bed beside Suzie Doll and waited for Mom to come home, so I could stop thinking about that moment she would walk in the door and I wouldn't be able to tell her what had happened, because I was pretty sure she wouldn't even think it was weird.

Chapter 7

2007
Halifax

On a dreary day in May, four months after I began writing my memoir, I pronounced it finished. I closed my laptop with a satisfied sigh. I'd read my manuscript over several times, edited it thoroughly for grammar and punctuation, and even come up with a catchy title: *North of Normal*. I was certain it would be only a matter of time before publishers were fighting over it.

The following week, I stamped and addressed query letters to forty-five agents. Then I walked down the street and stood in front of the mailbox. Though I'd sworn off *The Secret*, just for good measure, I took a moment to visualize every single one of those faceless people writing me back with a positive response. This would work. It had to. I slipped the letters into the slot and hurried home. There was someone I wanted to share this moment with.

"Mom?" I said over the phone.

"Cea. How are you, darling?" Her greeting was more subdued than usual. She wasn't stoned, I realized.

"I'm good. Hey, I finished my book!"

"Oh, honey, that's wonderful. Can I read it now?"

95

"Of course. But let's just . . . see what the agents have to say first. It might need a little more editing."

It wasn't the first time Mom had asked me this question, and as usual it brought on a twinge of guilt. When I first told her I was writing my memoir, she'd been as excited as me. She'd even taken hours to help me put the events of my childhood into chronological order and fill in some forgotten stories. But my mother's opinion of our shared past differed vastly from mine. While I saw my childhood as something I had survived and turned out relatively well in spite of, she saw it as the key to any success I'd had. It was my undisciplined upbringing, she claimed, that had given me the freedom to become whatever I wanted. It was pointless to enter into this debate with her, as our chance of seeing eye-to-eye was about zero.

I could hear water running in the background. It seemed like whenever I talked to her on the phone lately, she was taking a bath. "Are you in the bathtub?"

"Yes. Just . . . feeling a little under the weather."

"Mm. Mom, I need to ask you something," I began, knowing I was inviting an argument. "Are you refusing treatment because it's *really* what you want to do or because you think your parents won't approve? I mean, Papa Dick . . . he's dead now. He died of *cancer*, Mom. He refused treatment too. Do you see a pattern here? I mean . . . what about your grandson? Don't you want to be here for him?"

"Of course I do, Cea. I don't expect you to understand. We're very different in our beliefs—"

"Yes, we are. Like I believe in living, for example."

"It's not like that. I believe in that too, but for me, giving my body up to radiation isn't living. You know how my family feels about such things."

My family. It was a term that revealed so much. It was no secret that I, with my suburban dreams and weakness for McDonald's fries, had never fit in with my mother and grandparents. And that even though Mom had had a child of her own for nearly four decades, she still considered her parents to be her primary family members. I could accept that; it was the rest I couldn't. I thought of how happy she looked when she was with Avery, of the quiet weekends I'd always imagined we would have together one day—*one day*, after she left her boyfriend and got her life together and acted like a mother. When would the selfishness stop? Very soon, I knew. Because after all her self-centred choices throughout my life, she was now making the ultimate statement that her needs and desires were more important than mine.

"Mom, I don't want to lose you. Okay? You're kind of . . . the only person I can talk about some stuff with. Like James." It was true. I could share things with her that I couldn't with my friends, because she never outright told me to leave him or cast judgments. What I *couldn't* say was that her ability to really listen to me almost made up for the many times she'd failed me. She was the only person I knew who always assumed things would get better—which was part of the current problem, of course, because she also assumed that *she* was going to get better. "Listen, Mom. I just . . ." I had to say it. "You're going to die. You know that, right?" My voice had come out in a hoarse whisper.

"You're wrong, Cea. I'm going to go now," she said softly, and hung up.

After that I sat for a long while, staring at nothing.

The best thing about Halifax Atlantic Superstore was that it had a liquor department right inside it. With Canada's strict liquor-sale laws, such convenient one-stop shopping was practically unheard of elsewhere. As I piled my cart with cheap wine, a fact that I didn't want to look at directly lingered at the edge of my consciousness. In these bottles was my coping mechanism, my daily disconnector and my reward for getting through another day. I'd once seen an article on alcohol abuse—*If you use alcohol to de-stress after a bad day, you're an alcohol abuser*—and all I could think was, *What other reason is there to drink?*

In any case, this was not the time to try to kick my four-glass-a-night habit to the curb, because today the darkness of depression was threatening to obliterate me. I'd once seen a movie where someone got trapped in an elevator and the walls began closing in, threatening to crush its occupant; right now, I felt like I was just barely holding those walls at bay. As I pushed the shopping cart into the produce section, I caught Avery's eye and forced a smile. He was sitting in the toddler seat, contentedly playing with his plastic driving toy. *Vroom vroom, beep beep, urrrrrch!* Avery was happy, and he didn't know that Mommy was on the verge of a nervous breakdown—that was one good thing, I thought. My mother was still alive—that was two. We had a roof over our heads and enough money, or at least enough credit, for groceries—that was three. And we were moving back to Vancouver. That was a fourth thing to be grateful for, though the absurdity of it certainly wasn't lost on me.

It had all transpired within the past few weeks. Ten months after moving our entire lives across the country, James had been offered a job in the very city we'd left behind. I knew there wasn't any point in mourning the amount of money and energy we'd spent on our failed Halifax experiment, so instead I embraced the positive—the new job itself, a return to a city that was familiar to me, having friends again, being closer to Mom, maybe even a fresh start—*another* one, that was—for James and me. I didn't even complain when James told me he'd need to leave Halifax before me to start his new job, leaving me to finish off a small renovation we'd started, pack up the house and put it up for sale, all on top of my usual tasks of caring for Avery and running my business. I'd managed to keep a smile on my face through it all—until yesterday.

The previous day had registered sky-high on my scale of worst ever. The morning had started with my receiving the very last response to my literary-agent query effort. Great story, the agent had written tactfully, but my writing needed work. That assessment had been repeated often over the past two months in various agents' rejection letters, but with this last one, my reality was undeniable: my book wasn't good enough to be published, and perhaps it never would be. My life story was not going to rescue me from my current life after all.

And then, as if that weren't bad enough, James and I had had the most horrible argument of our relationship that night. One that it seemed to me a marriage couldn't—and even *shouldn't*—survive. I wasn't blameless. I'd certainly made mistakes in our relationship. But I'd also apologized, compromised, thanked and truly *tried*. I hadn't fallen in love with James, I realized; I'd fallen in love with the little boy inside of him that I wanted so badly to heal, as if by doing so I could also heal myself. It was all so obvious now, and so easy to trace this back to my own issues with my family.

I knew I had to get out. But leaving my husband now would put me in a position that frankly terrified me. I couldn't even afford to rent my own apartment at this point. I had a struggling business that I couldn't keep up with and no one to turn to. As it stood right now, James and my plan was to live with his mother when we returned to Vancouver. If he and I split up, I would have nowhere to go. And my mother was dying; whatever money I had now needed to be spent on visiting her in Calgary before the inevitable happened. As so often in my life, I was struck by the reversal of our roles, that right when I needed my mother's help the most, I was instead tending to her needs and dealing with the fallout of her mistakes. It wasn't as if she even had to be dying right now—she had *chosen this*. Just like me, I thought. There was no doubt in my mind that I'd brought this entire shit storm onto myself.

Tears sprang to my eyes, and I realized I was about to break down crying in the dairy aisle. I turned away from Avery and dabbed at my face. Shoppers glanced at me and looked away quickly, just as I did when I witnessed such a public display. My mind spun, looking for a way out. There had to be one, there just had to be. After everything I'd survived, this could *not* be the life I would end up in. I took several deep breaths to steady myself and made my way to the checkout.

The sunlight was blinding when I exited the store. I slipped my sunglasses on as I pushed the cart to my car, thankful for the mask. Just then I noticed a woman standing at the curb, holding out a cup for spare change. And I noticed something else: there was a baby carrier resting on the sidewalk beside her feet. I stopped, unable to pull my eyes away. I'd seen plenty of homeless people before, but I'd never seen one with a baby. I turned my cart in her direction and stopped in front of her.

"Is that your baby?" I asked, peering down at the carrier. My heart lurched. Inside I could see a small face, closed eyes, chest rising and falling. He couldn't have been more than a few weeks old.

The woman nodded. "Yeah. It's been hard, you know? Trying to keep things together for him."

I nodded back. As I dug my wallet out of my purse and emptied change into her cup, I noticed her looking at the contents of my shopping cart.

"They were having a sale on my favourite wine," I said self-consciously.

"Oh," she said with a shrug. "I don't drink."

I dropped my eyes and reached into one of my bins. "Here—" I handed her a bag of apples and a loaf of bread.

"Thank you. Thank you so much," she said quietly. Then she smiled at Avery. "Your little boy is so cute."

"Thank you," I choked out, and turned away before she could see the tears in my eyes.

Suddenly I hated myself for being so self-pitying. This woman had it so much worse than me, not to mention that *unlike* me, she didn't even drink to drown her sorrows. I loaded the groceries into my car, and then, instead of putting Avery into his car seat, I let him sit in my lap in the driver's seat and pretend to drive. It was one of his favourite activities, one that I allowed him sometimes when I was desperate to complete a task—I'd sit beside him in the passenger seat and work on my laptop while he played. He giggled happily and grabbed at the dashboard switches and dials. As I watched him, shame swept over me. Could I really not pull it together for my child? And if I couldn't, if I put my own needs and desires before his, how was I any different from my mother? I thought about myself at Avery's age and forced myself to recognize how far I'd come. I'd created the life I'd dreamed of as a child—a home with two parents, regular meals, plenty of toys and some semblance of stability. My son didn't need to know how empty it felt for me. I had chosen—no, practically begged—to have him, and I had no right to let him down. I may not always have made the best decisions, but practice had taught me to accept the consequences of them and sometimes even turn them in my favour. If there was any way my marriage could be salvaged, I would find it. One thing I'd never been was a quitter.

"My angel," I whispered to Avery, pressing my face into his hair. "I won't give up. I promise you, I will not give up."

1977
Gulf Islands, British Columbia

I liked David, and I was pretty sure David liked me. Sometimes when we sang songs at music time, we could use our classmates' names, and David used mine even though nothing rhymed with "Cea." He even looked at me under his eyelashes when we said the Lord's Prayer every morning, and I wondered if he thought it was as dumb as I did. *Our Father who art in heaven, how will it be Thy name.* What did art have to do with being a father, and how will what be whose name? It made big fat zero sense to me, and I hated how we all sounded like hissing snakes when we said "trespasses."

It was the autumn of second grade. Art the pervert had touched my privates just a couple months before, but it wasn't like I ever thought about it. I found it was a lot more fun to think about David. He didn't say much, but he had wavy hair that fell over his forehead in a way I found appealing. And plus, he was the only kid in the class taller than me. When I caught him looking at me, my tummy did a little flip that was both scary and thrilling.

David and I rode the yellow school bus together. I always sat with Vanessa Eastgard, who got off two stops before mine. David sat a few rows behind me, beside his own best friend.

"I heard David say he wants to kiss you," Vanessa told me one day, and I rolled my eyes as if the idea grossed me out. But the thought actually made me a little excited.

One day after Vanessa got off at her stop, I was staring out the window when I felt someone sit down beside me. I turned to look and jumped in my seat. It was David, and he was smiling at me. I turned away quickly, feeling my face burn. He leaned in close to me.

"Get off at my stop," he said.

"But how . . . ?" *will I get home*, I was going to ask, but then I decided it didn't matter. I got off the bus behind him, and together we watched it pull away. Eventually the five or six other kids who shared David's stop disappeared from view. Silence filled my ears. We were standing at the side of the road with a wooded area behind us.

"This way," David said, taking my hand, and I followed.

As we wound through the trees, I tried to calm myself. I knew what was about to happen, and I was terrified. I'd seen plenty of grown-ups kiss before. Mom and Barry did it all the time, and before that, Mom and Karl. I'd seen my grandparents do it, and some of the summer visitors when they had come to stay with us in our tipi camps.

David stopped near a picnic table. "In here," he said to me, falling to his knees and crawling under it.

I followed and sat beside him without touching. It was cozy under here, like a little fort. I could smell pine needles and wet wood. David turned toward me and placed his hands on my shoulders.

"I like you. You're pretty," he said.

I tried to smile back at him, but I realized I was holding my breath. "Um, I like you too," I finally replied.

And then it happened. His face moved slowly toward me. Just as my vision of him was blurring, his lips were on mine. His eyes closed, so I closed mine too. A strange feeling welled up from the bottom of my belly. It was a feeling of not wanting to do anything else in the world except stay here as long as I could, stuck to David's mouth. I parted my lips slightly and let my tongue touch his.

"What—?" He jumped back as if I'd burned him. His mouth broke away from mine, his hands fell from my shoulders, and the few inches of distance between us became a foot.

I looked at him in shock. "I—I have to get going," I said, scrambling out from under the table. My head bumped against it hard as I stood up, but I didn't stop.

I fled through the trees toward the road and finally stopped to rub my head, hoping David would burst out of the trees behind me. But he didn't.

The next day at school, though I glanced at David way more times than usual, I never saw him looking at me.

Two months later, on a night shortly before Christmas, Barry crossed the floor in the half-finished house from my mother's bed to mine. When he made me touch him, I hated it, wanted it and then hated myself for wanting it. But at least with him, I knew just what to do.

Cocoa, flour, sugar and butter. Baking powder and a splash of white vinegar. I stood beside Barry's mother, helping her make a devil's food cake. She baked one every time we came for a visit. I loved everything about Irma's house—the fruity wallpaper in her kitchen, the clean blue water in her toilet, the candy dish in the living room that was always filled with chewy white mints. We used to come here every Sunday, before Mom started looking all sad. But everything had changed a few weeks ago, after Barry asked me to touch him down there and then gave me a Barbie doll for doing it.

"So, young lady," Irma said, beating sugar and butter together by hand. "How is school going?"

"Fine, I guess."

"You guess?"

"I don't know. It's just kind of . . . useless."

She scowled at me. "*Useless?* What are you talking about?"

I shrugged without answering, and she shook her head unhappily. "I tell you, I just don't get you kids sometimes."

This made no sense to me, because how could a grown-up not get kids when they'd obviously been one themselves?

I took a rubber spatula from a drawer, wishing I could think of something else to talk about. Irma was exactly how I imagined a regular grandmother looked and acted—slightly stooped over, with silver hair that she got set at the beauty salon once a week. A stickler for good manners, she placed hand-crocheted doilies under every dish in her house. Sometimes I tried to imagine Grandma Jeanne in Irma's shoes, but the picture was ridiculous. My own grandmother would be topless with a joint in her hand and wouldn't give a fig about manners or doilies. All the same, I missed her. It was three years since I'd seen my grandparents, and Mom wasn't even sure where they were anymore. Irma was right here, actually caring what happened in my life—but I couldn't tell her the truth about anything, because her son liked to press me up against walls and rub himself on me until there was a wet spot on his jeans. If Irma ever discovered our secret, I was sure she'd think I was the grossest person ever.

Irma finished mixing her wet and dry ingredients together and held out the wooden spoon for me to lick. I took it.

"So, do you care to explain yourself?" she asked.

"Oh, I don't know. Just . . . I guess sometimes I wonder if I should even go to school. I mean, Mom dropped out when she got pregnant with me, and she always tells me how there's no point to it . . . and plus, she was the only mom who didn't come to my school Christmas play . . ." My voice trailed off. I wondered why I was saying all this stupid stuff. I liked school and had never even thought of not going until this very minute. And what did I care if my mother didn't come to the school play? I knew perfectly well such things weren't her cup of tea. Even though the words had never been spoken, I understood the deal between Mom and me. She had had me too young and didn't know what to do with a child. Still, she had chosen to keep me. In exchange I was not to expect anything more than simply having a mother who loved me. And that was fine. Except . . . sometimes I wondered if she knew about Barry and me—after all, it happened just a few feet from her bed. Maybe I was just mad that she didn't know.

"Now you listen here, young lady. Stop talking such nonsense. You are *not* dropping out of school." Irma scraped her batter into the pans and turned toward me. "You are not your mother," she added in a quieter voice. Mom was only a wall away; I could hear her and Barry talking in the living room. "You're a strong girl. I can sense it. Your mother—she needs a man. To approve of her, to support her. But you will find your own way. Mr. Peterson—my husband—has been dead and gone for ten years now. I miss him, but my life's a heck of a lot easier now. Trust me, I know how men can complicate things. You learn to stand on your own two feet, and nobody will be able to push you around. You are *not* a girl who gives up, ever. Do you understand?"

I nodded mutely, surprised that she was talking to me like a grown-up. But I *was* a grown-up, practically. A memory flashed through my mind of me, standing in front of Barry and waiting for a signal from him. As always during these moments, my greatest wish was for a smile, and my greatest fear was no reaction at all—his eyes turned away as he lit a cigarette or shuffled through his cassette tapes for something to snap into the ghetto blaster. When he said nothing, I walked toward him, placed my hands on his shoulders and boldly straddled his lap. It was a memory from just a few days ago.

I swallowed hard. "Um, Irma?"

"Yes?"

Your son told me he wants to screw me. I opened my mouth to speak. I pictured the words tumbling out and hanging in the air. What would she say? Would she laugh and say I was being ridiculous? Tell me I wanted it just as much as he did? Storm into the living room and confront him, throw him out of her house? And then what? He would throw Mom and me out of *his* house, and we would have nowhere to go.

Behind me I heard the living room fall silent and then a match striking.

"What is it, dear?" Irma asked sharply.

"I—um . . . could we play gin rummy tonight? After we clean up, I mean?"

"Of course, dear, of course," she replied with a smile.

I plunged my hands under the running tap, feeling the burning water wash cleanly over my skin.

Chapter 8

July 2014
Vancouver

A **middle-aged woman raised by counterculture** parents, grateful to find a story she could relate to so closely. Still struggling to forgive her family for their choices, reading *North of Normal* had given her the strength to finally have a conversation with her parents about her upbringing.

A young man who suffered a childhood of extreme neglect, doing his best to raise his children in a better way, even though he'd been given no tools to do so by his own parents. Encouraged that he could find his own happy ending after reading my story.

A man who knew me as a child in the Kootenay Plains, expressing the profound influence my grandparents had had on his life. Assuring me that I'd captured Papa Dick's charms and flaws equally on the page.

A woman who'd lost her mother to cancer two years ago, appreciating the mix of emotions I'd experienced over my own mother's death. Like me, still struggling to make sense of the extremely layered and complex relationship they'd had. How did I define forgiveness, she wanted to know, because she herself wasn't entirely sure what the word meant.

An elderly woman who'd always felt like an outcast due to the crippling rheumatoid arthritis she'd had since she was a toddler, finally convinced she needed to write her own memoir after reading mine. Realizing her story mattered and that the time to make her dream come true was right now.

A kindergarten teacher who'd also had a Suzie Doll when she was little, curious about my ability to overcome adversity and wondering why some people seemed to be born with more resilience than others. Did I have any tips for her in dealing with the children she taught?

I sat at my laptop, smiling as I read message after message in my inbox. My book had been out for two months, and the fear I'd initially felt about receiving letters from readers had long since left me. At first I'd opened them cautiously, scanning quickly for negativity before daring to read in detail. Those negative words had never come. Instead I read stories of other women's struggles to find acceptance in their families and society, young men who dreamed of a life off the grid, teenagers fascinated with the hippie movement and elderly women who had nothing in common with me but admired my "spunk." My own friends had read my book and reached out in full support.

I thought about the people I'd made assumptions about based on appearances. Many of them had told me their own stories since reading mine, and often the reality of their lives starkly contrasted to what I'd imagined it to be. I realized that by believing they would judge me by my past, it was actually me who was guilty of passing judgment. People who read my book had as much to teach me as my story had taught them.

I turned my attention back to the screen. A reader, someone who had known my family once upon a time, wanted to know if I had any contact with my uncle Dane. Really, it was impossible for me to think of my uncle without inserting the word *crazy* in front of his name, because that's what he'd always been to me. I thought about the last time I'd seen him, when I was nine years old. Papa Dick and Grandma Jeanne had taken me with them to visit him at the mental hospital. He'd shown me an old photo of myself and told me my mother died in a fire. Earlier, when he came to live with us in the tipis for a while, he'd told me stories that scared and fascinated me: he had no bones in his body, the FBI was after him. "Do you know why we die?" he asked me once. "It's because of our skin. We only have so many layers, and eventually they all peel away. You can't live without skin to hold your organs in." I'd pictured myself old, lying on a bed with bones and heart exposed. That was the first inkling I had that he might be lying to me. Dane's mental illness had started young; according to my aunt Jan, he'd even molested Mom when they were just kids. All of this I'd written in my book, but I hadn't told everything about my uncle Dane.

I stared into the middle distance, trying to recall the words I'd written and then deleted. It was one of the last scenes in the book—right after Mom died, when my aunt Jan delivered my mother's apology to me for what had happened with Barry. There was something else she thought I should know, she said.

"The night in the cellar. When Dane snatched you from your mother and locked you in the laundry room with him . . ." Her voice told me something big was coming.

"Yes?" It was suddenly hard to breathe.

"There was . . ." She placed her face in her hand, avoiding my eyes. "Some blood. Down there, I mean."

Her words made my legs go weak, and I collapsed onto the bed. After I caught my breath, I looked at her as a new member of a club that no one ever wants to belong to—that of adults who'd been sexually abused by a family member. *That makes three marks of shame,* I thought. *Art, Barry, and now my own uncle.*

"Did Mom know? Papa Dick and Grandma Jeanne?"

She nodded. "Yes. I think they just thought—well, that you wouldn't remember it, so it wouldn't really affect you."

I shook my head in disbelief. That in itself was bad enough, but that they'd all known and yet let him back into our camp to live with us was inexcusable. All those weeks in Morley, they'd allowed him to be alone with me. Sure, Mom had asked me to stay away from him, but she'd been too busy with her lover to enforce it. My grandfather had gone on a hunting trip, and Grandma Jeanne had stayed in their tipi, doing her chores and whistling away as if it were nothing to be concerned about that her granddaughter was outside cavorting with the man who had molested her as a baby. This, I had decided, was not a story I could reveal to the world.

I grabbed the copy of my book that sat beside my computer and found that conversation with Aunt Jan. I could see exactly where the deleted passage would have been, among others in my book—holes in my story that no reader would notice, because they'd been skilfully patched over by the processed truth of memoir writing. Like the Darcy story, another I'd written and deleted. Darcy, my fourth mark of shame.

No wonder I still felt haunted. Worse, I felt like a fake. Readers went out of their way to thank me for being brave enough to tell my story, and I smiled right back at them, knowing full well I hadn't told the worst of it. What gave me the right to be so selective about the truth?

I put my book down and looked at the message about Dane again. I certainly didn't want to have any contact with him, but he was one of only a few living links to my past. If there was something someone could tell me that might give me some insight into my family's history, I wanted to know it.

Thank you so much for writing to me, I typed. *I don't have any contact with Dane, but I'd be curious to hear your take on him . . .*

I finished my message and sent it, my mind still spinning. Sometimes readers would ask me which memories had been the hardest to write about. Most people guessed it would be Barry molesting me, but writing about Barry had been easy: he was a man nearly four times my age who'd made me touch him, and in hindsight, I saw clearly that he was the abuser and I the victim. The hardest things to write about were the times in my life I felt I didn't matter, that I wasn't heard by my family, that I wasn't allowed to feel shame or modesty or have an opinion that differed from that of my freedom-obsessed family. Trying to navigate my way through the minefield of

Person beliefs—homeopathy, astrology, health food, artificial mood enhancers, freedom, nonconformity—and non-beliefs—religion, politics, consumerism, attachment, guilt, regret, expectation, obligation, education, authority, government, discipline—had left me with little room to form my own opinions other than "whatever's the opposite of theirs."

I still remembered the frustration of trying to make the adults around me see that their way of thinking was often outlandish and that my disagreeing with them didn't make me wrong. Especially when it came to fear.

1978
Yukon

I ran. Arms pumping, breathing laboured, rocks and shale cascading down the mountainside behind my panicked footfalls. I could hear the bear behind me, crashing through the bushes. *Papa Dick, Papa Dick, save me, save me,* my mind shrieked. Beyond that, there was no time to think. I was eight years old, and I was certain I was about to die.

Fear is the only enemy. It was something my grandfather always said to me, and I had believed him. Until this very moment.

"Go go go!" I heard Mark shouting behind me, sounding as terrified as I felt.

That only scared me more. After all, Mark was practically a grown-up and from the big city. I'd only been to a real city once, but I knew it had lots of calamity and traffic and people on every corner just waiting to beat you up or steal your purse. I could only imagine that it was a whole lot scarier than a tipi camp in the middle of the Yukon wilderness. At least until today.

Mark was a summer visitor. In the couple of months since I'd been living in the bush with my grandparents again, Mark had become my friend in a world with no other children. Mom and I had moved here after she and Barry finally broke up—at least I'd *thought* Mom and I were moving here, but as it turned out, she didn't stay. Shortly after we arrived at my grandparents' camp, Mom had told me she wanted us to start a new life in Calgary, but she needed some time to find a job and a place for us to live. It was decided that I would stay with my grandparents for a year, while she got things set up. I'd bawled as I watched her paddle away in her canoe. I hadn't expected to be so upset, because when she first told me the news, I'd been sort of relieved. The thing was, I now knew for sure that Mom knew about Barry and me. Worse than that, she wasn't even mad. I felt like throwing up every time I thought about it. But as I watched her go, another more terrifying thought crowded into my head: maybe she was leaving because she was secretly disgusted by me, and she was never coming back. As I gave her a last wave and watched her canoe round the point and disappear from view, there was only thing I wanted to do—chase after her and hug her and tell her I was sorry, so sorry. But it was too late.

My battling emotions about Mom made the chores of tipi life a welcome distraction. The amount of work to be done to keep the camp running was an endless cycle, and plus, I had my third-grade homeschooling to do. Coming back to the wilderness had seemed natural to me, but it also made me into a weirdo all over again. In the Gulf Islands, I'd begun to feel a little normal. Even though Barry was making me touch him, and we lived in a half-finished house, at least we lived in a *house* instead of some canvas shelter, and I went to a regular school with nice teachers and even had a few friends. Now I'd become the freak from the wilderness once more—and if I really did go to live in the city with Mom and if I wanted to have any friends, I'd have to act like this year hadn't happened. Because who was I going to talk to about hunting bears and eating fried grouse and mushing sled dogs and a grandfather who insisted I do my yoga naked and the way I knew it was morning each day by how the sunlight slanted into the tent I slept in all by myself? Nobody, that's who.

So it was Mark, my one connection to a world outside my tipi life, who made me feel a little better. I would tag after him while I did my camp chores, badgering him with questions about life in the city. He never seemed to mind, and sometimes he would play cards or hide-and-seek with me. We fished and hunted together with our bows and arrows, and he told me I was a good shot. He said he was planning to become a wilderness guide just like Papa Dick after he finished university, and I secretly wondered if we would still be friends then.

And that's how it happened that a bear was chasing us. This morning Mark had announced that he was taking a hike up the mountainside behind our camp, and I had run and put on my hiking boots without being invited. He just laughed and messed up my hair like he always did.

"Okay," he said to me. "But you better keep up. I'm not waiting around for you."

"No problem." I smiled happily. I loved hiking the mountainside. If I climbed high enough, I could see right down into the lake and feel like I was standing at the top of the world.

An hour into our hike, Mark said it was time to go home. I reluctantly pulled myself away from the berries I'd been picking and followed him back down the hill. It was late summer, but there were still a few flowers in bloom.

"Come on," Mark said each time I stopped to pick them, but I was intent on collecting the perfect bouquet to bring home to Grandma Jeanne. She hardly ever smiled anymore these days, and I thought flowers might cheer her up.

"Cea. Let's *go*," Mark said to me for the tenth time, clapping his hands together.

By then I was busy plucking rosehips off a bush. Grandma Jeanne loved making tea out of them.

Suddenly I heard a noise in the trees, a little up the hill. I stood up and looked, then I glanced at Mark, who shrugged. I turned back to my rosehips. Another sound, this time louder and closer.

"Probably a deer," Mark said. "Or a bear."

I nodded. Bears were nothing to be afraid of, I knew, as long as you didn't scare them, threaten their babies or run away from them. I'd run into them a number of times by myself and never had a problem.

"Let's get going. Just in case," Mark said.

"But even if it's a bear, we should just—"

Another crash, much louder this time. I looked at the treeline, expecting a large animal to come bursting out. A memory washed over me of Mom rushing out of our tent, yelling and screaming at an unknown enemy. That time it had worked out perfectly okay. I turned back to Mark.

"There's nothing—"

"Bear! Run! *Run run run!*"

Electric fear charged my body. I dropped my rosehips and tore down the hill as fast as I could. As I dashed around trees and jumped over fallen logs, I could hear Mark racing behind me.

"Don't stop!" Mark yelled. "It's coming! Don't look back! Don't stop, don't stop!"

I wouldn't look back, I told myself. But I had to. Just for a second, long enough to see Mark's terrified expression. He was running so fast the wind was pulling his hair back from his face. Then my foot caught on a rock. I tumbled to the bottom of the hill like a log and scrambled to my feet again, bruised and scraped. I was pretty sure my knee was bleeding, but I didn't dare stop. I set off again. I was almost back at camp. The ground was level under my feet now, but I was slowed down by my injured knee. I pictured the bear's jaws closing around my leg and pulling me to the ground. We were doing exactly what attracted bears most—running—and though my brain screamed at me to stop, I simply couldn't.

Up ahead through the trees, I saw the best sight in the world: Papa

Dick. He was at the chopping block, swinging his axe over his head as he split wood.

"Papa Dick!" I shrieked as loud as I could. "There's a bear! It's chasing us! Get your rifle!"

He turned to face me, axe held over his left shoulder with both hands, as if ready to swing and attack if he had to. I shot past him and finally stopped, safely behind him, turned and braced myself. But there was no bear. And the crashing had stopped, replaced by another sound: laughter. It was Mark, shaking his head as he gripped his sides. There was a rock in his hand. He threw it into the trees, and it made the same sound that had chased me down the mountain.

"Your face! You should have seen—"

In a flash, Papa Dick was in front of him. He grabbed Mark hard by the upper arm. Mark stopped laughing and looked at my grandfather in shock.

"What the hell is the matter with you?" Papa Dick hissed.

"But she was taking forever—"

"I don't care!" Papa Dick roared back, and I realized how seldom I'd heard my grandfather raise his voice. "You think it's a *joke* to make someone think a bear is chasing them? Leave your fear-mongering in the concrete jungle. You're lucky I don't make you pack your bags right now."

I looked at both of them in shock. I was embarrassed over Mark's joke, not to mention that my body was bruised and battered because of it, but I didn't want him to go home.

Papa Dick turned to face me. "What Mark did was wrong, Cea, but let this be a lesson to you too. Fear is nothing but perception, and often perception is far worse than reality."

"What does that mean?"

"It means what I've always told you. Fear is the only enemy, and only in weakness can it attack. Strength is the opposite of defeat."

I nodded, but really I didn't understand. Wasn't it normal to be afraid if I thought a bear was chasing me? Would it have been better if I'd stopped in my tracks and yelled at it that I wasn't scared? Was I really weak because I hadn't? In Papa Dick's eyes I was, because in this case I would have come face to face with the truth. But what if it *hadn't* been a joke?

A dark cloud fell over me. I didn't know what my grandfather expected of me, but if there was one thing of which I was certain, it was that I'd always disappoint him.

Mark walked over to me and took my hand. "Come on," he said quietly. "Let's get that knee bandaged up."

For a while after that day, I lost my easy comfort with the wilderness. Snapping twigs made me jump, and I rounded each bend along our lakeshore with my senses on alert for danger. But despite my confusion over my grandfather's words, they stayed with me. I wanted his approval. I wanted to be fearless, and I wanted to choose strength over defeat. But even more than that—and this was something I could never tell Papa Dick—I wanted to be flawless like my Barbie doll, who had an outfit for every occasion and never lost her smile. That doll had planted a seed in me that was now in full flower.

I'd first met Barbie when a summer visitor's daughter brought her to our tipi camp in the Kootenay Plains. Her perfect plastic face had stirred something in me. Something that had to do with female beauty and how beholding that beauty made me feel—awestruck, admiring, more curious about faces. And then when I was five, Mom and Karl had taken me to Calgary for a day, where I'd seen something at a department store that would change my life: two models walking a ramp for a fashion show. They were tall and skinny, just like me, and it was this observation that made it all click—the extra height I'd always hated could actually work in my favour. And Mom had told me I had the looks for it too. When I saw photos of myself, I saw green eyes, long eyelashes, a straight nose that seemed the right size for my face, a full lower lip. I wasn't certain I was going to be pretty enough to be a model when I grew up, but I knew I'd at least want to try. And I could only imagine the look of disgust on Papa Dick's face if I were to tell him so.

A few weeks after the incident with Mark, I was bathing in the lake. It was early autumn, and the water was freezing, but I still preferred washing out here to washing in the tipi. At least here I could have some privacy. I always bathed with my underwear on, just in case Mark or Papa Dick should happen by, though I knew he would give me hell for wearing them. Papa Dick had no patience for modesty.

I was rinsing the shampoo from my hair with an empty coffee can when I heard a sound. I turned and saw a male moose swimming toward me. Other than the *V* in his wake, the water around him was perfectly flat. His antlers, hung with long pieces of grass, loomed above the surface of the water. I froze, wondering if I should run up the trail to tell Papa Dick. We were due for a big game kill to store for the winter, and this animal was the perfect target—convenient, large and, most important, male and adult. Hunting had little effect on my emotions. We did it to survive, and I'd watched my grandfather shoot countless animals. I'd killed them myself, with my bow and arrow, and I knew that alerting him now would make me the hero of the day. But I wasn't so sure anymore that I wanted to be my grandfather's hero.

Not long ago, I'd been sitting in the tipi when a mouse skittered across my legs. Without even thinking, I'd shot my arm out and was probably as surprised as the mouse when I caught it in my hand.

"What should I do?" I asked Papa Dick, though I already knew I wanted to let it go. Its fur was soft, and its tiny black eyes were filled with terror as it squirmed helplessly in my hand.

"Kill it, of course," Papa Dick answered.

I looked at the mouse again, imagining my grandfather's disappointment if I let it go. He'd shake his head at me, throw out a line about ignoring the cycle of nature and then hide his face behind his book.

I squeezed the mouse as hard as I could, until I felt its tiny heart stop beating in my hand. Papa Dick smiled approvingly, but that didn't cure the sick feeling I had over what I'd done.

I watched the moose. When he reached the shore, he found his footing on the lake bottom, heaved himself to a standing position and scrambled onto the beach. He was less than twenty feet from me, with his head turned away toward the water. I took a step in his direction, and then another. He didn't move. I sucked in my breath and held it, and then I took another step. His massive head swung my way, and I jumped and dropped my eyes. When he didn't move, I slowly raised my gaze to his face. I knew I was being stupid, but I couldn't help myself. And what I saw in his eyes was so gentle, I felt almost as if he were smiling at me. I knew all too well what terror felt like, and I was happy not to see it in this animal's eyes.

We looked at each other for a moment, and then he turned away and walked down the beach in the opposite direction from our camp. A minute later, he turned and disappeared into the trees. I smiled to myself, feeling a little triumphant. I had challenged my grandfather's teachings, and nothing bad had happened. Maybe following my instincts was okay sometimes, instead of listening to the relentless storm of opinion that rarely seemed right to me.

Chapter 9

2007
Halifax

Sweetie. *Please,*" I said to Avery desperately. "Please just let Mommy do this. Then we can go to the playground, I promise."

I unwrapped my son's arms from around my legs and placed him on a chair. He started to howl. I turned away, fighting my instinct to sweep him up again. I'd been trying to get him occupied with something for the past hour, and nothing was working. He'd even ignored the TV when I put on his beloved *Cars* DVD, no doubt sensing my urgent need to be free of him. We were leaving for Vancouver the next day, James was already gone, Doris wasn't available, and I had a million things to do. We had started a renovation on the sunroom before we knew we were moving, and the trim still needed to be painted. There was clothing to be packed, my car to be returned to the leasing company, the refrigerator to be cleaned out, some last swimwear orders to be filled, and the promised trip to the park—and it was already two o'clock in the afternoon.

I grabbed my paintbrush and paint can, went to the sunroom and started slapping white semi-gloss on the windowsills as fast as I could. Avery fell onto the floor in a heap, screaming indignantly. I kept working, my blood pressure rising. Twenty minutes later, the job was finished and Avery was still howling. I plucked him from the floor and placed him in his high chair with some snacks. He threw them at me, flailing in his seat. My eyes welled up with tears. I sat on a box beside him, talking quietly and trying to soothe him. When it became clear nothing was going to work, I placed his sippy-cup back on his tray and walked to the basement to fill orders.

As soon I opened the door, I saw it: the floor was flooded. "Oh, *shit*!" I ran down the stairs, glancing at the culprit window and cursing myself for not having replaced the glass. It was broken when we moved in, so we'd covered it with plastic as a quick fix and forgotten about it—and yesterday it had rained in torrents. I lifted one of my swimwear boxes and inspected the bottom. Water crept four inches up the sides of the cardboard. Cold dread coursed through my body. I could still hear Avery yelling upstairs. I slipped my hand down the side of the box and felt the swimsuits along the bottom. They were damp. *Fuckfuckfuck*—

I heard a thud from upstairs and a blood-curdling scream.

"Avery!" I dropped the box and took the stairs two at a time.

He was lying on the floor with a sizable red bump on his chin. I snatched him up and hugged him to my chest.

"Oh, honey, I'm sorry. I'm so sorry."

I sank down on the floor with him, listening as his screams slowly turned to hitching sobs. When he was calm enough, I cradled him in my arms and looked down at his face, thanking my lucky stars he'd landed on his chin instead of his head. His eyes were fluttering closed. I took a few deep breaths, trying to still my mind and reset my panicked mood. As I stroked his cheek, I found myself wishing that Mom were here. She'd come to Halifax shortly after we moved, so she could watch Avery while I unpacked, and she'd wanted to help again this time but was too ill.

Avery's arrival in our lives had changed my relationship with Mom in a way I'd never imagined. Our frustrations with each other and tremendous differences of opinion were still there, but her love for my son and the effort she made to be with him made all of that less important. I'd seen the difference in her from the very beginning. I had allowed her to be present for Avery's birth, and for the first time in a long while, she didn't disappoint me. She flew into town, waited days until I went into labour and then helped me through it. I had handed Avery to her when he was a few minutes old. She gazed at him lovingly and then met my eyes with tears in her own. "I wish I could do it all again," she whispered. It was a kind of apology, I guessed, but also so much more. I realized then how sad it was that she'd never had a chance to experience motherhood with at least a little preparation and confidence, or to share her life with a caring man who could have helped her with me.

Months later, I'd needed someone to watch Avery while I did a swimwear trade show in Las Vegas. Even though she was already weakening from the cancer, she volunteered immediately. I flew her to Vegas, and she spent her days playing with Avery at the hotel while I worked my booth. One time I let myself into the hotel room to find them sleeping. Mom's body was curved around Avery's, and he was holding her thumb in his hand. He'd always been a fussy baby, unwilling to let anyone but me and sometimes James hold him. But he'd never hesitated to go to my mother, as if he understood the deep purpose he was serving both her and me. My son was the thing I'd always hoped would be important enough to bring Mom and me together again. That closeness would be snatched away when my mother died, but at least we had it for a little while. I realized in a way I had James to thank for that, because if we'd never had Avery, maybe Mom and I wouldn't have had our moment of harmony.

Avery was asleep in my arms. I carried him upstairs and placed him carefully in his bed. Then I grabbed a couple of buckets, put on my rain boots and went to the basement. As I bailed water under the dim glow of the hanging light bulb, a feeling of acute loneliness swept over me. Was I destined to face all of my life's trials alone, without support or guidance? Was I even *worthy* of such things? Even if Mom and I had managed to create some peace between us, the constant tumult of my unsettled thoughts guaranteed that I was rarely at peace with myself or my choices. Sometimes, I felt like I was at war with the life I myself had created.

1979
Calgary

I exited the city bus and walked fast, pretending the sidewalk was snapping at my feet like a hungry crocodile. Four blocks between here and safety. Cars rushed by, horns honked, crowds of people swarmed the busy intersection. I scanned the street for military vehicles; the coast was clear. Relieved, I hurried on.

I was nine years old, and city life was still new to me, and more than a little scary. Just six months ago, my grandfather had saved my life by pulling me out of the frozen lake at our Yukon tipi camp. One year ago, I had been shooting porcupines with my bow and arrow, chopping wood for the stove and helping my grandparents winterize our tipi for the long, dark, freezing months ahead. The years before that had been spent running from the cops for drugs and theft, living in the forest and squatting in abandoned summer cottages. Still, I felt almost nostalgic about those memories in comparison to the anxiety my new reality caused me.

Maybe it would have been easier if Barry hadn't been living with Mom when I first arrived. Mom and I had been apart for nearly a year, and I craved reconnection with her, but there *he* was, the most unwelcome face from my past. How could my mother not know that her taking him back was the worst humiliation of my life? I guess it didn't really matter, because a few weeks later, Barry packed up and left.

I came home from school one day to find his car missing from the curb and Mom moodily smoking a cigarette beside our lone window. I would have liked to think it was because of me that Barry left, that the pointed effort I'd made to show him I wasn't the same eight-year-old he'd coerced into touching his privates in exchange for a Barbie doll had had an effect. I'd scowled at him, refused to make eye contact and then finally outright told him he wasn't welcome in our home. I found this new side of myself both exhilarating and depressing. Tough Cea felt powerful, but also not who I wanted to be. I didn't like that life was requiring this new Cea, whom I didn't much care for, to emerge. I liked being nice. I liked to laugh and be happy. And when I was being Tough Cea, the happy, optimistic part of me got buried so deep I wondered if it would ever come out again.

It also occurred to me that I was doing the job my mother should have been doing. "What's wrong with *you*?" I asked her flatly when I found her crying at the window. It was obvious, of course, but I wanted her to think that Barry was so unimportant I hadn't even noticed his absence.

"Nothing for you to worry about, darling," she said with a sniffle, as if she'd spent her life shielding me from life's hardships.

For both my mother and me, Barry's departure meant shifting concerns. Since Mom's part-time waitressing job barely kept a roof over our heads, after he left there was very little to eat. I spent most nights staring into the darkness, wondering what would happen to us if we were tossed out of our home. It wasn't so long ago that the concept of homelessness equalled little more than another day on the road, another tent in the forest or another tipi camp. But now the thought was as hard and unyielding as the concrete at my feet that my grandfather had spent years warning me about.

I stopped at the intersection, looking around nervously for teenagers as I waited for the light to turn. Just a few days before, a gang of them had tackled me to the ground and spray-painted my hair green, guessing that I was a seventh-grader in need of a good froshing. They let up, even apologizing a little, when I started to cry and told them I was only in fourth grade. But the fear had been planted. Each day I spent my entire ride on the city bus to and from school watching closely for teenagers. The only thing worse than spotting them was seeing anything of a military nature.

The light changed, and I scurried quickly across the street toward home. For me, home was a basement suite with red shag carpeting. The single room featured a hot plate and minibar fridge in one corner, a wobbly table and chairs in another, and my mother's bed at centre, doubling as a sofa. With no space for a second bed, Mom had negotiated a room upstairs for me in the main house for an extra fifty bucks a month. That level of the house was occupied by three bachelors who came and went on mysterious schedules. One of them was rarely seen, another always gave me a wide berth when he happened upon me, and another, named Mike, was friendly enough to let me come upstairs to watch TV sometimes while Mom was at work. I didn't mind sleeping in the main house, because at least I had my own space where Mom couldn't have sex right beside me. She found me a faded floral bedspread and lamp at a thrift store, and I put an old sheet over a cardboard box to make a coffee table. Then I placed a dish of mints on it; I wanted people to feel welcome when they visited my room.

The last of the season's autumn leaves crunched underfoot as I strode up the walkway to my house. As always, I let myself in through the back entrance, dumped my school bag on Mom's bed and opened the tiny fridge. It would be another few hours until Mom was home, and I was hungry. I found some pickles, peanut butter and some of Mom's homemade bread, and I made myself a sandwich. Then I sat down at the little table, did my homework, tapped my pencil for a while and finally picked up my latest book, *Fear of Flying* by Erica Jong. I'd found it on Mom's bedside table and loved it from the first page, but today I couldn't seem to concentrate. I gave up and trudged upstairs to see if Mike was around.

"Hey," he said when I appeared in his living room. He was sitting on the sofa, eating cold pizza from the box and watching TV. Mike was a photographer, but he didn't seem to work all that much. I liked him though, because he always had a smile and a joke for me. "Why so glum?"

I shrugged. "Dunno. Just, um . . . have you ever heard of ABBA?"

"ABBA the band?" he asked, and then suddenly launched into "Dancing Queen."

I looked at him blankly. "Yeah, I guess so."

"Swedish. Two guys, two gals, top of the charts. Why?"

"Just . . . I was at school today, and everyone was talking about them. Jessica and Debbie and Nicole and Karen were, anyway, and then they asked me what my favourite ABBA song was. But . . . I'd never heard of them."

"Well, hey," he said with a grin, putting his pizza down. "We can fix that." He moved into a corner and started flipping through his record collection, muttering as he pulled each one out and gazed at it. "Bjorn and Anna . . . weird thing going on . . . got bored with each other or something . . . switched partners . . . " Album after album landed in the centre of the room, forming a messy pile, but my attention had been drawn to the television. I walked over and stood in front of it. I'd never seen the news before. A balding man with a deep voice was speaking, and there was a picture of a mushroom cloud beside his head. *Experts debate the threat . . . Soviet Union . . . nuclear fallout*, he was saying. I swallowed hard and turned back to face Mike.

"Um, I gotta go."

He tipped his head at me questioningly, ABBA record finally in hand. Four good-looking, bell-bottomed people smiled at me from the cover.

"What's the rush? Don't you want to hear 'Waterloo'? It's my personal fave."

"No. Sorry. Maybe later."

I fled down the stairs as fast as I could and lay on Mom's bed curling myself into a ball. Tears soaked my collar and Mom's pillow. I couldn't stop shaking.

Ten minutes before Mom was supposed to be home, I dried my

eyes, brushed my hair and started getting food out for dinner. Just picturing the confused look on my mother's face if she were to catch me crying was almost as terrifying as a nuclear war. First, Mom wasn't exactly an encyclopedia of knowledge—she probably wouldn't even know what a nuclear war was, so I'd be stuck trying to explain something to her that I barely understood myself. And second, she would have no words to comfort me. She would hug me, tell me I was being ridiculous and then light up a joint. No. The last thing in the world I needed was for my mother to ask me any questions about my current state of mind.

Thursday at school was my favourite, because it was library day. Not only did I get to escape into my lifelong salvation, reading, but since everyone else in my class was forced to do it as well, it was the one time each week I didn't feel like a total freak. I would glance around at the other kids and feel a hopeful sense of belonging. If they were losing themselves in the same worlds as I was—*The Secret Garden*, *Anne of Green Gables*, *The Black Stallion*—could we really be so different?

Mom had chosen my first city school based on its name, the Saturday School, thinking it made the whole concept of what she saw as forced education a little more fun. The kids there might be more like me, she explained, into health food and crafts and reading versus the latest program on TV. "I'm sure they'll be fascinated with your wilderness past, sweetie. You should be proud of it," she said to me on my first day. I nodded back at her, knowing very well I'd never tell a soul where I'd come from.

As it turned out, the kids at the Saturday School were just as into Wonder Bread and television as anyone else, and the only thing that seemed different was that we got to call our teachers by their first names. As for the other kids, they didn't hate me, they just thought I was weird and mostly ignored me. I always raised my hand in class.

I brought bulgur soup and peanut-butter-and-garlic sandwiches for lunch. I wore clothes that looked like they'd been retrieved from a trash bin, which in some cases they had been. I felt the power of my classmates' rejection as if it were a physical force. I saw their world as a mysterious and impenetrable fortress of normalcy that I would never have access to.

One library day, I finished the page I was reading in *The Secret Garden* and glanced up at the clock: twenty minutes left until the dreaded lunch hour, when I would eat my lunch alone and then sit on the swings by myself. I placed my book face-down on the table. Then I looked around for Rose, my teacher, thankful that she was nowhere to be seen. There was something I had to do, and she was another person I really didn't need any questions from.

At the beginning of the year, the librarian had shown us how to use the Dewey Decimal System to look up what we wanted to read. I went to the catalogue cards and flipped through *W* until I got to *War*. Then I found the correct shelf and withdrew one of the only books on the topic: *Understanding Nuclear Threat*. The book was thin, with the usual picture of the mushroom cloud on the cover, and it was aimed at preteens. I'd been hoping for a grown-up book, but this would have to do. I read it cover to cover right there and then placed it back on the shelf. The last line of the book stuck in my head: *It is unlikely we will see a nuclear war in this lifetime.* I took a deep breath, trying to draw comfort from that.

After library, Rose ended the class early by telling us she had something important to tell us. There had been an incident with a female student, she said. The girl, who went to another school, had been walking through the park next to our schoolyard when a man scared her. That was as much as we got.

"Don't walk by yourself," Rose instructed us. "Get your parents to pick you up in front of the school, or pair up with a friend."

Neither of these options was available to me, and I needed to cross the park to get to my bus stop. After debating whether to take the long way around and add fifteen minutes to my walk, I went ahead and hurried straight through the park. There were plenty of people around, including families with kids on the playground equipment.

But the next day it was snowing, so the park was nearly empty. Halfway across, I stopped in my tracks. *What if that guy showed up right now?* I wondered. *And what if he did something really bad to me? Would people like me then?* I thought about the kids from school who would gather around me sympathetically when they heard the news. It would be so different from the things that had *really* happened to me, like Art and Barry and . . . the other person I wouldn't let myself think about. Everyone at school would be in on it, just happy it hadn't been them, and it would have nothing to do with my family. It would just be bad luck, and bad luck was so much less shameful than the scars of my family's mistakes, which seemed an unwavering reflection of who I must be.

Against every imaginable odd, I was invited to Karen Harrison's sleepover birthday party in late winter. I knew that every girl in the fourth grade had been invited, so I debated with myself for days over whether to go. I knew I would be the outsider there, as always, but I also realized it was probably my only chance to try to make friends with them. I decided to go.

Karen had a pink canopy bed piled high with stuffed animals. I sat on the frilly bedspread shuffling through a stack of ABBA records while "Fernando" played in the background. Karen, her sister Debbie and three other girls were dancing crazily around the room, pretending to be girlfriends and boyfriends. To buy time, I held each record cover up one by one, acting like I was studying it carefully. The truth was, their antics made me feel a little yucky.

The doorbell rang, and all the girls screeched and took off down the hall. I stayed put. Chatter chatter, gab gab, and then Jessica and Nicole were in the room. They both stared at me for a moment, probably surprised to see me, but they didn't comment. Nicole was carrying something that looked like a toolbox. She broke it open and started taking out eyeshadow palettes, powder jars and lipstick tubes.

"You first," she said, pointing to Karen, who sat down in front of her in a vanity chair with a plushy pink backrest. Nicole began applying makeup to her friend's face, rattling on about spring and summer colours. One by one, she called each birthday guest to sit in front of her in the makeup chair. At the end of each session, the girl would look in the mirror and smile happily. I watched anxiously, wondering if I'd be included.

When everyone but me was done, Nicole put her hands on her hips and looked around the room with satisfaction. Then she jabbed a finger at me. "Your turn."

I got up from the bed, trying not to show my relief. She slipped a headband on to hold my hair back and stared at my face for a moment.

"My mom works for Mary Kay," she said, applying thick foundation to my skin. "Do you trust Mary Kay?"

"Um . . . yeah. Of course," I replied with a smile.

"Good. I'm going to be a makeup artist when I grow up."

"You should be. You're super ex-el at it," I said, copying the cool kids' word for *excellent*.

Nicole continued chatting away, doing something mysterious to my eyelids and then to my cheeks and lips. I tried to make interesting comments, but it was like someone had locked my personality away in a box and thrown away the key.

"You're done," Nicole said finally, whipping my headband off, and suddenly I had an awful thought.

What if she had made me up to look like a clown, just to be mean? She seemed so nice—but had I only been invited here today to be the brunt of a horrible joke? I glanced over at the other girls, but they were gathered around a jewellery box. Suddenly I found it hard to breathe. My heart kicked into triple time.

"Are you okay?" Nicole asked.

I nodded and jumped up and ran to the bathroom. After locking the door, I looked at myself in the mirror. I needn't have feared; Nicole had done my face up exactly like the other girls', with frosty baby-blue eyeshadow and sparkly pink lipstick. I looked older, and kind of pretty. My eyes were greener than usual, my lips rosier and my face grown-up in a way I'd seen it only once before: two years ago, when I had dressed up as a princess and won Barry's attention.

Trying to calm myself, I sat down on the toilet and put my head in my hands. They were sweaty. I wanted to stay in here all night, but I knew I couldn't.

"Thanks for the makeup job," I said to Nicole when I finally returned to the bedroom.

All the girls were staring at me. For a moment, I was certain they were all thinking the same thing: that the weird girl from their class didn't belong here with them and that I should just find a reason to go home. Then Debbie spoke.

"Wow. You look really . . . different," she said to me, and it didn't sound mean.

It was a compliment, I realized.

"Yeah," Nicole added. "I think you're maybe, like, the prettiest girl here."

"Thank you," I said shyly, turning away as my cheeks burned. I couldn't believe how nice they were being, and it took me a moment to realize something that was probably obvious to everyone else here: looks mattered. A lot. If you were pretty enough, people would want to be your friend. I'd heard that I was pretty before, but it had always been from the wrong people—Mom, who didn't really count because she was supposed to tell me so; my uncle Dane, who was crazy; Karl, who wasn't exactly Mr. Honesty; and Barry, when he'd been getting me to touch him. This was different. This meant that maybe I could actually realize my dream of being a model. The thought gave me an odd little surge of hope that I'd never felt before.

Karen got up from her bed. "Here," she said, holding a hand out. In her palm, two gold stud earrings with pink stones glittered at me.

"Thank you," I breathed. "But . . . I don't have pierced ears."

"Wow, really?" She pushed my hair away from my ears to see for herself. "Why not?"

"My mom won't let me."

"Really? She must be really strict."

"Yeah," I replied, smiling ironically. "That's my mom, all the way. Super strict."

Mom had always loved to party, and now that we lived in the city, she had plenty of opportunities to do so. She had no shortage of pot-smoking, free-loving friends who enjoyed a good time just as much as she did, so it seemed like nearly every weekend she and I would be out at some potluck or another. I was always the only kid there, which made it both fun and dull for me. The beginning of the evening was the fun part, because all of Mom's friends would fawn over me and bring me food and special drinks without alcohol in them. It was after the drugs came out that it got not so fun. People who had chatted with me an hour ago suddenly didn't even seem to know who I was. Others rubbed their bodies together on the living room dance floor, and sometimes more than two of them would start kissing together. Guys stumbled and fell, and ladies laughed too loudly. The worst was that every now and then, I'd get cornered by someone—usually a guy—who'd want to talk to me all night about something really boring, like good communication or human sexuality or the beauty of life or blah blah blah, and I'd practically fall asleep while they were yammering away at me. A few times, I'd even been passed the joint or hash knife as it went around. "I'm only *ten*," I'd say hotly, folding my arms over my chest with a scowl. For whatever reason, this would get a really good laugh out of whoever was offering.

After a few of these parties, I figured out my best strategy was to find an empty bedroom and lie down with a book. I'd usually fall asleep, only waking up as Mom was piling me into some guy's car for a ride home. He would almost always still be there when I came down for breakfast the next morning, passed out beside Mom in her bed. Though I'd pretend to not even notice them, the guys were pretty nice to me. And I didn't mind them too much either, because for the time they were there, Mom was happy. And even better than that, since I had my own bedroom, I didn't have to listen to them going at it all night long.

A couple of weeks after Karen's birthday, Mom and I went to a party at her friend Eva's house. Eva was my favourite of all of Mom's friends, because even when she got really stoned, I could barely tell. I headed for the food table, ate some quiche sprinkled with sunflower seeds and settled on the sofa next to a guy wearing a turban. His eyes were as twitchy as his fingers as they plucked at his orange robe. Just as I was wishing I had a book to hide behind, Mom passed by, joint in hand, and plunked down beside me.

"Sweetheart," she said in a breathy voice, planting a wet kiss on my cheek. Her skin smelled like pot smoke and patchouli. "Are you having a good time?"

"Sure." I drew my legs onto the couch and reached up to touch my earlobes. "Can I get my ears pierced?" It was a question I'd asked at least twenty times, and I'd told Karen the truth when I said my mother wouldn't let me. Naturally the only thing in the entire world Mom forbade me to do was the one thing every other girl was allowed to. That and cutting my hair, which I'd all but given up asking for. It currently reached past my elbows, because Mom hadn't so much as trimmed it for a few years. I'd been dreaming of a sassy bob for just as long.

Mom cocked her head at me. "Sure."

My mouth fell open. "*What?* Seriously?"

"Sure."

"Thank you, *thank you*!" I threw my arms around her, already envisioning the glittery rhinestone studs I was going to pick out at the piercing place in the mall.

"You're welcome, sweetheart. But just one, okay?"

"One what?"

"One ear. That way you can, you know . . . try it out."

"But I—"

"Darling, please. This isn't easy for me. I need to do it in small steps. You can choose, left or right."

I gazed at my hands, wondering how I would explain this at the piercing place. "Okay."

"Fantastic!" Mom clapped her hands together as if the whole thing had been her idea. "Now, where's Eva? Have you seen her? I'm sure she has a needle and cork around here somewhere."

"Needle and . . . what?"

Mom was already flagging Eva down from across the room and pointing at my ears. "Darling, there's no point in paying for it when we can do it for free. And I'm sure it won't hurt a bit. It's not like we haven't seen it done before, right?"

It was true. Mom had taken me to a party several years ago, during the brief time we'd lived in Nanaimo, and I'd watched a lady pierce her friend's ear with a needle and a cork. And just a few months ago, we'd seen a guy get his lip pierced the same way.

Eva floated over to me, dark curls spilling over her long turquoise caftan. "Mom finally relented, huh?" she said, smiling at me. "So, which ear?"

I pointed to my right, and she clamped an ice cube on either side of my earlobe. I watched as she threaded a needle with black thread.

"Sorry I don't have an earring to give you, but this should do. Ready?"

I nodded.

"Okay, here goes."

She placed the cork behind my ear and lifted the needle. I clenched my teeth. It hurt, but just for a few seconds. I felt the thread pull through, and then Eva cut the needle off and knotted the thread into a small hoop. I touched the new hole gingerly.

"It'll heal in about a month," Eva said. "Don't forget to pull the thread back and forth every day, or it'll get stuck in there. When it heals over, I'll give you a nice earring to put in."

"Thank you," I said happily, giving her a big hug. In my head, I was already planning how I would hide my makeshift earring from the other kids at school. In four weeks, I would be just a little bit closer to normal.

Nicole had a waterbed and three rollerball lip glosses that tasted like fake grapes, cherries and something called root beer that I'd never had before. We sat on the floor of her bedroom, applying the gloss, licking it off and then applying it again in an endless cycle. Between us sat a paring knife from her kitchen and two unopened Band-Aids.

"I can't believe Mom said you were a winter. You're totally a fall," Nicole said, circling her lips until gloss dribbled down her chin. "Brown shadow goes on green eyes, duh."

"Yeah."

"Not like me, I'm a summer. Brown eyes, they can take pink and blue shadow. Who do you like better, Anna or—?"

"Anna," I said immediately.

Naturally, ABBA was playing in the background, because Nicole also had her very own record player. I loved everything about Nicole's bedroom. I'd come over to her house a couple of times since Karen's birthday, and tonight was to be my first sleepover. I was still secretly glowing from the compliment her mother had given me at the dinner table. *See that, Nicole? Cea eats all her vegetables, and she doesn't even ask for ketchup.* While it was true that growing up in the wilderness had made me the world's least picky eater, I would never tell

Nicole's family that, because I wasn't about to do anything to ruin my official best night ever. The fun seemed to never end—Nicole's mom was in the kitchen making us popcorn right now, and after that—not that her mother knew about it—Nicole and I were going to cut our fingertips with the paring knife and become blood sisters. All the girls at school were doing it during lunch break.

Nicole had come to my house once, and I'd kept her out of the basement by sweeping her immediately into my bedroom. It was only when I sat her on my bed with a mint that I started having regrets. Running downstairs for a snack would be awkward, as would explaining the bachelors. As she looked around the room, I saw questions in her eyes. My bed was just a mattress on the floor, and besides Suzie Doll, I didn't have any toys. But when she didn't say anything and still talked to me at school the next day, I knew she was a true friend.

"Hey," I said to her suddenly. "Do you know if they ever caught that guy?"

"What guy?"

"You know, the one in the park. The one who scared that girl."

Nicole shrugged. "Dunno."

"Hmm. Because . . ."

"What?"

I looked out the window. Cars slid by over the slushy pavement. "I don't know. Do you ever, like, wish you could just get it over with? Because you know it's going to happen eventually anyway, I mean?"

Nicole was looking at me blankly. "Get what over with?"

"Like, *sex*. You know."

She frowned, and I realized she had no idea what I was talking about. How could you be ten years old, I wondered, and not know what sex was? I'd known since I was two.

Just then I saw a military truck through the window round the corner and pass Nicole's house. I could see two soldiers in uniform through the truck's windshield. *No*, I thought. *Not tonight.* My heart slammed in my chest. I clasped my hands together, but they wouldn't stop shaking. Finally I stood up from the floor on shaky legs.

"Um, I'm really sorry, but I have to go home."

"What? You're *leaving*?" Nicole asked incredulously.

"Yeah. Sorry. I forgot to tell you that I'm not allowed to spend the night."

"But you brought your sleepover bag—"

She was looking at me like I was crazy. I should have been embarrassed, but I felt too sick to care. "I'm sorry," I said again with some effort, grabbing my bag. I had to get out of there.

"Dad!" Nicole yelled, her eyes still on me. "Cea has to go! You need to take her!"

Her father appeared at the bedroom door.

"It's okay," I said to him. "I'll take the bus."

"Of course you won't. I'll drive you."

Twenty minutes later, I let myself into my house. Mom was out, probably for the whole night, but I had already known she would be. That was okay. The bachelors were upstairs in case I needed anything. They were having a party tonight, with loud music thumping through the ceiling. I decided to sleep in Mom's bed, where it would be a little quieter. I lay down and waited to stop shaking. Eventually I did, but the music wouldn't let me sleep. After tossing and turning for a while, I finally got up and walked into our tiny bathroom.

I stared at myself in the mirror. Nicole had done my makeup tonight, so there was mascara smudged under my eyes. I soaked a washcloth, cleaned my face off and brushed my tangled hair. Parted in the middle, it hung straight down on either side of my face. Exactly like Mom's, except lighter. I hated it. I didn't even know exactly why I hated it, except that I wanted to cut it and Mom wouldn't let me. For men, she'd said, because I was supposed to be pretty for them.

I opened the drawer, found some scissors and held a handful of hair away from my neck. The scissors made a dry snipping sound as my hair fell to the ground. Since I couldn't reach the back very well, I just did the sides. I knew Mom would be furious, but she'd have little choice but to finish off the job tomorrow. I put the scissors down and ran my fingers through one side. It felt strange to reach the end of my hair so quickly, and my neck felt bare and cool. It wasn't the style I'd imagined, but I didn't care. In the mirror, I saw the me I wanted to be.

Mission accomplished, I went back to bed. As I lay there, I thought about Nicole lying asleep in her gurgling waterbed. I should have been there right now, but I'd ruined it. As I drifted off to sleep, my last thought was to wonder if Nicole would still talk to me at school on Monday.

I wasn't much of a television fan, but every now and then I liked to watch *Three's Company* on the bachelors' TV set. One day after school, I was doing just that when Mike sat down on the sofa beside me.

"Hey," he said, handing me a large yellow envelope. "I thought you might like to see this."

I took it and reached inside, pulling out a black-and-white photograph. It was a picture of me sleeping, lying on my side with the faintest smile on my lips.

"Your mom asked me to take it," he explained. "To capture your innocence."

"Really?" It seemed like a strange thing for Mom to say, but it was getting harder and harder for me to understand her at all these days.

"Anyway, you're very photogenic," Mike continued, looking down at the photo. "That means you take a good picture."

"Thank you." I smiled at him, but I only had eyes for one thing. A few weeks before, my ear had finally healed, and as promised, Eva had given me a small silver hoop to replace the thread. The hoop was lying against my jaw, and there was something about it that made me feel incredibly normal. I was Cea Person, and I had . . . well, one pierced ear at least. Nicole still talked to me at school, even if she looked at me a little differently. And despite Mom's utter distress over it, I had a decent-looking bob that fell just below my chin. Maybe I wasn't completely powerless over my life, and maybe everything was going to be just fine.

"Mike," I said quickly, before I could stop myself. "Is there going to be a war?"

He tilted his head at me questioningly. I rushed on.

"Like . . . I mean a nuclear one, or whatever, that's going to kill us all? Or maybe just some, and then the rest of us will have to live underground for a long time until the mushroom cloud goes away and stuff?"

"Of course not." He looked upset. He put a hand on my back and patted it a little. I stiffened, then relaxed again. "Where did you hear that?"

I shrugged. I really had no idea. Mom had never talked to me about war, and my grandparents certainly hadn't. Any topic of a political nature was either forbidden or completely ignored in my family. I hadn't heard anything in the news other than the one time on Mike's TV, and we hadn't talked about it at school. I hadn't really known what the word *nuclear* meant until I'd read that book in my school library. All I knew was that since a couple of months after I moved to the city from the Yukon, I'd been plagued by images of a nuclear bomb going off, sending the earth's population running for cover. I wasn't even sure if I wanted to be one of the lucky few who survived it. Yet admitting that I was scared didn't seem an option. If Papa Dick didn't even think a bear attack was worthy of fear, how could *anything* be?

"I . . . I don't know," I said honestly. "It just seems like . . . Couldn't it happen? I mean, for real, right now?"

Mike shook his head. "No, Cea, it's not going to happen. Okay?"

"Okay," I replied, wanting desperately to believe him. "Yeah. Okay."

Mike's hand was back on my shoulder, patting it like I might pat a kitten with a broken leg, and I knew right then that Mike wasn't Barry. I fell against his shoulder and sobbed, holding his arm until his sleeve was soaked through with my tears. All the stress of the past six months came spilling out of me—the loneliness, the rejection, the relentless fear of war, and the discovery of my shameful past by others. Mike was a good man, a normal man, a man my mother would never look twice at. And he had been a friend to me, as had Nicole. I could make friends. Normal people could like me. There was hope.

Chapter 10

2007
Calgary

Mom," I said, hugging her. "It's great to see you."

"You too, sweetheart."

I stepped through her open door and smiled, even though the sight of her pinched my heart. My mother's skin and eyes looked sallow, and her bones were closer to her skin than I'd ever seen. Clearly she was on her way out. The whole thing still seemed surreal. Mom was fifty-four years old, and until just recently, she had always looked a decade younger. People were forever mistaking us for sisters.

"Hey," I said, taking Avery's coat and shoes off. "What do you want for dinner tonight? I'll make you whatever you want."

Avery trailed after me into Mom's kitchen. I glanced around the corner into the living room, praying Sam was still at work. Coming to visit my mother was always so awkward. It was all I could do to swallow my resentment and smile—just like I'd been forced to do with him when I was a teenager.

After dinner Mom read a book to Avery in the living room, while I cleaned up. Seeing them play together always filled me with an odd mix of joy and sorrow. When I thought about where she and I had been when I was Avery's age, living under canvas, me chasing after her while she chased after her dream of love and romance, I wondered if she ever reflected on the different choices she could have made for both of us.

I refilled my wineglass and joined them on the sofa. After a few minutes, Avery slid onto the floor with his bulldozer.

"How's James?" Mom asked after a moment.

"Okay. We're trying. But ever since we moved back to Vancouver . . . well. Let's just say living at his mother's house hasn't made things any easier. Nothing to do with her, just—I feel like we need our own space and, well . . ." *I can't leave him until you die*, I didn't add, *because my sanity just won't take it.*

Mom squeezed my hand but said nothing. One thing I'd always admired about her was that she insisted on seeing the good in people. Though it was obvious to me now how mismatched James and I were— that we'd even made it past the first date seemed unfathomable— she'd never criticized him to me. Indeed, my marriage was like a wounded animal lying in the snow, just waiting for the life to bleed out of it.

But we had Avery.

"Gamma 'Shell?" he said from the floor. "Pay wif me, okay?"

Mom lowered herself to the floor and zoomed his bulldozer across the rug a few times, and then Avery threw his arms around her lap and hugged her. Mom's eyes filled with tears.

"Mom," I said softly. "You're a great grandma." Then I snapped a photo of them, trying not to know this might be the last picture I would ever take of them together.

The next day, Mom said she felt well enough to go shopping, so I helped her into the car and drove her to the mall. Shopping together was the one activity we seemed able to engage in without finding a reason to argue. But by the time we pulled into the parking lot, she was already looking exhausted. I walked her slowly to the customer service desk and rented a wheelchair. Avery insisted on riding on her lap, which she allowed for a few minutes until it became too uncomfortable. A sense of surrealism returned, as I pushed my mother past Aldo, Smart Set, Le Château. I was only in my thirties—how could the woman who had given birth to me at age sixteen possibly be in this state?

At lunchtime I parked Mom at a table in the food court. "Sit side Gamma 'Shell," Avery said, scrambling up on a chair beside her.

I passed Mom's handbag over. She pulled out an alfalfa sprout sandwich, a sliced avocado and a handful of Chinese herbs. I got sushi for Avery and myself and tried to eat, but I had no appetite. I watched as Mom crammed too much food into her mouth, licked her fingers and wiped her hands on her pants. In the past, I'd been humiliated by so many of my mother's unacceptable habits, but now I just studied her in a detached sort of way. She'd always lacked basic life skills—and who was to blame for it? Her parents seemed to be the obvious answer, for out of a stubborn determination to buck societal expectations, they hadn't taught her such things. But nobody had taught me either. As usual, whenever I tried to puzzle out questions about my family, the hows and whys of their eccentric traits left me feeling even more confused.

I cleared my throat. "So . . . I've been working on my book lately. It's going well. I'm almost ready to query agents again."

"That's wonderful, Cea," Mom said with a smile. "I can't wait to read it."

I nodded, drumming my fingers on the table. "Mom. Do you ever hear from Jessie or Jan?"

"Not Jessie," she replied through a mouthful of food. "Jan comes around every now and then, but she's not doing well. Drugs and such, you know."

"What about Dane?"

"Still in the loony bin, I guess." Her eyes dropped, as they always did when my uncle's name came up.

"Mm. Papa Dick—you talk to him sometimes. Didn't he come through Calgary not long ago?"

"A few weeks ago, yes."

"And did he see Jessie and Jan? Did he even *ask* about them?"

She fixed her eyes on her sandwich. "It was just a short visit—"

"Okay, so no. Does he *ever* see his other kids? Has he ever tried to help them?"

"Not that I know of."

"Not that you know of—so that means no too." I cradled my head in my hands. Not for the first time, I wondered what my grandfather's true motivation had been for moving his family to the wilderness. Had he really believed he was doing something helpful for his kids, or did he do it just because that's what he wanted to do, and his children were a burden he was forced to bring along?

"Mom. Do you think he's ever stopped to think that he might be responsible for some of his children's problems?"

"Cea, don't be so hard on him," Mom said. "He loves them, he just can't—"

"—be bothered with them," I finished for her. I gazed up at the ceiling, feeling agitated. "You know, Mom, I've been working through a lot of stuff since I started writing, and remembering a lot of stuff. About Karl, for example. He was pretty nutty, but he was a good guy. He tried to be there for me. And then there was Barry." I watched her face carefully.

"Yeah. Crazy Barry." She shook her head and fell silent.

I thought of my eight-year-old hand landing on her boyfriend's penis, only to meet her fingers as they rested at the same place. Was she really never going to admit to me that she'd known, that she should have stopped it? Was it possible that she'd even *forgotten*—that it had been such a non-event to her that it had faded from her memory?

"Mom," I said, folding my hands in front of me and locking my eyes on hers. "I'm really trying to come to terms with a few things here. You and me—we've never been better, and I'm grateful for that.

But it doesn't change what happened in the past. So much went on, and I have questions. I mean, why do you think all your siblings are so messed up? And do you think Papa Dick ever thought about the consequences of raising a child—me, I mean—outside of society? And—"

"*Cea*," she said urgently. "Why do you have to dwell so much on the negative? Your childhood was beautiful. You were raised in the wilderness and given every freedom you could ever have wanted. You had a mother who loved you, and that's so much more than a lot of children had. Be grateful for that. So many kids had it so much worse than you did."

"Yes. And so many kids had it so much better."

My sentence hung in the air, suspended over a background of mall chatter. It was the first time I'd said such a thing out loud, and I was instantly filled with guilt.

"Listen," I continued calmly. "I'm not trying to judge here, I'm trying to understand. All I know is that I feel depressed and disconnected and like I can't make sense of anything, and I think I've felt like this my entire life. I don't know what anything means. I don't understand why I went through so much as a child, and why now I'm going through a completely different kind of hell." I could hear my voice rising again. "Because that's what it was sometimes when I was a kid, Mom, it was hell! I get that you don't want to accept that, but it was!" She was looking at me with big, sad eyes, but they just fuelled my rage. "And you know what? It's still hell between us, because you're still with *him*, and it reminds me every single day that the men in your life have always been more important to you than me! And now here we are, sitting in a goddamn *food court*, of all places, and now that you have a grandson and we're finally getting close again, you're freaking *dying*, and you refuse to do anything about it! None of it makes any sense, and I just don't know what the fuck to do!"

Avery was staring at me, and I could feel the scornful eyes of passing shoppers.

"Cea. Stop it," Mom said softly.

She's right, I thought. *This is not the place.* But I didn't care. My mother could be dead within weeks. If there was anything left unsaid, I had to say it now.

I leaned forward in my seat and lowered my voice. "Mom, you don't even know everything I went through. I couldn't tell you, because you were so caught up in your *freedom*, and I didn't fit your image of it. How many times did you dismiss me as being uptight just because I wanted you to protect me from things a kid shouldn't experience?"

She stared at me, and for a moment I thought I'd gotten through to her. Then she picked up her sandwich again.

"I did the best I could, Cea," she said quietly, and she went back to eating.

I shook my head angrily. So this was it, I thought. My mother would die, and with her any answers to my burning questions or any hope that she would take responsibility for her mistakes. Because apparently, my family's ways were a burden only to me.

1981
Calgary

My youngest aunt looked exactly as I remembered her. Seven years had passed since I last saw her, a span of time that had brought me to the threshold of my teen years and Jessie into womanhood. Her face looked the same—long and thin, teeth thick with yellow plaque— but she was chunkier now, which wasn't surprising considering the current circumstances. I stood awkwardly beside Mom in Jessie's doorway, wondering if she was going to invite us in. I could see her husband behind her, smoking a pipe as he sat in a worn armchair. He hadn't even glanced our way yet.

"Jessie," Mom said with a smile. "It's wonderful to see you. Are you going to let us in?"

"Oh. Sorry, I forgot," she said, stepping aside. Her voice—loud, slow, each word enunciated with great effort—had not changed either. My aunt had been born mentally handicapped, but she managed, just barely, to look after herself and her like-challenged husband.

We made our way into her tiny living room. Her husband finally looked up at us, gave us a stiff salute and went back to his pipe. The place was a shambles. Dust bunnies resided in every corner, the carpet looked like it hadn't been vacuumed in weeks, and dishes were piled on every surface of the tiny galley kitchen.

"Jessie. Do you have some dish soap? Let's just do up these dishes here," Mom said, moving toward the kitchen.

I followed, and Jessie trailed after me.

"But . . . don't you want to see the baby?" she asked disappointedly. "I named her Grace, you know. After Dad's sister. The one that died."

Mom nodded. Jessie had called us just a few days ago to deliver the news about her baby, and I could still hardly believe that I finally had a real cousin.

"Yeah, Mom," I said, grabbing her hand and tugging on it. "Let's go see her now."

Jessie led the way into her bedroom. The blinds were drawn, and the room was lit only by a dim night light. Beside the double bed, a crib had been set up with a Winnie-the-Pooh mobile dangling above it. I saw a lump on the mattress, but I was distracted by the sight of poster boards taped around the room. Each had a single sentence written on it in large black block letters. GRACE NEEDS A NEW DIAPER AFTER EACH MEAL, read one. DON'T FORGET TO FEED GRACE EVERY THREE HOURS. GRACE NEEDS TO BE PICKED UP AND HELD EVERY DAY. IF GRACE CRIES, REMEMBER NOT TO GET ANGRY WITH HER.

"Who made these?" Mom asked, waving at the signs.

"Carol. At the health place."

Of course. Given Jessie's and her husband's mental states, a provincial health facility would be monitoring Grace closely. The thought gave me some comfort. If there was a system in place for situations like this, they couldn't be all that uncommon, and that meant that everything might be okay. I'd already been babysitting for a few years. I pictured myself coming over to Jessie's apartment on a Saturday night, playing patty-cake with my baby cousin while my aunt and her husband went out to catch a movie. I would even tidy up the apartment for them as a surprise. It could happen, I thought. It could really happen, and not too long from now.

Jessie walked over to the dresser, picked up a bottle and shook it vigorously at Mom and me, as if she were teaching us a lesson. "This is formula. I have to warm it up, you know, so it's not too cold for Grace's tummy."

Mom nodded encouragingly, and I smiled. Jessie moved to her baby's side with the bottle. Finally I crossed the room and looked inside the crib.

I hadn't paid a lot of attention to babies, but this one looked like none I'd ever seen. It wasn't much bigger than a doll, its eyes were wide and unfocused, and it was lying much too still. Even when Jessie pushed the bottle into its mouth, it barely moved. *She*, I reminded myself. *She. It's a girl, just like me.* Slowly Grace began to suck at the bottle.

When the baby had finished feeding, Jessie walked over to the dresser again and held something out to me.

"Here. A picture for you," she said, and I took it. It was a hospital photo of Grace. Her face was red and wrinkly, and she had a green plastic bracelet around her wrist.

"Thanks," I mumbled, stuffing the photo into my back pocket.

After we left, Mom and I walked to the bus stop in silence.

"Mom," I said after we took a seat on the bench. "What—what was wrong with Grace? What do you think she has?"

"Has? I don't know, sweetie. I think she's just inherited a lot of problems from Jessie and John. Their mental state, you know." She sounded tired.

I gazed up the street, pretending to search for the bus. I felt pissed off. I was eleven years old, and I didn't want a cousin with huge mental problems. I wanted a normal baby who would coo at me and grab my nose and scream when she was hungry. I wanted aunts and uncles who had engagement parties and weddings and baby showers, and birthday parties for their kids that they invited me to, just like my school friends who complained about all the stupid family gatherings they had to go to. What I didn't want was one severely mentally challenged aunt, one drug-addled bipolar aunt and one paranoid schizophrenic uncle who'd ended up in a mental institution because he'd tried to kidnap me as a baby and hide me in a cellar.

But then I thought about Grace, lying helplessly in that crib with no idea of what life had in store for her. I wondered if she would ever have any friends. I knew what it felt like to be the outsider, the weirdo. Maybe Grace and I weren't so different after all. I pulled her photo out of my back pocket and stared at it for a minute, and I held it in my hand all the way home.

A few weeks after we visited Grace, I was reading in my bedroom when Mom came in and sat next to me on the bed.

"What's wrong?" I asked when I saw her face.

"It's Jessie, she just called. They . . . they took Grace away."

"They—what? What do you mean?"

"I mean the authorities. The—I don't know, whoever was in charge of Grace's case. They were monitoring Jessie carefully, and they decided the baby had to be taken away."

"But . . . why?"

Mom shrugged. "A baby is a lot of work. Jessie tried, but . . . I think she just wasn't able to look after it."

"Her," I responded dully. "Look after *her*." I met my mother's eyes, already knowing the answer to the question I was about to ask. "Mom. Did Grandma Jeanne ever meet Grace? Did Papa Dick?"

"No. I mean . . . not that I know of."

"So, no. Their first grandchild since I was born. And Jessie named her after Papa Dick's sister. And how old is Grace now? About eight months?"

"Cea, you know how it is. Mom is—"

"Busy with her new boyfriend, yes. And Papa Dick is too busy living his wilderness dream to be bothered. Yes, I know how it is." I snapped my book closed and brought my fingertips to my forehead. "You know what, Mom? They make me sick."

Mom rose from the bed. "I don't like hearing you talk like that, Cea. My parents are wonderful. They gave us everything we needed when we were growing up—love, acceptance—"

"Yes!" I said, jumping up beside her. "They gave that to you, but they can't even be bothered to meet their own grandchild? There's something not right about this family, Mom, but I guess I'm the only one who cares!"

Mom pursed her lips and shook her head, and then she left. I closed the door forcefully behind her and paced the room a few times. After I'd collected myself, I went to my bookshelf and took down the photo of Grace. I hadn't really looked at it since Jessie gave it to me, which made me feel deeply ashamed. Really, was I any different from the rest of them? I tucked the picture into the corner of my mirror and stared at it. No. I was crying, and that alone was proof I was different. I knew what happened to kids who went into the foster system. I pictured her landing at someone's home, someone who didn't really care about her, and then getting slowly sucked into a black hole of misery. I cried because Grace would never know that she had a cousin somewhere in the world, a cousin who loved her. And I cried because I knew, without a doubt, that I would never see her again.

Chapter 11

2007
Santa Fe

Two weeks after my showdown with Mom at the food court, James and Avery and I flew from Vancouver to Santa Fe to visit my father. It wasn't the best time to travel—after all, I might get the call about my mother practically any day—but Dad had bought us tickets as a surprise for my birthday. "I bet you could really use the break," he'd said, and I knew he understood what I was going through.

Though we'd grown close in recent years, we still engaged in a dance of ambiguity when it came to his role in my life. As a father who'd been mostly absent from my childhood, he didn't feel he had the right to offer me his opinions or advice, so often his help came through other sources—books or online articles he sent to me, carefully told stories of his friend's daughter's divorce or move to another city.

At the airport, we piled into Dad's car for the one-hour drive to his house. I took the back seat beside Avery, while Dad and James made small talk, and then I fell silent. As he drove, Dad's eyes flicked toward me in the rear-view mirror, but I gazed resolutely out the window at the flat-topped hills. It was pointless for James and me to try to mask the tension between us—we hardly said a word to each other anymore—but in small spaces, it was almost unbearable.

Me riding my stick horse in the Kootenay Plains, 1973, shortly before Apache died.

This is one of the only photos I have from when we lived in the Gulf Islands with Barry. I was seven.

Mom and me in Calgary when I was twelve. One of my all-time favourite pictures. I mean, *those pants*! Notice how my mom (*left*) is just loving the camera and how nonplussed I look. Our expressions say a lot about where we were in our lives at the time.

Me (*left*) and Carleigh in tenth grade. We met in fifth grade and are still very close friends.

My high school graduation photo. Why, oh why did I have to graduate in the '80s? By the time I saw a copy of this picture, I'd already escaped school to go live in Los Angeles.

In the Caribbean for a photo shoot, in 1990.

With Mom and Grandma Jeanne at my wedding to Kevin. This was the first and only time I saw Grandma Jeanne wearing makeup.

On holiday in Jamaica, age twenty-one.

Out with friends in Munich, 1994 (I'm on the far right). Heather (*far left*) is still one of my best friends in the world.

Shooting a catalogue in Guadaloupe, age twenty-five.

On location for a magazine shoot in Mauritius, age twenty-seven. Because don't we all wear full jewellery to the beach, ladies?

Me and Mom in Hawaii in 1995 on the one and only vacation we ever took together. Despite our smiles, the trip was a trying experience for both of us as we attempted to mend our relationship.

Me on my wedding day to James, 2001.

Just after Avery's birth, July 2005. I knew I'd love him, but I never imagined how much.

Mom came to visit with Grandma Jeanne after Avery was born. Mom was so excited to have a grandchild, and she was a wonderful grandmother during the short time she had with him before she died.

Avery and me in Halifax, 2007. He was my bright spot during that very difficult year.

The day this photo was taken was the last time I saw Papa Dick—
I was glad he got to meet Avery. He died about a year later.

Remy and me
not long after
we met. We were
inseparable from
our very first date.

Avery and me on my wedding day in 2009. I was five months pregnant with Emerson. Avery helped Remy propose to me, and also walked me down the aisle.
Photo credit: S. Nieuwenhuijsen

Remy and me with Emerson shortly after he was born. That little guy has brought us so much joy!

A family photo taken in 2012, shortly after my daughter, Ayla, was born.

Since *North of Normal* was published, I've had some wonderful speaking opportunities. Here I am just before giving a TEDx talk in Vancouver.

I love the way these two photos show how far my father's and my relationship has come. The picture on the left is of me and my dad meeting for the first time when I was two, and the one on the right is of him with my daughter, Ayla, at age two.

Finally, Dad cleared his throat. "Cea, I have a surprise for you!" he said enthusiastically. "I've booked a chart reading for you tomorrow with Guthrie."

"Chart reading?" I repeated blankly, not because I didn't know what he meant, but because I hadn't realized he was into astrology.

My mother had lived her entire life by it for as long as I could remember, and for that reason alone I'd rejected it. I remembered sitting beside her with my legs splayed out to the sides, listening to her predictions. "The moon's in Gemini next week, which means money will flow freely. Maybe Karl should sell his pot plants." "Saturn's in my second house, so it's a bad time to make decisions. Let's hold off on looking for a new camp till next week." And then, much worse, the explanations: "The moon's in Capricorn, Cea—no wonder you're out of sorts." I'd glare at her, knowing it was pointless to make her see that I was upset not because of the position of the planets, but because I was sick of her having sex in front of me or being made fun of at school for my pot-smelling clothes or trying to convince her that her married lover would never leave his wife. The last thing I wanted was someone telling me that everything that was happening to me right now was the result of something I had absolutely no control over. Besides, I was pretty sure that unless Guthrie the astrologer told me that my pot of gold was waiting at the end of the next rainbow, I didn't know if I'd be able to handle it.

That night Dad and Lara offered to take Avery for a sleepover with them. I returned to our suite with James at my side and dread in my heart. I realized how much I'd been using Avery as a shield, a perfectly legitimate excuse to avoid being alone with my husband.

It was too early for bed, but I brushed my teeth and got into my pyjamas anyway. I lay on my side facing the wall, and a few minutes later, I felt James lie down beside me. This must be what purgatory feels like, I thought. It was so clear that James and I were finished, but my mother was dying, and it occurred to me that James was probably putting off the inevitable out of consideration for my situation, just as

I was putting it off for my mental state. I needed to be grateful. I reached behind me and gave his arm a little rub, and he placed his hand over mine for a second before dropping it again. It would be the last time we touched in any purposeful way.

The next morning, I sat in Guthrie's office waiting for him to arrive. A gift was a gift, after all, and I had to admit to being a tad curious. The door opened, and I watched him enter. I had pictured a long-haired hippie wearing a tie-dyed *Legalize Today, Get High Tomorrow* T-shirt, but I couldn't have been more wrong. Elderly, handsome and clean-cut, this man could have been a tax accountant or a family doctor. He shook my hand and sat down across the desk from me, then produced a large piece of paper covered in lines criss-crossing over a large circle. He studied it for a few moments and then let out a low whistle.

"My, my. How are you doing?" he asked, meeting my eyes.

"Well, I, uh . . ." I didn't know what to say. His voice had sounded almost grave, and I was pretty sure he wasn't making small talk. "Not so good," I answered honestly.

"I'll say. You see this?" He traced a line with his finger. "You've been under the heavy influence of Neptune for the past six years. And all the while, Uranus here has been tripping up your every effort at turning things around. This is a very powerful combination of dark forces. These have been some trying years for you, I imagine? About six of them?"

"Yes. Very trying." My cynicism evaporated, and to my embarrassment, tears filled my eyes.

He smiled gently at me. "I assure you, there is good news ahead. But I'm afraid your hard times are not over yet. I see a time of great turbulence and loss. The coming eighteen months will be very difficult for you. You will survive it, of course, but it will take all of your strength."

"Mm. Well, I can't say that surprises me much," I said, pushing down the knot of fear in my stomach. I took a deep breath. "My mother. She's very ill. I assume . . . she will die?"

He didn't hesitate. "Before the year is through, I'm sorry to say. She is beyond the point of return."

I nodded resignedly, as he looked down at my chart again.

"And I see here . . . another death, although this one is more metaphorical. The death of a long-held dream or a vital relationship. A divorce or separation, perhaps? Are you attached?"

"Yes. We're having problems."

He nodded again. "It is all but over. Your spirits are highly incompatible. I see another man in your future, and you will be very happy together. And children—I see children. This man will be your soul mate, for lack of a better term."

It was a nice thought, but the last thing on my mind right now was a new relationship. "What about work? Career, I mean? I'm running a business right now, but it's not going well."

"It is not your true calling."

"No. It never was."

"There is a very strong creative streak in you. But it's raw. Unsharpened, if you will. Acting—? No, writing. Are you a writer?"

"Well, I'm *trying* to be," I said, hoping I didn't sound too pathetically eager. "I mean, I've been writing this book, a memoir about my childhood, but it seems I don't have much of a talent for it. It got rejected by forty-five literary agents." I paused nervously and then plunged in again. "But I just finished another draft. It's *so* much better than the first one, almost like a new book!"

He nodded. "I truly hope it works out for you. But I must tell you that I think your talent needs time to develop. A few years."

"A few *years*? But—I need to get it published now! It's my only chance to make enough money to leave my marriage! And I have a son to think about . . ."

"You will need to make do in other ways for now. Serve in a

restaurant, work in a shop, but know your time is coming." He looked me straight in the eye. "There are many, many people who come to me wanting to be artists, Cea. Most do not have the chart to support it. But the lines I see here are so powerful, so clearly geared toward your success as a writer, I swear to you I've only seen this a few other times in my four decades of reading."

"Seriously?"

"Seriously. But I also see a long-running theme of powerlessness in your life. Does that ring true for you?"

"You could say that. My mother . . . she made a lot of bad choices when I was growing up. I was always trying to make her see her mistakes, get us on a better path, but she was too focused on her own needs. I felt like I had no power over my own life. That's why I started modelling so young—to escape."

He nodded. "Keep writing. Hone your craft. But don't give up. I say this to you specifically because I've noticed that people who've experienced a lot of powerlessness often give up before they should. They doubt themselves and their abilities."

"Okay," I said with a bright smile. "I won't give up, I promise."

"Excellent. Now, I see you reaching your goal of publication in"— he peered down at my chart again—"2012."

I felt like I'd been punched. "In 2012? But that's five years from now!"

"Indeed. At that point, your writing will have reached the skill level necessary for success. From then on, your chart clears to welcome mostly sunny days. Never again will your life be as difficult as it has been these past six years. One more year of hardship, one and a half at most. You're almost there. Hang in there, have faith, and you will prevail."

I felt like crying. "But . . . I was just about to start looking for an agent again . . ."

"I can only tell you what I see here. But please, prove me wrong. I would love nothing more."

I gave him a soldiering-on smile and thanked him. As I waited in the reception room for Dad to pick me up, Guthrie's words echoed in my head: *have faith.* For the first time in my life, I actually found myself wishing I did have a faith to lean on. Though I disliked religion intensely, I'd always straddled the line of believing in *something* that I couldn't quite name. Spirituality was a subject I gave a lot of thought to, perhaps because my family hadn't. After all, my entire childhood's teachings on God had been one conversation I'd had with my grandfather at age five.

"What's God?" I'd asked him, after hearing one of the summer visitors' kids talk about praying.

"A doctrine created by folks desperate to find meaning in their lives," he replied, and that had been that.

Nature had been my grandparents' religion, and astrology had been my mother's. That I couldn't pinpoint my own beliefs frustrated me—because to so many, it seemed like the most obvious thing in the world.

1982
Calgary

When I was in sixth grade, a teenage girl who lived half a block away from me was raped. I remember coming home from school and seeing three police cars with flashing lights in front of her house. I didn't know the girl, but I went to school with the son of the people who lived next door to her. I found him in the small crowd gathered on the sidewalk and stood beside him, both of us trying to make sense of what we were seeing.

It was the kind of rape that you heard about in the news: the middle of the day, a teenager at home alone—apparently she'd been sick so hadn't been school—a broken window and a brandished knife. I watched as her front door opened and two medics escorted her to a waiting ambulance. She had a blanket over her shoulders, and her hair swung like a dark sheet in front of her face. What struck me the most was her posture. She was hunched over like an old lady, her eyes cast down at the sidewalk. At first I wondered why she was walking like that, and then it occurred to me: she was ashamed. Curling her body inward, as if doing so could protect her already violated private parts. It stirred something in me.

That night at home, for the first time ever, I wished we had a TV. I hadn't had a television in my whole life and had only noticed its absence since moving to the city a few years before. Despite my schoolmates' daily talk of *Diff'rent Strokes* and *The Dukes of Hazzard,* I'd never wished for one. But tonight I wanted to see the report on the news about the girl down the street who had been raped. I wanted details.

When I told Mom that night, she gazed at me steadily for a moment. "*Raped?* What do you mean?"

"I mean some guy broke into this girl's house today and raped her. And now I'm kind of scared, because what if he comes back? Looking for someone else to rape, I mean? And I'm, like, at home by myself all the time . . ."

"Mm. Yes," Mom said, moving toward the back door and turning the flimsy safety lock on the knob. "There, all safe now," she declared. "And anyway, sweetie, don't worry. I'm here to protect you."

I nodded stiffly.

But the next night, Mom didn't come home from being out with Sam until after midnight. I lay in my bed, unable to sleep. It wasn't just that I was afraid of someone breaking into the house. Lately there was a blackness that seemed to shadow my every thought. It felt dark, hopeless, almost like a physical presence, like nothing in the world could ever make me happy again. Sometimes it would lift for a while, but it always settled back in—especially when I felt powerless to change my circumstances or make my mother see reason, which was almost all the time. I was twelve years old, and I understood all too well that I was at the mercy of her choices until I could escape them.

If only, I thought, I could find a way to do so without waiting until I'd finished school.

The front door opened. I heard Mom's voice, and then long strides crossing the hardwood floor behind her. A moment later, opera music blared from our cheap Hitachi stereo system. Great, I thought—he was here. I pictured him sending my mother to the kitchen to make him something to eat, which she would scurry along obediently to do, and weighed the potential price of reminding her of her duty to protect me from lurking dangers outside: a confrontation with Sam.

I got out of bed, pulled my door open and entered the kitchen. Mom was at the sink peeling potatoes, the only food Sam ever seemed to eat. I guessed there was always hope he'd drop dead of malnutrition.

"Mom," I said, looking pointedly at the clock as I leaned against the counter. "Did you forget what I told you yesterday? About a rapist being on the loose? That lock on our door wouldn't keep out a two-year-old."

"Of course I didn't forget. I'm home, aren't I?"

I shook my head in disbelief, but she kept her eyes glued to her task. I looked at what she was wearing: a blazer and skirt with nylons. "Nice outfit," I said, looking for a jab. "Very *proper*."

"Shush," she replied tightly.

I shook my head again and went to the fridge. My mother's willingness to become whoever her current lover wanted her to be had always boggled my mind, but with Sam she'd really pulled out all the stops. Everything about her changed when he walked in the door—clothing, musical taste, manners, even values. It did occur to me that this other person she became was more like the "normal" mother I would have liked to have, but that it was a big put-on just made me feel all the more distant from her.

One year before, Sam hadn't walked into my life but rather crept into it under cover of night. I'd hear him walk in the front door after dark, or see Mom talking furtively on the phone, or occasionally see his retreating back when he left before dawn. Eventually, after I'd inquired into his identity several times, I found myself sitting in an Italian restaurant with the two of them. I'd only been out for dinner a few times in my life, so I noticed everything—the candles glowing in the yellow-tinted glass holders, the words on the menu that I'd never seen before. Mom seemed nervous, picking up her fork and then dropping it again. I ate buttered dinner rolls and spinach cannelloni and said nothing.

After we had finished eating, Sam lit a cigarette and grinned at me. "So. Your mother tells me you are in fifth grade. Do you enjoy school?"

I shrugged. "Sure, I guess." I kept my eyes down, unable to meet his. I knew that no matter how nice he was to me, I would never be able to like or respect him. And without a doubt, my feelings were far from opaque.

Beside me, Mom dropped the potatoes into a pot of water and walked away, her nylons swishing together. I opened the fridge and reached for the orange juice. Just then I heard Sam's footsteps approaching from the living room. I grabbed a glass and poured the juice too quickly, splashing it onto the counter.

"You should be more careful. Your mother has better things to do than clean up after you," Sam said.

A hundred retorts came to mind, but, of course, I couldn't say any of them. Plain and simple, I was a prisoner of my mother's taste in men and her eagerness to please them. I returned to my bedroom, closing the door hard behind me.

Back in my bed, I tried to banish the anxiety that had washed over me, but it was little use. My mother was lost to me, I was stuck under her roof, and now there was a rapist on the loose to worry about. I flipped onto my back and gazed at the ceiling as my mind drifted backwards. I thought about the warning my teacher had issued our class the year before about the dangerous man, the one who had scared the little girl. I thought about walking through the park that day, standing in the snow and almost daring him to find me. And that's when I got the idea.

"I have a surprise for you," Carleigh said to me, smiling big. "It's about this summer. You know that camp I went to last year? Well, guess what. My grandmother has paid for us *both* to go this year. Isn't that awesome?"

"Wow, really? That's so amazing," I replied with a smile I didn't feel.

Carleigh was my best friend, the first girl who had talked to me when I started the new school in fifth grade and, truth be told, my only real friend. I'd always been the follower to her leader, and happily so. I would have done anything for her. She was more popular, more outgoing and a whole lot more normal than I was. I could talk to her about my mother and Sam and even count on her to make me laugh about them. But ever since I'd broken open my lie several weeks ago about being raped, our friendship had shifted. Now Carleigh was the one who would to do anything for me.

She wanted details, of course, and I had supplied them. It had happened in the schoolyard of the school I'd gone to the year before, I said. A drifter, some random guy that parents were all warning their kids about. Walk in pairs, they said, and stay away from parks and wooded areas. I had obeyed until one day when I'd left school a little late with no one to accompany me. Beyond that, the details got a little sketchy.

"So then you're not, like, a virgin anymore, right?" she asked, and I hesitated.

"Well, I think I still am *technically*, since I didn't want him to do it, you know?"

"Oh. Yeah, of course." She took her bolo bat from her back pocket and started smacking the ball, *whack whack whack*. "So . . . was he cute at least?" she asked finally. *Whack whack whack.*

I looked down as if I were traumatized by the memory of it. "Um, sort of," I replied, and then I backtracked. "I mean . . . I don't really remember what he looked like and stuff. He, like, pushed my face into the ground, so I sort of couldn't see him."

"Wow. That's, like, totally harsh."

"Yeah." I brightened, hoping to change the topic. "You want to go for a Slurpee?"

"Sure." She switched the position of her bolo bat and whacked it upward as we walked. "Anyway, so my grandma, she thought this would be really good for you, because you get all cleansed by Jesus and stuff—"

"Wait a minute. You *told* her?"

"Of course not! I just told her it would be awesome if you came. And it's really rad at this camp. You get to ride horses and—"

"*Horses?*" I scoffed. "I don't know how to ride a horse. And besides, I don't even like them."

"How can you not like horses? Everyone likes horses."

"Not me," I said. What flashed through my mind was a vision of Apache, lying on his side with blood oozing from the hole in his head. I whipped my own bolo bat from my back pocket. *Whack whack whack.*

"You're probably just scared, that's all. The first time I—"

"Not scared. Just don't like them."

"Well, okay, whatever. Geez, touchy much?" Carleigh gave me a perplexed look.

"Sorry," I said, meaning it. I was always nice, agreeable, smiling, grateful to even have a friend. What was wrong with me?

"It's okay. Anyway, my grandma's even going to pay for it, 'cause she knows your mom can't afford it."

I nodded but didn't say anything. It wasn't just the horse thing that had put me off but the mention of Jesus. Though I would never have admitted it to my best friend, I wasn't even entirely sure who Jesus was, or what God was all about, for that matter. The only time I'd heard Mom mention their names was when she was cursing, so until recently, my knowledge had been limited to one Sunday school visit a couple years ago. A friend had brought me, and we sat in the church basement, colouring in pictures of three guys carrying presents for the newborn baby, while the teacher read from the Bible. Her words swam around me like puzzle pieces I had no hope of fitting together. After she finished reading, she gave us a quiz, and for the first time in a classroom, I had no answers. I just didn't get it. I gathered that Jesus was a real living person, but his dad was a spirit who lived in the sky and who no one had ever seen. I didn't understand how someone invisible could have a real live baby, and plus I was confused about the whole Mary thing. I knew very well how babies were made, and I thought that if I was walking around with my new husband, and I suddenly found out I was pregnant with some other guy's baby, I'd be pretty ticked, and I figured my husband would be too. And if God had that kind of power, then why couldn't he just go and find his own wife up in heaven and get her pregnant and then send her down to earth? Why did he have to go and use someone else's wife?

One year ago, my answers had miraculously shown up in the form of a tiny red Bible handed out by a visitor to our school. I kept it under my pillow, so Mom wouldn't find it, and committed myself to reading two pages every single night. I was a good student, so after I finished reading, I would review in my head what I'd learned and try to relate it to my own experience, but my mind would drift as I stared at my model collage. I'd made it shortly after we moved into this house, using a large and ornate frame I'd found in a back alley and filling it with images of the current hot models: Carol Alt, Iman, Kim Alexis. It didn't take much for me to admit that staring at those photos and imagining my future filled me with a lot more rapture than Jesus ever could.

After six months, I finally gave up and stuffed the tiny Bible into the bottom of my drawer. But even if I was unable to understand what it was all about, there was one thing I was pretty certain of: normal people believed in God.

"Sure, that sounds great. Thanks," I said to Carleigh. "It'll be awesome."

I stood with my feet solidly planted on the ground, placed the arrow on the withers and raised my bow. It was all I could do not to laugh at my target. Hijinks at Circle Square Ranch were not much tolerated, but someone had drawn a picture of Satan, complete with horns and a pitchfork, on the paper target. I held my bow arm steady and let the arrow fly. It hit the bull's-eye with a loud *thunk*. The girls around me stopped talking, but I kept my face expressionless. It was my second bull's-eye in a row, and I had one more turn. I took five steps backwards and fired again. *Thunk*, right into the centre. There was a smattering of grudging applause, and a counsellor stepped forward to present me with the gold medal.

"Congratulations," she said with a tight smile. "Right through Satan's heart. Jesus is celebrating with you."

I grinned back at her. It was the last day of camp, and this moment represented the single highlight of the past seven days.

Over the last week, the darkness had plagued me worse than ever. Every fear I'd had about going to this camp had been realized. Right off the bat, Carleigh and I had been placed in different cabins, leaving me the lone Jesus ignoramus in a sea of fervent believers. Though I'd tried to be friendly, not a single girl—or counsellor, for that matter— seemed to want anything to do with me. It was as if I were doused in a perfume called Doubt that repelled everyone. Much of our day was devoted to Bible study and talk of mortal sin, during which I would smile and nod pleasantly and contribute exactly nothing. Our evenings were spent in the dining hall listening to lectures about the evils of makeup and *Self* magazine, followed by the screech of records being played backwards to reveal mostly illegible lyrics that the counsellors insisted were satanic. And, of course, the best was saved for last—cautionary tales of girls and women who had engaged in premarital sex and whose souls were marked to burn in hell for eternity. All I could think about was my mother, who was likely at that very moment screwing her married lover. Despite all Mom's shortcomings, I had a hard time believing she was hell-bound.

My only solace as I traipsed back to my cabin with my gold medal was that it was finally, finally over.

It was not over. In fact, the worst was yet to come.

That night after dinner, we were all directed to the recreation hall, which had been converted to a temporary theatre. We were instructed to sit, and I took a seat in the back row. The room began to buzz with electric energy, and it soon became apparent what was going on. It started off with three counsellors selecting a girl each to bring onstage. Once there, they sat on folding chairs while the counsellors stood behind them, lightly gripping their shoulders. The counsellors spoke loudly above the campers' heads, and after a while, each of the girls began to emit a bizarre stream of gibberish. The counsellor would then give a rapturous hoot and send the camper off the stage to tag one of her friends. I'd learned a lot about praying in the past seven days, and at this moment, I prayed harder than I ever had in my life that no one would call me onto that stage.

It was much too hot in there. I itched to escape from the room, but both exits were blocked by counsellors with crossed arms. I glanced at the girl beside me. She had her eyes closed and was slowly swaying from side to side on her seat. I recognized her from my cabin; she was one of the horsey girls who spent all their time in the stables. I hadn't gone near the horses all week.

I glanced back at the stage in time to see a girl descending the stairs and coming straight for me. She weaved slightly as she walked, as if she were tipsy. I ducked down in my seat, but it was no use.

"I think *you* need this more than anyone here," she said, pulling me up from my chair.

From the stage, the counsellor was beckoning to me, patting the back of her chair. *Shit.* Filled with dread, I pushed myself forward and took my seat onstage. I spotted Carleigh, who was seated in the audience with her cabin mates, and caught her eye. She gave me an encouraging smile.

The counsellor, a woman in her twenties, crouched in front of me. Her pupils were huge. "You know Jesus loves you. Right?"

I nodded, petrified.

"Say it."

"Je—Jesus loves me," I stammered, feeling like a complete moron.

Two chairs down from me, a girl stopped spewing gibberish and slumped off her chair onto the floor. Two counsellors swept in and carried her off the stage.

"And what do you want his forgiveness for tonight?"

"Forgiveness?"

"Yes. For what sins?"

"Sins?" I thought fast, trying to remember what they were. "Um, for, like, thinking unpure thoughts, I guess, and, like, maybe for disrespecting my mom and stuff, and wearing mascara and lip gloss?"

She nodded solemnly. "Very good. Now, just relax and let his love flow through you. You want to make the ultimate connection with Jesus here. So when you feel like you want to speak to him, just open your mouth and let it out."

I gazed at her with dread, but she was already moving to the back of my chair and placing her hands on my shoulders. Around me the fervour continued, and everyone seemed so *happy*. Maybe the counsellor was right, I thought. I was unhappy too much of the time, and maybe Jesus's love was just what I needed to change that.

I closed my eyes and tried to focus. I pictured Jesus on the cross and tried to get sad about it. When that didn't work, I prayed to him in my head to help me start a modelling career. Then I remembered that modelling involved makeup and magazines, so as far as mortal sin went, I might as well ask him to drop a boulder on Sam's head. My eyes popped open.

"Speak! Let it out! Speak!" the counsellor was urging over my head.

I closed my eyes again and started over. This time, I just asked to be happy.

"Speak! *Speak now!*" The counsellor was working herself into quite a lather.

What if I couldn't do this? I switched tactics, asking Jesus to just please say something to me so I could give the counsellors what they wanted and get this over with. When a couple more minutes passed and I didn't feel anything, I knew it was hopeless. Jesus and I apparently had nothing to say to each other, but that didn't help my current situation. Not one girl in this room had gotten off the stage without first proving her connection with Christ.

I opened my mouth and, imitating the girls who'd gone before me, let a stream of nonsense escape. As soon as I heard the counsellor whoop behind me, I stood up and ran off the stage as if I were energized by Jesus's love. Then I pushed my way past one of the exit guards to the bathroom. I was pretty sure I was going to throw up.

Carleigh and I were both quiet on the ride from Circle Square Ranch back to Calgary. We sat in the back of the RV, while her grandmother sang along to country songs up front.

"I still can't believe we weren't in the same cabin," Carleigh said finally.

I nodded. I'd noticed that Carleigh had not suffered for friends as I had this week, but I also knew I couldn't blame her for her popularity. I stared out the window at the passing fields of cows and horses. My already foul mood was plummeting. I hated where I was leaving, but I hated what I was going back to even more.

"So, do you . . . feel any better now?" Carleigh was asking me. "I mean, because of the, you know . . ."

"The rape."

"Yeah."

I looked her in the eye, suddenly emboldened. What did I have to lose? "It never happened."

"*What?* What are you talking about?"

"I mean it never happened. I lied. No one ever raped me."

"Wow. Really? But . . . why?" Her eyes were huge.

"Dunno. I guess I just . . . really wanted the attention." I crossed my arms defiantly. It was the best answer I could come up with on short notice, but it was nowhere near the truth. What I felt was that I was caught in the middle of a massive tangle of questions to which I had no answers. One of these questions involved Carleigh herself, who had every right to be angry at me but wasn't. I should have been relieved or grateful, but for some reason, even though I was the one who had lied, I felt betrayed. I didn't want people to accept where I came from without question. I desperately wanted someone to know the truth about me, and yet I was so afraid of exposing it that I could only reveal my pain through lies. I wanted someone to dig and insist and demand that I tell them the truth, but I knew this was way too much to ask of a twelve-year-old friend.

I slipped my hand into my jeans pocket and touched my gold archery medal. The darkness was pushing in on me hard, trying to take over, and right now, this little reward was the only thing that assured me I wasn't a total loser. I should have been grateful to have something, at least, but all I could think about was the irony of where this validation had come from: an environment far removed from everything I knew and yet similar in its extremity. I thought about my own childhood, the over-the-top freedom and insistence by my family that nothing existed outside of what we could see with our own eyes. So opposite to the world of anyone who'd grown up God-fearing, rigid, forever trying to please an intangible being by preparing for a time and place in another realm.

Why did people need to go to such extremes? Did a happy medium even exist, or was everyone's life marred by some extreme or another, even if it were only extreme ordinariness? I wasn't sure. All I knew was that if that normal place existed, I was still an unbearable distance from finding it.

Chapter 12

2007
Vancouver

Like a stuck record, the date ran around and around in my head. *December seventeenth, 2007, December seventeenth, 2007. Please get out of here. Please just open the door and leave.*

I sat on the edge of the hotel room bed, watching as James tied Avery's shoes, put on his own coat, patted his pocket for his wallet. My need to be alone right now felt like a physical force. My mother had been dead for five hours, and I'd been holding it together for just as long.

Just two days ago, I'd seen her at the hospice after flying in from Vancouver to Calgary to say my last goodbye. Ever since, I'd been waiting for the phone to ring with the news. It had finally been delivered this afternoon.

And, of course, as befitted the story of my life, it couldn't have happened on a normal day. James, Avery and I had been living with James's mother since our return to Vancouver, during which time she also happened to be renovating her house. This morning workers had shown up to lay new flooring, forcing all of us to decamp to a hotel for the night. On any other day it wouldn't have mattered a bit, but today it did. As I looked around at the cheap Holiday Inn furnishings,

167

I thought of the many unusual shelters my mother and I had occupied in my childhood and found it sadly fitting that I would grieve her passing here. After all, right now I was almost as far removed from my childhood dream of a normal life as I had been then.

James had the door open now. "I'll take him for as long as you need," he said. "And, hey . . . I'm sorry," he added gently.

I nodded my thanks, and the door finally closed behind them. I picked up the wine bottle at my side and poured myself a full glass. All I hoped was that I could get my tears out before Avery came toddling through the door again with his eyes in big questioning circles, asking why Mommy was crying.

I collapsed back on the bed. The last time I saw Mom, she'd been so far gone she could barely speak; I'd laid my favourite childhood book beside her and thanked her for being my mother. So why did the memory of that do nothing to stir my emotions? *She's gone*, I thought. *She's gone forever.* I knew I held a hundred things inside—devastation and relief, forgiveness and blame, anger and love—but I couldn't actually *feel* any of them. My eyes remained as dry as the deep, empty well of my heart.

Of course, I thought as I stared up at the spackled ceiling. *It's survival.* If I started crying now, I might never stop, and I had way too much to get through to afford such a luxury.

Christmas Day of 2007 was, for me, one of a horrible in-between. My mother's death was a week behind me, her memorial two weeks ahead. My marriage lay in ruins that both James and I pretended not to notice because of the season and circumstances. James's mother poured me wine and tried not to look pitying. Random friends of James's family dropped in throughout the day, oblivious to my pain as they cracked off-colour jokes. Everyone laughed, even me.

"A fireman jacket!" Avery squealed delightedly, lifting it from a pile of shredded paper.

I forced my lips into a smile. More than anything about today, it was the sight of my young son that pained me. At this point, his life revolved around his parents, and he had no idea his world was going to be ripped apart when they separated. I pulled him into my lap and hugged him too hard. He squirmed away, wanting to play. As I watched him, I imagined myself in a hospital, surrounded by friends and what was left of my family. They would finally see that I was not okay and wonder how they'd missed that I had been on the verge of an emotional breakdown. For the first time I could ever remember, I didn't give a flying fuck about being strong.

I knew of people whose worlds had fallen apart for various reasons, but my situation was different, because in order for a life to fall apart, it must once have been together. I could see clearly that mine never had been. Sure, I'd pretended—spent years exuding a persona of success and competence, making myself pretty and surrounding myself with pretty things, filling in the husband slot to complete the happy picture, and smiling, smiling, always smiling. But the contrast to my inner world—depression, restlessness, uncertainty of my boundaries or even my right to have them—was like a single black storm cloud in a clear blue sky. And the thing was, I couldn't remember a time I hadn't felt that way. Rather than starting out whole and unravelling, my unprocessed past had slowly closed around me until I was left with nowhere to run. Now, immobilized, I was forced to look at myself and see the truth.

I got up from the sofa and descended the stairs to the bedroom I was sharing with James and Avery. I was quite certain the adults wouldn't miss me, but I probably didn't have long before Avery would come searching. I sat down on the bed, then I took out my laptop and started to type.

I endure. I persevere and I take it on and I chomp through problems like Ms. Pac-Man, because my life isn't that bad compared to others'. I have never given myself licence to complain, because complaining would make me a victim. I am defined by my ability to endure and my will to survive. It doesn't matter what you pile on to me physically, mentally or emotionally, because I don't know how to set boundaries or define acceptable behaviour. No one ever taught me how. I had a mother who loved me, and that's more than a lot of kids had, so I had no right to expect anything more. So bring on the stress, the issues, the problems, the shit. I will take it and say nothing at all, because I am gagged and muzzled by my own unfailing and insistent smile.

I closed my laptop and collapsed onto my side in a sobbing heap. Deep within, I recognized that though I hadn't been able to cry for my mother, I could cry for myself. It was a little shameful but also revealing. My history may not have been a happy one, but at least I'd always *tried*. I'd truly believed that if I tried hard enough, I could create the happiness and the reality I craved. But it hadn't worked, so somewhere along the line, I'd stopped taking control of my life and become a spectator in it. And though I'd always promised myself it wouldn't happen, a victim mentality had slowly squeezed its way into my mindset. If I had any chance of surviving, I would have to change that, and fast. I knew very well that self-pity and courage could not co-exist.

1986
Calgary

I sat at my desk, tapping my pencil and glancing up at the clock every few seconds. My teacher gave me a sidelong glance. Normally eleventh-grade English class was the highlight of my school day, but today I couldn't wait to make my break. I had a modelling job for a local mall after school, and it was going to pay me enough to help Mom make rent this month with money left over for a new pair of jeans.

Maybe I'd been wrong about Jesus, because one year after the holy-roller camp, where I prayed to him to make me a model, my request had been granted in the form of a modelling competition. That was three years ago, when I was thirteen. I'd walked into an agency after spotting an ad in the newspaper, and as soon as the photographer saw me, things happened quickly. Within a few months, I moved to New York, and I spent the following two summers working in Paris. As it turned out, I *had* found a way to escape my mother, even if it was only within the parameters of school breaks. The downside of my career was that it was an isolating choice. I spent every school holiday away and most weekends working, which didn't give me much in common, or anything really to talk about, with my schoolmates. And then there were the misconceptions. My few true friends had cheered for me and treated me no differently when I'd started modelling, but I'd noticed changes in others. I saw judgment—groups of girls I hardly knew who suddenly found reason to giggle or comment snidely, eyes averted, when I walked past. I saw appraisal—boys who looked at my makeup-free face and flat chest and likely wondered what the big deal was. I saw envy in some, not so much for my career but for my independence. I knew it was pointless to tell them that they were the lucky ones, because they didn't have anything at home they needed to escape from. And forget the parents who, when they found out I conducted my career without adult supervision, looked at me like I was some wild child. "What about your mother?" were always the first words out of their mouths, to which I'd learned a simple "What about her?" to be a more effective response than any explanation. But of course it was all worth it, because I'd turned my long-held dream into a career, and in doing so I'd realized that my life was within my control.

I gazed out the window as the wind blew up a swirl of leaves on the cracked sidewalk. Just a few weeks ago, I'd been clicking my way through photo shoots in Paris, all the while navigating the tricky game of refusing invitations to party with the crew and still getting a second or third booking out of them. Sometimes I wondered what was wrong with me—all the other girls were happy enough to party, and most of them seemed to live for it, but even the idea of it made me squirm. On the few occasions I'd consented to being dragged out, I'd sat alone at my VIP table with a bottle of Perrier, while my friends drank, danced, flirted and sometimes snorted coke or left with a photographer or client. I saw accusation in the other girls' eyes when I didn't join in— *there goes Little Miss Boring, home to bed early again.* What I didn't want to explain to them was that while I understood their unbridled antics, freedom wasn't exactly new to me. And even more than that, their behaviour was too close to my mother's for my comfort. In a way, these nightclub outings were just another version of the parties she used to drag me to when I was ten.

The bell finally rang, and I snapped my book closed and made a dash for my locker. As I was scooting down the hall, I spotted my friend Tiffany waving at me frantically through the crowd. I pointed at my watch and kept going. I'd actually been furtively dodging her since my return from Paris. Tiffany loved to party, shoplift and make out with random guys, none of which were top priorities for me—at least not anymore.

I grabbed my schoolbag and headed for the exit. As I was pushing through the doors, someone grabbed my shoulder. I turned.

"Hey. Are you avoiding me?" Tiffany demanded.

"No. I'm just in a bit of a hurry. I have a job today."

"Oh, okay." She pushed her lower lip out sulkily. "It's just that we've barely talked since you got back. And I've got some news." She smiled slyly at me, and I knew her news could only be one thing. Tiffany had been dying to lose her virginity ever since I'd met her a few years ago.

"You—really? Wow, that's . . . I mean, how was it?"

She glanced around and lowered her voice. "*Totally* amazing. Derek Stevens. He's *so* hot."

I smiled, uncertain what to say. I hadn't taken that step yet, and I wasn't in much of a rush to. Though I wouldn't have admitted it, the whole idea of sex made me squeamish. It seemed impossible to even think about it without seeing my mother entangled with some lover, and if that wasn't a turn-off, I didn't know what was.

"Well. I better get going, I have to catch the bus," I said, and walked quickly away. When I turned back once to wave at her, she was staring at me as if I'd just ruined her birthday party.

When I got home from school, Mom was sitting at the dining table with a long-haired couple in their forties. The man grinned and stood up when he saw me.

"My word, you've gotten big. And so pretty too."

"Thanks." I glanced at Mom uncertainly, then back to him. "Do I know you?"

"Collin spent a summer with us on the Kootenay Plains," Mom explained, and my smile faded.

I hated it when people from my past came barging into my present, wanting to reminisce about the wilderness days. I gave him a quick nod and turned toward the kitchen.

As I started making myself a sandwich, I could feel the man's eyes on me. I did vaguely remember him, and I was pretty sure he had been nice to me. So why couldn't I be nice back? Because he probably remembered things about me that I didn't even know myself. Because it was highly possible he'd had sex with Mom while I was in bed beside them. And because being nice to him was the equivalent of being on good terms with my past, when I didn't even want to admit where I'd come from.

I took my sandwich to my room and started doing homework, thankful to have a closed door between me and the world. My bedroom walls were a monument to the models I idolized, the only trace of my past being Suzie Doll placed high up on my bookshelf. I sat down on my bed and opened my books. My high school had the Pace Program, which meant I could choose how quickly or slowly I wanted to complete my classes, and my goal was to finish school a year early.

Not that anyone but me cared if I graduated, least of all Mom—which was exactly why I intended to do so.

I was deep into my chemistry textbook when I dropped my pencil on the floor. As I leaned off the bed to pick it up, I noticed a bottle of Love's Baby Soft perfume under my bookshelf. I crossed the room and picked it up. When Tiffany and I were into shoplifting together a few years before, this had been one of her favourite targets. As I slipped it into my schoolbag, I caught a glimpse of Suzie Doll, the only remnant of my childhood that I kept visible, sitting on the shelf. I gave her a little smile. *Just one more year*, I thought. *One more year and we'll be out of here. We can do it.*

"Turn right at the stop sign," said the driving tester beside me. "At the top of the hill, you're going to do your parallel park."

"Sure thing," I replied, as the car rattled loudly beneath us. Mom's Chevy Nova was an embarrassing heap of crap, but I didn't even care, because my driver's test was almost over, and my licence seemed so close I could already imagine my smiling photo on it. Just in time too. I was due to go to Los Angeles for a modelling job in a week, and I'd need a car to get around. Since I was only sixteen and too young to rent a vehicle, my agent George was going to lend me one of his. It was all set up.

I drove to the top of the hill, signalled and began backing up. Luckily I was confident enough in my parallel parking skills not to worry about messing up.

Just then, I heard a loud *crunch*, and the steering wheel went loose in my hands. I hit the brake. "What the—?" A cloud of smoke rose from under the hood.

"Oh, shit," I said. "I cannot freaking believe this."

I popped the hood and got out of the car, goose bumps rising on my arms in the chilly autumn air. My driving tester stood beside me, staring down at the engine and scratching his head with his pen.

"Looks like your mom's engine blew. I can call for a ride back to the branch, but you're going to have to get a tow truck for the car."

I covered my face with my hands and leaned against the bumper. What the hell was I going to do? Los Angeles was practically impossible to get around without a vehicle, and I certainly couldn't afford to take cabs everywhere. And there was no way I could cancel the job, which was paying me more than I could make in six months modelling locally. I thought about showing up at the airport and telling George he'd have to chauffeur me around for a week. George, who had plucked me from my tiny local agency and sent me off to New York, who'd made sure I made it to the finals for a modelling competition the year before, who'd put me up in his house in L.A. and never made any moves on me, who'd always sung my praises to my bookers. It was bad enough that I was still trying to get over the last time I'd seen him in Calgary. He'd asked me out for dinner, and, to my dismay, insisted I bring my mother. I gritted my teeth as she ordered the most expensive meal on the menu, ate it like she'd been raised in a barn, got drunk on Kahlúa and then, just to top off one of my worst evenings ever, proceeded to put the moves on George. She hadn't even had the decency to be discreet about it, instead running her tongue around the rim of her glass while gazing into his eyes, like some sort of porn star. I wanted to die, but George smiled at her politely and patted my hand like it was no big deal.

"I seriously can't believe this," I said to the driving tester. "I—I have to go to L.A. next week. I need to be able to drive . . ." I stopped myself, thinking how ridiculous I must sound to this middle-aged man. Like not being able to drive around sunny Los Angeles was such a huge problem for some spoiled little teenager. But to my surprise, he looked at me with interest.

"L.A., huh? Holiday?"

"No. Work," I said quietly.

His forehead crinkled. "At your age?"

"Yeah. I still go to school and everything," I added quickly, not wanting him to think I was a dropout. "I just . . . work too."

"Huh. You an actress or something?"

I shook my head, pasting on a smile I didn't feel. The judgment of my schoolmates was one thing, but that of strangers was even worse. I hated telling anyone I was a model: the word was so heavy with connotation. Just saying "I'm a model" felt like the equivalent of saying "I'm so beautiful," because that's how others perceived it. I'd even had people react by saying, "Well, *la-de-da*," as if I were bragging simply by stating my profession. The reality was completely different. Modelling to me equalled hard work, sacrifice and perseverance. I definitely wasn't about to explain all that to the stranger standing beside me, but then I noticed the sympathetic look on his face.

"I work as a model," I said, taking a chance. "And I just really need to be able to drive. Would I . . . if I can borrow a car from someone, would I be able to come back and finish the test in a day or two?"

He gave me a small smile and then looked down at his clipboard. "You were only one point away from passing. If you had completed that parallel park and gotten us back to the branch safely, you would have had it. So . . ." He took his pen out and placed a check mark in a box. "I'm just going to assume you would have nailed it. Now, we better get walking. We need to find ourselves a pay phone."

"Oh my god. Oh my god, thank you so much!" I babbled. I wanted to hug him, but I stopped myself. "You have no idea how much this means to me."

He grinned. "You're obviously a very determined young lady."

I realized that this man had put the pieces of the puzzle together for himself. Very likely he'd observed my mother's junker car and my ambition, understood that I was a girl in desperate need of escape and handed me a gift.

The day after my driver's test, I found Tiffany beside her locker at school.

"Hey. Guess what?" I said excitedly. She looked at me with a devilish smile. "Not *that*," I continued quickly. "I got my driver's licence!"

"Oh." She looked disappointed. "Good for you. I still haven't gone for my learner's yet."

I nodded, wondering if it seemed strange to her that she was having sex before she even knew how to drive. This seemed to me like a corruption of the natural order of progression to adulthood.

"Here," I said, holding out the perfume bottle. "You must have left this at my house."

She stared at it, her eyes widening into pretty green circles. "Thank you," she squeaked.

I cocked my head at her. "What's wrong?"

"Just, um . . . you're cool with it, right?"

"Cool with what?"

"Just that . . . well, your mom said it was okay and everything, so I figured you wouldn't mind."

"Mind? What are you talking about?"

She brought her hand to her mouth in sudden realization. "You don't know."

"Of course I don't!" I replied impatiently. "What are you talking about?"

A few students turned to look at us as they passed, so Tiffany leaned in close to me. "Me and Derek. We needed a place to do it. You were away, and I know how your mom is, like, super cool about sex and stuff, so . . . well, I kind of asked her if we could borrow your bedroom—"

"You *what?*"

My mother was a never-ending source of embarrassment. She smoked pot in front of my friends, talked about sex like it was the weather and held her boobs with her hands when she ran for the bus because she refused to wear a bra. Her table manners were so atrocious that I didn't dare have a friend over around mealtimes. But this was different, and wrong on so many levels.

"I—I know it sounds kind of lame now, but it didn't seem that way at the time. And your mom said no problem. She was going out that night anyway, and—It's not like we used your bed or anything. I do have class, you know. We brought a sleeping bag."

"A sleeping bag?" I stared at her.

"Yeah. I mean, no big deal, right? We cleaned up and everything—"

I held up a hand. "Listen. Just . . . don't worry about it, okay? It's fine." I forced a smile, turned and hurried away.

Damn it, why do I always have to smile? I thought. *Why do I always have to pretend everything's okay when it's not? Why do I always forgive before I'm ready?*

Except, of course, when it came to my mother.

"Mom!" I burst through the front door, ready to unleash.

The house was quiet. I did a quick check of the rooms and then stood in the middle of the kitchen, seething. Where she might be was anyone's guess. My mother and I were like fruit suspended in Jell-O, sharing the same world but never connecting. Out with her new boyfriend was the best probability. Though she and Sam had finally broken up a year or so ago, she'd quickly taken up with another prize—this one being unemployed, substance-addicted and emotionally remote. I heard the front door open and jumped slightly.

"Hey," our current roommate said, passing through the kitchen.

"Hey." I watched her disappear into the bathroom. We had so many roommates passing through our home to help us make rent that I could barely keep their names straight.

I went to my bedroom and shut the door. I had to do something, or I would explode. I grabbed my notepad and pen. *Michelle*, I began, feeling empowered by the use of her first name. *I hate you right now. Really fucking hate you . . .*

I finished the letter and wrote my name at the bottom, and then I placed it up on my bookshelf. Tomorrow I would put it somewhere she'd find it and then spend the day with a friend—let her wonder where *I* was for a change. I lay down in bed and stared at my collage. Tonight, one year seemed longer than forever.

The next morning, I got up and went into the kitchen in search of breakfast. The fridge was nearly empty. I sighed. If there wasn't food in the house, it meant either that one of us—usually me—hadn't done the shopping or that Mom had run out of grocery money. In this case, it was probably both.

I got dressed and stood in front of Mom's closed bedroom door. "Going to the grocery store," I said loudly, not expecting a reply.

"Cea?"

"No, it's *God*," I said sarcastically. I heard movement, and then her door opened.

"Hi," she said with a weak smile. Her face was red and puffy.

I crossed my arms angrily over my chest. Mom's new boyfriend had about as much power to make her cry on a weekly basis as Sam had. How many times did she have to allow a man to devastate her before she stopped going back for more?

"What's up?" I asked harshly.

"Oh, you know." She flapped her hands. "Anyway, I wanted to, you know . . . say sorry for not being around more. I'm . . . I'm going to try to do better. I want to be here for you. Okay?"

"Yeah. Sure," I said with a smirk.

"When are you going to L.A.? I was thinking I could give you a ride to the airport."

"That would mean your car would have to be fixed. And for that, you would need money. Don't worry about it—I'll find a friend to take me." I walked down the hall and left, shutting the front door hard behind me.

At the grocery store, I cruised the aisles, trying to collect my thoughts and emotions. *Okay*, I said to myself as I threw juice, bread and tomatoes into my basket. *Okay. At least she's trying. She knows she's screwing up, and if she really means it this time . . . maybe it's not such a big deal after all . . . I'm probably just being uptight . . .*

I would not give my mother the letter, I decided. If nothing else, I couldn't afford to give her a reason to try to send me away, as she and Sam had once done. Just months after I'd started modelling, the two of them had sat me down and told me that if I couldn't accept their relationship, they would put me on a plane to live with my father. The thought horrified me—not because I didn't think he was a far healthier parental choice than my mother, but because I had no interest in being forced on a family I barely knew. And most of all, because my new career would be over almost before it began—there was no modelling agency in the small town where my father lived, and I doubted he would allow me to go to New York and Europe by myself.

When I got home, I was putting the groceries away when Mom walked into the room behind me.

"Cea," she said quietly, and something in her voice made me turn. "Is this for me?"

I stared. She was holding the letter I'd written. *Impossible*, I thought. She hardly ever went in my room. "Where—where did you get that?"

"In your bedroom. I ran out of eyeliner."

"It's not a good idea to share eye makeup. Modelling 101, duh." I snatched the letter away from her, instantly regretting my last remark. It was childish and unnecessary, but sometimes I couldn't help reminding her that while she'd never even *tried* to have a career, I already had one at the age of sixteen. I softened my voice. "Of course it's not for you. There's a girl at school I'm having issues with. Her name is Michelle too."

"Oh. Okay, because . . ."

"Because what?"

"Nothing. I just didn't think we were that far gone. I mean, what could upset you that much?"

I suddenly felt like I was looking through the right end of a telescope for the first time. Writing that letter had made me feel like I was in control, when really Mom was the one with the power. She still had no idea how her bad choices affected me, because she never questioned them. While she lived in a protected bubble of oblivion, I dealt with the reality she'd created for both of us.

"Nothing," I said, shaking my head. "Don't worry about it, okay? It wasn't for you." I gave her shoulder an awkward little pat.

And then, of course, I smiled.

Chapter 13

December 2014
Vancouver

Okay, okay!" I said to my dinner guests, glancing at my watch. "It's almost midnight. Quick, we need to go around the table and tell our best and worst moments of 2014."

"All right." Fiona laughed. "You first!"

I smiled and laced my hands together in front of me, a nervous habit since my first day of kindergarten, when I'd wanted to make a good impression on the teacher. That's what normal kids did at school, I'd noticed in books.

Across from me sat Remy, surrounded by the ten close friends who had joined us to ring in 2015. Everyone at my table tonight had come into my life through different avenues—my kids' schools, mutual acquaintances, a high school reconnection. Knowing they would all read my book when it came out, I'd secretly fretted over their reactions—after all, I'd rarely shown them the cracks beneath my magazine-page veneer. But I needn't have feared. If anything, my story had brought us closer, spurred interesting conversation and even inspired them, if their claims were to be believed. My life wasn't perfect—the darkness still threatened me sometimes, but at least I could be honest about it now. I had a wonderfully supportive husband

182

who put his arms around me when I cried and reminded me of my value. As grateful as I was for that, I could also see that all those times I'd cried by myself had taught me something important: it's when there's no one to comfort us that we experience growth. And because of that, my lifelong apprehension at revealing my true self was fading. The person who'd felt shut down by both her ex-husbands' responses to her past, who had refused to share it with her closest friends for so many years, seemed almost like another woman.

"Seriously, you all know me," I said. "I never thought I'd have a year like this. Amazing friends, husband, kids, new house, best-selling book. I'm the luckiest person ever." I sipped my drink, realizing I could say this aloud because everyone at the table knew what I'd been through. In a way, telling my story had given me permission to be happy—at least in my own mind.

As I often did, I wondered what Mom's life would be like now, had she lived. A day didn't pass that I didn't think about her, but I had to admit that it was a relief to not worry about her future. Really, there were only two ways I could have imagined it going, and either one would have brought its own world of problems. Given her inability to provide for herself, she likely would have landed on my doorstep or stayed forever with Sam. The first option would have compromised the peace in my family, and the second would have compromised the peace within myself. Though I'd tried to talk to her about it before she died, Mom had never acknowledged that her affair with Sam had made me feel unwanted, expendable and powerless in the years when I needed her the most. As a result, I'd questioned the most fundamental of parental duties, uncertain if I really had a right to expect a mother who was present, supportive and protective. I knew the answer now, of course, but it had taken me decades to arrive here. Though it wasn't always easy, I was able to put aside my own desires in my kids' best interests, and it never ceased to amaze me when others didn't.

I brought my attention back to the present and turned toward Dianne, who was about to describe her worst moments of the year in her typically funny way. Dianne knew my history better than anyone else at the table. I'd met her at Avery's preschool, and of all the outlandish coincidences, she had known Papa Dick in the Yukon decades ago when she'd lived there herself. *Yes*, she'd said with a big laugh when we made that discovery, *you certainly have an interesting story to tell with that one!* We'd become friends soon after my split with James, and she'd seen me go through some dark times as I struggled to get back on my feet. Sitting here now, I couldn't help but notice the contrast to my last New Year's Eve with my second husband. It had marked the end of 2007, the worst year of my adult life.

My mother had been dead for two weeks, and my split from James loomed three weeks in the future. I hadn't wanted to do anything except watch *The Hills* and get plastered on Freixenet, but I'd grudgingly accompanied James to a house party. Besides a couple high on ecstasy, we turned out to be the only guests there, and James promptly fell asleep on the sofa beside me. I drank too much wine, sitting in front of *Dick Clark* with the host and his girlfriend.

"What was your best moment of 2007?" the host asked me, making polite conversation, and I came up blank.

"Finding my son after I thought he'd been kidnapped at Old Navy," I said dramatically, not bothering to elaborate.

Later, as James and I rode home in a cab, I watched streams of revellers pour through the downtown streets, thrilled at the prospect of another year. All I could think about was that with the holidays over, James and I would be free to drop the pretence and go our separate ways. But I had nowhere to go, no money, not even a car to drive. It was a lifetime low, but it was also the tunnel I needed to enter in order to see how much lighter it was on the other side.

And Remy was now a big part of that light. Something I'd learned since being with him was that our value is determined by ourselves, not anyone else—the more you expect, the more you get. With Remy I was able to be myself fully, to ask for support without fear and to be appreciated for the role I played in our family. Just by believing I was worth more, I'd attracted a partner who believed the same. In a way, I had James to thank for this, because without the lessons I had learned by being with him, I wouldn't have seen how much I needed to move forward toward my own fulfillment. Trying to become the person I thought he needed me to be wasn't much different from my mother's approach to Sam and her other lovers, but finally I had put an end to the pattern. And it had turned out well in the end—James and I worked together much better as co-parents than as a couple, managing to put Avery's well-being above all.

I caught Remy's eye across the table and smiled, thinking about the signs I'd been given so many times when I was making a mistake. Had I not ignored those warnings, it was quite possible I wouldn't have ended up right here. And I felt truly grateful that I hadn't sacrificed my values to create an easier, but less meaningful, life for myself.

1988
Los Angeles

When I started modelling, I promised myself I'd never be one of them—one of *those girls* who'd made it by sleeping with someone just because his opinion mattered to the right people. Sex in exchange for a prestigious booking seemed to me no better than prostitution—something my mother might have done, perhaps, if she had been given the opportunity.

And then I met François. I was eighteen years old and living in Los Angeles. Since getting my driver's licence two years ago, I'd lost my virginity to Kevin, my first real boyfriend, graduated from high school and moved away from home. Back home in Calgary, I now had a decent enough boyfriend named Jason—serious enough to do long distance but not serious enough to invite him to L.A. with me—and I was getting as much work in this city as I could handle. So when an overweight man smelling of sweet cologne and French cigarettes passed his number to me at an industry party, I barely took notice. I was already annoyed after fighting off a handsome but relentless black man who had followed me around all evening, drunkenly insisting we find a hotel room. "Do you know who I am? I'm the *Juice*. O.J. Simpson," he kept saying to me, but the name would only register when I saw him on trial on TV a few years later. I threw the cologne-soaked man's number into the restroom trash bin and forgot all about him.

But the fashion world in any given city is a tightly knit one, meaning that anyone with influence or money can easily get whatever information they need. A few days after the party, one of my roommates at the models' apartment where I was living held the phone out to me. The phone at the apartment rang day and night—back-home boyfriends looking for reassurance, bookers bearing career-making-and-breaking news, mothers urging their daughters to eat more or less, to call their grandmothers on their birthday, to come home. I received plenty of calls from the first two but rarely from the third.

"It's for you," my roommate said. "François something."

I took the handpiece, irritated. I never gave my number out. "Yes?"

"You never called me," an accented male voice boomed. "I've been waiting by the phone for three days."

"As if," I scoffed after a beat, drawing a total blank.

"It's the truth. You haven't left my thoughts for a moment."

I let the line fall silent as I tried to remember. French accent, deep voice, no shortage of confidence. It finally came to me.

"I met you at a party the other night, right?"

He laughed good-naturedly. "Why, yes. I'm glad I left such a memorable impression."

I laughed back. "It's not that you *didn't*. It's just—"

"Sure, I know. You have a stream of admirers. Around the block, just hoping for a glimpse."

"Well, not exactly. Not even close. I just . . . I was distracted that night, I think. Um, what was your name again?"

"François de Legare."

"Oh. Right." It was all coming back now. This one had bragged about royal connections, homes in three cities, a best friend who was the beauty editor at French *Vogue*. *You should be a great big star by now*, he had said to me without a trace of insincerity, and I had completely ignored him.

"We talked about dinner," he continued. "I hope you remember that, at least? How about the Ivy on Friday night?"

"The Ivy on Friday night. Um, yeah, okay . . . I mean, why not?"

"I couldn't ask for a more enthusiastic response. Very well, then, I will pick you up at eight o'clock."

"I can just meet you there. I do have a car."

He chuckled softly. "Indeed. The little blue Rabbit, yes?"

Though François couldn't see it, my face reddened. In a land where what you drove equalled how much you were respected, my car was a serious source of humiliation: old, rusty and banged in on one side from a recent accident. I didn't want to spend the money to replace it until I knew I would be staying in L.A., and lately my agency in Paris had been asking me to come back. Besides, I would rather drive my own cheap wheels than sell out. Two years before, while I'd been here for a modelling job, I had accepted a coffee date with a wealthy businessman I'd met at a dim sum restaurant. Two days later, he showed up at my hotel claiming he'd bought me a car. I never did see the actual vehicle—just some dangling keys—but the whole thing had creeped me out.

"How—how do you know what kind of car I drive?" I asked François.

"I saw you leaving the party. I waved at you, remember?"

"Oh, right. Um, okay, do you have a pen, then? I'm at—"

"Darling, please. I know where you live. Until then?"

I paused. Something about this was totally grossing me out. I remembered perfectly well what François looked like, and there wasn't one living cell of my being that was attracted to him. And if I wasn't attracted to him, what other reason was there for going on a date?

"Yes," I said finally. "Until then."

One thing was certain: François knew how to pull out all the stops. He picked me up in a white Rolls-Royce, and though I was initially embarrassed by the thought of getting into such a pretentious vehicle, it took me a humiliatingly short amount of time to get used to it. Inside, I found a single pink rose waiting on my seat. There was a telephone resting in the console, something I'd never seen before. When I commented on it, François held it out to me.

"Go ahead. Call your mother," he said with a grin, but I just laughed. Mom was the last person I could imagine discussing with the likes of François de Legare.

By the time François pulled up to the restaurant an hour later and handed his keys over to the valet, I felt like I was stepping out of his vehicle into a completely new life. Paparazzi clogged the guarded entrance, hopeful for a glimpse of a movie star or two. "What have you been in?" a short man asked me as his camera flashed in my face, but François put his arm around me protectively and guided me inside.

Once we were seated, he ordered martinis for us.

"Um, I'm not much of a drinker," I said, holding my hand up, and it was true. My efforts to avoid the partying model lifestyle meant that I'd only had alcohol a few times in my life, and each time, I got raving drunk within an alarmingly short time.

"Very well. Champagne, then."

Our drinks arrived, and I sipped the bubbles slowly; it tasted more like grape juice than booze. I didn't protest when he refilled my glass, even though my head was already beginning to feel wavy. At the end of my third drink, I leaned forward and mustered up the courage to divulge the truth.

"Just so you know, I, um . . . have a boyfriend. Like, back home and stuff."

"Of course you do. How could you not?" he replied lightly.

I smiled back at him, but even through my drunken rose-coloured glasses, I had to admit that the sight of him repulsed me. His skin was so deeply tanned it looked like leather, he wore fake-looking blue contact lenses over his naturally brown eyes, and his jowl was firmly residing in double-chin territory. Not to mention that he had to be at least fifty years old. But François seemed at peace with his physical shortcomings, maybe because he wasn't truly interested in me.

"Seriously," he said, throwing his hands up in sincerity. "You may find this hard to believe, but I am only here to help you. I see in you a potential that comes along very rarely. The thing is, my best friend is the beauty editor at French *Vogue*. We grew up together, went to the same school. We went in our own directions, but I always gave her my word that I would send the best of the best her way should I come across it. Beautiful girls, but more than that. True beauty, true talent. And you have both. Your body is thin, long, lithe like a young filly. Your eyes . . . they sparkle, the colour of the deepest green seas. Your lips are the shape of sensuality itself. Your hair is thick and heavy, like silk. Your teeth . . . they could use a little work, but with a little effort could be perfect too. You are the whole package. Do you know how often I come across someone like you?"

"Uh, no." I ducked my head, both embarrassed and disconcertingly charmed by his words. Teeth thing aside, none of my boyfriends had ever described me as flatteringly as François just had. And neither had any of my bookers, which, if I were honest, would have meant a whole lot more.

"I'll tell you how often. Almost never." He leaned back in his chair and smiled at me. He wasn't so bad when he smiled. "I have helped others, you know," he went on, and then named two top models of the moment. "Have you heard of them?"

"Of course," I replied, trying not to look impressed.

He nodded. "I discovered them. Sent them to the right people. And look where they are now."

"Wow," I said, feeling my eyes widen. For any model, landing a booking for *Vogue* magazine, whether it be American, French, Italian or British, was the pinnacle of success. The type of modelling I did—clothing and lingerie catalogues, TV commercials, advertisements for everything from skincare products to banks to holiday destinations to ironing boards—paid well, but it lacked glamour and wasn't the gateway to top-model stardom. I'd always been realistic about my potential as a model, and to me a booking as prestigious as *Vogue* had seemed out of reach. My face was just a little too ordinary, my nose and hips not quite narrow enough; and of course there was the issue of my teeth. While they weren't horribly crooked, a single jutting top tooth meant my smile didn't meet the standard of perfection required for me to really go far. If there was one thing in the world I wished my family had been able to provide for me—besides a completely different childhood, that is—it was braces. There wasn't a day that passed when I didn't think about what a difference that one thing would have made in my life. But sitting here across from François, I wondered if maybe I'd set my career sights too low.

"Anyway," François said abruptly, tearing into a new piece of bread. "Your boyfriend. Lucky man. Tell me about him?"

I glanced away. The last thing I felt like talking about right now was my boyfriend, whose university lifestyle and hometown charms suddenly seemed ridiculously unsophisticated compared to François's high-rolling reality.

"How about . . . we don't," I replied, lifting my glass, and François grinned at me.

Apparently François didn't believe in wasting time. The day after our dinner, he called me again.

"I faxed Helene your photo," he said. "She called me back right away to say how beautiful you are."

"Wow. Really?" I responded, hating the hopeful leap of my heart.

"Really. May I take you to lunch to celebrate?"

"I don't know. Is there . . . something to celebrate?"

He laughed. "My dear, one of the most influential people in the fashion world thinks you've got what it takes. I would say so."

"Okay. Yeah. Thank you. How about tomorrow?"

"Tomorrow it is."

This time there was a yellow rose waiting on the passenger seat. "For friendship," François said with his Aspirin-white smile.

After lunch, he was driving me back to my apartment in Westwood when he veered off toward Beverly Hills. My belly jumped nervously.

"Um, is there an errand you needed to run?" I asked lightly, suddenly aware that the man beside me could very well be a serial killer. A cold memory from my childhood swept over me, of riding beside a man who had picked Mom and me up when we were hitch-hiking. He put the moves on Mom and then refused to pull over when she rebuffed him, making both of us certain we were seeing our last day. It was fear that saved us; I was so terrified that I almost had an accident on his seat, so he was forced to pull over, and we made our escape.

But François laughed reassuringly. "Don't worry, darling, just taking a little detour. If you're going to meet Helene, you'll need something to wear. Don't all girls love to shop?"

I looked down at my outfit. I was wearing my Levi's 501 jeans and favourite black eyelet Anti-Flirt bodysuit, bought in Paris the year before. I thought I looked fine, and besides, I wasn't interested in being in debt to François.

"But I don't—"

"No buts. Your birthday is coming up, right? Think of it as an early birthday gift."

A minute later, he pulled up to the Azzedine Alaia store and parked. My jaw dropped. Alaia was *only* my favourite designer in the whole world. As I waited for François to open my door—I was already getting used to his ways—I ran through the gamut of justifications in my head. We went into the shop together.

Half an hour later, I emerged wearing a tight black dress with straps that crossed over my back. I had wanted to take it off to bring home—after all, it was a little on the sexy side for daywear—but François had insisted I keep it on. After catching a glimpse of the twelve-hundred-dollar price tag, I figured it was the least I could do.

It wasn't long before François and I were talking on the phone daily and going out a few times a week. It never moved beyond friendship, and I almost always met him on his turf. I tried my best to keep him away from my apartment, which currently housed eight models and was a mecca for gossip. But one day, I agreed to let him pick me up for lunch. I was ready for him when the doorbell rang, running to get it in hopes of escaping before the other girls saw him. I knew exactly how the scenario looked, and though I'd seen all of them doing versions of the same thing, I still prided myself on being the one who wouldn't be sucked in by lofty promises and expensive dinners. I breezed out the door, shutting it quickly behind me.

I kissed François on both cheeks, trying not to inhale the scent of his sweet cologne. He pulled back and looked at me.

"Hey. You okay?" he asked.

"Yeah, sure." I wasn't actually, because that morning I'd heard from my booker that a client I'd recently worked for had gone bankrupt. They owed me several thousand dollars I knew I'd never see. But when I thought about telling François about it, in my head it just sounded like I was hinting around that I needed money. "I'm fine."

"Good," he replied, smiling at me and shaking his head.

"What's wrong?" I asked self-consciously.

"Nothing. Just that I haven't seen you in nearly a week, and I can't believe that you've grown even more beautiful."

"Yeah, right." I turned away to hide my pleasure at his compliment, making a big deal out of scanning the street for his car. "Where did you park?"

"Right here," he said, gesturing to a shiny red Golf Cabriolet parked at the curb.

"Oh. Brought the casual wheels today, did you?"

"Yes. I noticed you like Volkswagens." We were standing in front of the passenger door, but he didn't move to open it.

"Um, yeah," I said awkwardly, wondering if I should just go for the door handle myself.

"So you like it?"

"Like it? It's only my dream car. I mean, not that your Rolls isn't great, but a *convertible* . . ."

He was holding out a key attached to a Century City VW keychain. I stared at him blankly.

"Good thing," he said. "Because it's all yours."

"*What?*" I clapped my hand over my mouth in disbelief. "Are you *kidding* me?"

"Why would I kid? I see that you need a new car. Here. Get in, let's go for a ride."

My mind was racing. This was an awesome car, no question about it, but I could only imagine the strings that came attached to it. And besides, how would I explain a forty-thousand-dollar car to my back-home boyfriend? No. I had refused a car from a man once, and I would do so again.

"François, seriously," I began. "There's just no way I can accept this. It's so sweet of you, really, but I mean—"

"What? That you don't want to sleep with me for it?" His face was serious. I giggled nervously, and he broke into a smile. "Only joking. I already told you, I just want to help you. All I ask is you be my friend. Now, let's go out for lunch—and you're driving!"

Certainly François knew how to be a gentleman, and the reality was that I enjoyed his company. We ate fantastic meals, went to the movies and Universal Studios, even had drinks at his penthouse apartment a couple of times, and he never made a move on me. I tried to think of ways I could make myself valuable to him to ensure that our current situation continued. I was always at my most witty and upbeat when we were together, and I even offered him dating and fashion advice. I'd never had a male friend before, and I wanted to believe that such a relationship between a man and woman was possible. But my weakness was likely obvious: I desired success. When he asked me about my childhood and family, even though I didn't supply much detail, he quickly gleaned my escapist desires. And each time we met, he would feed me a tidbit about how crazy Helene was for me. I always took it with a grain of salt, being savvy enough about my own industry to know that if she really loved me that much, she could have called up my agency and booked me at any time. But as much as I wanted to be, I was not immune to the lure of easy success.

One night François and I went out for dinner, and he told me he had a surprise for me. We were at Spago, sitting at one of their best tables after François, on a whim and with a single phone call, had jumped the queue of a one-month waiting list.

"So," he said. "I have some news for you. But I must tell you, I am hesitant to reveal it."

"How come?"

He smiled. "I've grown accustomed to your company. But I know it is not mine to keep."

"What do you mean?"

He paused dramatically, sipping from his wineglass. "I heard from Helene this morning. She has a big beauty editorial coming up, and she wants to book you for it. You would fly to Paris next week. She just wanted to see a couple more headshots, which I faxed to her already—the Gorman job you did last month."

"Are you serious?" Suddenly my disbelief was erased, and it made perfect sense: she had just been waiting for the right job to book me!

"Completely. You deserve this. Only, it means I will miss you when you go."

"But—you could come and visit me. I mean, you're from France, after all, so why not?"

He shrugged and waved a hand in the air. "My home is here now."

"Wow," I said, staring down at my spaghetti. "I'll . . . I'll miss you too."

Later, when we went back to François's apartment for a drink, it didn't even seem unnatural when he leaned across the sofa to kiss me. I realized that I had known all along this was coming, and my efforts at fooling myself into thinking otherwise had been pathetically vain. Did I really believe he had bought me a car and offered to help my career because of my bottomless supply of wit and intelligence? As his hand made its way under my top, I held my breath and told myself it would all be over soon. *Just this once. Next week I'll be on a plane to Paris, and I'll never have to do this again.* I let him take my hand and lead me to his bedroom.

Twenty minutes later, I was quietly throwing up into François's toilet. My skin reeked of his cologne. I knew I would never be able to erase the memory of his massive body on top of mine. But it was *I* who was making me ill. Not only had I cheated on my boyfriend, but I had just done the one thing I'd promised myself I never would. And now my ambition was exposed for the shallowest of reasons: a car I could look cool in, and a job I would probably never even get.

When I emerged from the bathroom, François was smoking a cigarette in bed with the TV on. He smiled and patted the mattress beside him.

"Stay with me," he said.

I lay down, careful to keep our bodies apart, and pretended to be exhausted so I could feign sleep. *Just one night. Just tonight*, I kept thinking. But sleep would not come.

How many times did I have to ignore my instincts to have them proven correct? Of course, I never did work for French *Vogue*. Time after time, François postponed his promise with one excuse or another: Helene really wanted me, but she was required to book another girl to return a favour. Helene loved me, but she was a little concerned about my teeth.

"I'm so sorry if my mother couldn't afford braces," I once replied defensively to that one. "Weirdly enough, I guess groceries took priority. And I can't exactly get them straightened now, can I? I might as well just wave goodbye to my career."

I'd like to say I walked away when I saw the writing on the wall, but I didn't. The affair lasted half a year. I never lost my feeling of revulsion each time I slept with François. He was my first experience with cheating, but I figured it didn't really count, because (a) I didn't enjoy the sex, and (b) I wasn't planning to marry my back-home boyfriend. The decent thing to do would have been to break up with my boyfriend, but thinking about how he would cry and tell me that he couldn't stand losing me made me feel like I was actually doing the right thing by staying with him. I started lying to him about where I was in the evening, and then I'd lie awake, eaten away by guilt and worry that I'd forget my own fiction.

One night, after tossing and turning for too long, I picked up the phone and called Mom. We didn't often speak, and I hadn't planned on telling her about François, but the moment I heard her voice, I let it all spill.

"So . . . I just feel really guilty. And I don't know what to do, because I really do like him, but I'm grossed out by . . . you know, the other stuff."

"You say he bought you a *car*?"

"Yes."

"Wow. Wish I had that problem. Darling, don't fret so much. You're both getting something out of the deal, right? Just think of it as . . . a fair trade."

"Fair trade," I repeated. "Right. Okay."

I hung up and lay back down on my pillow, trying to feel better. But it was no use. After all, my mother wasn't exactly known for her sound judgment—not that it seemed to bother her much. Sometimes

I thought my life would be so much easier if I could just be a little more like her.

Perhaps François was feeling a little guilty about our relationship too, because after six months passed and no booking from Helene had materialized, he did the next best thing: took me to New York and got me the best agency in the city, a highly selective one known for its top editorial girls—the ones who got the bookings with the best magazines. The owner seemed thrilled to have me and predicted great things for my future. François and I went out for dinner to celebrate, and it was later that night, in bed in our thousand-dollar-a-night hotel suite, that I finally realized I was in over my head. I was discreetly tucking the covers around me to try to separate our bodies when François turned toward me.

"I've fallen for you," he said matter-of-factly, and then he hesitated. His eyes, naked-looking without his blue contacts, gazed deep into mine. "Do you think you could ever love someone like me?" he almost whispered.

"Oh, François . . ." I tried to formulate a kind but noncommittal reply as I looked back at him. How stupid I'd been to never anticipate the possibility of this moment. I knew the answer, of course, but was I ready to lose everything that François represented to me?

"Don't answer," he said quickly. "It's because of Helene, isn't it? You are disappointed in me. I promised you would work for her, and you haven't." He sat up and lit a cigarette. "I have been selfish. She really did want to book you, but I told her you were thinking of quitting the business. That you wanted to get married and have babies. I wanted to keep you for myself. Will you forgive me? First thing when we get back to L.A., I will call her and tell the truth."

"Oh . . ." I said again, lost for words. "It's . . . it's okay. Really, I understand. Can we just . . . can we talk about this tomorrow? I'm really tired."

"Of course." He nodded, and I turned onto my side away from him.

My heart was a little broken for him. It was clear to me now that François was lonely, and I was filling a need for him. But I knew I would never be able to complete the circle of emotion needed for an equal and genuine relationship. And if that were true, no matter what my mother said, if I stayed, I was no better than a whore selling my body and company for wealth and success.

The following day, François and I flew back to L.A. and drove to his apartment. "I'll call Helene in the morning," he said again before we went to bed, but the smile I returned to him didn't touch my heart. The nausea I'd felt since the night before hadn't left me.

I lay staring at the ceiling for a long time, and then I reached out and placed my hand on François's shoulder. He turned toward me in the dark.

"I'm sorry," I said quietly. "I just can't do this. You deserve more. Someone who can really love you."

I switched on the lamp, got out of bed and began to dress. François lit a cigarette and blew smoke into the air, saying nothing. I looked at him, but he wouldn't meet my gaze. I turned away.

"I'm sorry," he said to my back. "Again, I broke my promise to you. We can just be friends, okay? Just go back to being friends."

I turned around to him and shook my head. "François. I just don't think that's going to work. I . . . I'm sorry. Really."

He nodded and looked away from me again. "Keep the car. I bought it for you."

I went over to him and hugged him and then walked to the front door. Just before stepping out into the hallway, I placed my car key on his entrance table, and then I left, quietly closing the door behind me.

I'd given in to the lure, broken my promise to myself, and just as I'd anticipated, I was filled with regret. But the thing about regret, I realized, was that each day presented a fresh opportunity to start putting it behind you. As I'd done before François entered my life, I would make things happen on my own—whatever the results.

Chapter 14

2008
Vancouver

A few days into 2008, I was at the swimming pool with Avery when my cell phone rang. I had no intention of answering—I was changing him back into his clothes, and he was on the verge of a meltdown because I was having trouble getting his shirt on over his damp skin. I glanced down at my phone. *New York, NY*, it said under the number, and my stomach did a little flip. *Could it possibly be?*

"Avery," I said quickly. "Be really good for Mommy, and sit here quietly for a few minutes, and then we'll go for an ice cream cone. Okay?" He nodded through his tears, and I took a deep breath and picked up.

"Ms. Person?" a male voice said.

"Yes?" My throat clicked closed nervously.

"It's Arnold Lassiter at Lassiter Literary Agency."

Yes! "Oh. Hello!"

"Hello there. I've just finished reading your memoir, and I have to tell you that I'm completely blown away by it."

"Wow. Really?" My voice was high and squeaky.

"Yes. It's an incredible story. I'd love to work with you on this. Are you still seeking representation?"

199

"Um, well . . . yes! I mean . . . I was hoping to work with you."

"Well then, I couldn't be more pleased," Arnold replied. "What do you say I email you the contract this afternoon, and we'll be on our way?"

"That would be *fantastic*!" I replied, too eager as always. "I'll read it over and get back to you. Until tomorrow, then?"

"Yes. Until tomorrow."

I hung up the phone and literally jumped for joy. Avery giggled and copied me, and I grabbed him up in a giant hug. This was it—I had an agent! Guthrie the astrologer had been dead wrong! It was only a matter of time now before I got a publishing deal, and best of all, I could leave James without my future being a huge and terrifying unknown.

James hadn't offered to attend Mom's memorial with me, and I hadn't asked him. A week after I signed on to have my book represented by Arnold Lassiter, I stood in Sam's living room preparing to read a poem I'd written for my mother. Her death had forced Sam and me to communicate during the past couple of weeks. Over the phone, we'd stiffly discussed food and flowers and guest lists. He'd wanted it held at their home. We agreed that I would plan it, and he would pay for it. At the end of our last conversation, he told me that Grandma Jeanne was staying at his house; would I like to sleep in the guest room? I didn't want to, but I also couldn't afford a hotel. It was convenient. I'd be with my grandmother. Yes, I replied, wishing I had the nerve or the pride to say no. Thank you.

Walking into Sam's house, I'd felt like I was stepping back into my past. A few roommates from the house Mom and I had lived in when I was a teenager were there, as was Aunt Jan. For me, the saddest sight of the day was Grandma Jeanne. She had four children, and each of them had carved a painful path through her life. I realized I might be the only person in the room who understood that my grandmother's grief wasn't just for her lost daughter; it was for all her family. The Persons were over. Some of them may still have been alive, but they, along with their admirable but questionable ideals, were all but finished. It felt like the official end of my history.

I stood at the front of the living room and read:

"In my dreams we hold hands again
And run through the meadows of my youth
Abundant with wildflowers
Jutting grey mountains rising from the west
Streams gurgling around our feet as we splash
And fall, tumbling and laughing, under a cloudless sky
For so very long it was just the two of us
I felt your wings spread around me, warm like an angel's soft embrace
You were a wildflower yourself
Rolling over the landscape and smiling into the breeze

"What I will miss the most
Are the moments that can now never be
The careless Sundays I thought we would spend on the sofa
The light in your eyes as you watch your grandson hike his first
*   mountain*
And fly him around by his ankles like the spinning wheels of time,
Time that I thought we would have forever
'I love you, Grandma Michelle,' says my son
'Please won't you do it just one more time
Sprinkle your fairy dust on me and kiss me good night.'"

Smile, nod, hug, nod, hug, smile. As soon as I could politely manage it, I escaped to the basement guest room. Footsteps crossed the floor above my head, and I hoped upon hope that Sam wouldn't come downstairs. As grateful as I was for his recent kindness, I still wanted to crawl out of my own skin at the discomfort of staying in his home.

I lay down on the bed and closed my eyes, arms spread at my

sides. I thought about my still-faceless agent, who was poised to release the story of the Persons into the world any day. I had now lost most of my family without ever really understanding them, and my mother's death had left me with questions that would never be answered—questions about my family's mental health, especially Mom's. Her traits were far less defined than those of her three siblings. Why hadn't my mother been able to help with my most basic homework? Why did she forget my boyfriends' names after she'd met them twenty times but remember details from her short time with my father like they'd happened yesterday? And why was she always *so* inappropriate?

Everyone thinks their mother is weird, my high school friends used to reassure me, but I looked at theirs and I looked at mine, and I saw a truth I could never clearly explain to them: there was something off about my mother. She'd escaped her siblings' schizophrenia and bipolar disorder and extreme mental challenge, but she still acted brain-damaged half the time. Perhaps it had been too much to ask, that writing would bring it all into focus for me. I'd seen my book as a life raft that would rescue me from my financial hole and, at the same time, bring me understanding about my family. Though I still believed it would, I also had to admit that it wasn't the most logical or direct way to address my issues. In that way, I had to recognize that I was a true Person, with dramatic ideas and solutions to problems that I only admitted were mistakes after it was too late.

1989
Paris & Calgary

My life as a model was everything and nothing like I thought it would be. I got to dress up and feel beautiful, I loved the work itself, and most important, the money I made ensured my continued freedom. But my career came with a price.

After leaving Los Angeles and the memory of François behind, I moved to Paris. With its sky-high standards, party lifestyle and deadly competition, Paris was like bootcamp for models with dreams of making it to the top. Girls cut their teeth there and then went one of three ways: they made it and suddenly had the industry bowing at their feet, did well enough to move to less competitive but still lucrative markets like London, Germany, Sydney or Tokyo, or went home and hung up their portfolio. I would eventually fall into the second category, but for a time, it seemed like I'd fall into the third.

I'd been to Paris many times before, but this was the first time I'd committed to actually living there indefinitely, and somehow that changed things. Rather than just passing through, I was now fully absorbed in the make-or-break modelling culture. And this time, I learned a few things about myself that weren't entirely pleasant. One was that I could go without consuming a single thing other than grapefruit juice for five days straight. I'd done it twice to get super skinny for an important job, and it had worked like a charm. Never mind that my arms had lost almost all feeling, and that by the end of it, my head swam with dizziness. At five foot eleven and 121 pounds, I'd never looked better—or so my agency assured me.

Another thing I learned was that I could reinvent myself: because no one knew where I'd come from, I could show up as whoever I wanted to be. The persona Paris brought out in me was Tough Cea. The part of me that had emerged as a result of my unsavoury experiences with Barry a decade ago had grown into an even tougher and more cynical nineteen-year-old, only now I didn't dislike her so much. She could walk down the street without paying any mind to the swarming gypsy children and masturbators in the doorways. She was the pessimist to my natural optimist. She dealt with shit and kept me safe, reminding me of every possible scenario that could go wrong. She also had no problem saying no to the regular flow of drugs that most models got caught up in.

But if I had no interest in drugs, I'd slowly but surely warmed up to alcohol. I felt safe in the knowledge that no one in my family was much of a drinker and that therefore my drinking made me nothing like them. I only drank when I went out, which still wasn't often, but when I did, I didn't stop until I blacked out. This was something else I learned about myself in Paris. One night, I was at a nightclub when a man tried to hit on me. He grabbed my ass, so I gave him the finger and left the dance floor. That seemed to be the end of it, until a while later when I woke up in the restroom with a very sore right hand. My roommate informed me that after I'd had a few more drinks, the guy had walked by me again and called me a nasty name, so I hauled off and slugged him in the face. I had no recollection of it whatsoever.

The last thing I learned in Paris was that I hated it. Not the city itself but everything it represented to me. I couldn't enjoy a chocolate croissant without experiencing modelling-induced guilt. Every bar or nightclub I passed held a memory of some industry creep trying to lure me in with drugs or sex. I lived in a two-hundred-square-foot apartment—with a roommate. The grocery stores were as big as 7-Elevens, everyone pretended to not understand a word of my school French, and, despite my remaining ambiguous about my back-home boyfriend, I found myself missing him. I was working regularly, which was a lot more than many models could claim, but it wasn't the calibre of work I had moved there to do.

I remember the night I decided I would go home. I was sitting on the futon sofa in my tiny apartment. My roommate was out for the evening, and even though I didn't smoke, I was smoking a cigarette from her forgotten pack. I was thinking about an important casting with a French magazine scheduled for the next morning. I'd seen them today, but they wanted me back so their editor-in-chief could meet me. I knew what getting the booking would mean: my first editorial with a top magazine, a trip to the Seychelles, eight tear-sheets for my portfolio that could elevate me to the next level in an industry that judged a model by the magazine name printed in the corner of the page. And it would also mean a week of starvation, a high possibility of fighting off the photographer's/client's/art director's advances and an even deeper sense of the emptiness I'd felt since coming here.

I pulled on the cigarette, inhaled tentatively and choked. Tried again and managed to exhale without coughing. I didn't want to feel cool when I smoked, but I did. It matched my new persona. Smoking a cigarette and contemplating such a high-calibre booking reminded me that I was a real, successful model. I'd been working for five years at a career that was the product of a lifelong dream. And now that victory was literally around the next corner, suddenly I didn't want it anymore. What the hell was wrong with me?

But of course, in the deepest part of my consciousness, I knew exactly what was wrong with me. I'd been trying to ward off the darkness since I'd arrived here, but it was winning. The escape I'd found through modelling was not what I'd hoped for. My past was still my past, and it could not be blotted out by any amount of evasion or success. It followed me around like a stray animal, begging to be picked up and examined and accepted. Or if not accepted, at least acknowledged. I'd started my career in search of a more normal life, and modelling was anything but normal. It was a portal into a world that revealed its dark side the further you travelled into it.

What I really wanted was to go home—which, in Paris, was practically a dirty word. All of us models were homesick, every single one of us, but admitting that to our bookers was like putting a black mark on the booking charts we longed to see filled with confirmed jobs. I'd seen it happen before—the girls who came into the agency in tears, and the reaction they'd get from their booker, which was some variation on how lucky they were to be there, but if it wasn't what they wanted, they were free to run home to their mama and/or boyfriend. From then on, they were considered ungrateful, and the bookings would start to dry up. And now I was under contract with my agency. If I told them I needed to go home to regroup, I'd be breaking my contract and I would never be invited back.

The next morning, I got dressed in my regulation black leggings, bodysuit and leather motorcycle jacket. I made sure my hair looked perfect in a way that seemed like I hadn't even glanced in the mirror that morning. As far as my face went, I had little choice; models weren't allowed to wear makeup to castings, and I had learned my lesson after an editor smeared her thumb across my cheek and then wiped the offending grime on my white T-shirt.

I arrived at the magazine's office, changed into a swimsuit as instructed and handed my portfolio over to the editor.

"*Oui.* Very versatile look. Small breasts but good figure. A circle, please," she said, indicating for me to turn around. Standard issue.

I did so, letting her take a long gaze at my ass. In my daily life, my every body part was appraised by both eyes and hands. Fingers poked, prodded, pinned, cinched and tugged at me all day long. Whenever I felt the urge to complain, I reminded myself how hard I'd worked to become a model and how easy my job was compared to so many other people's.

When I faced her again, she was smiling.

"Your skin," she said, holding my arm up and turning it over like an alien specimen. "It's very pale, no? I hope it will not burn in the hot sun?"

This was my chance. I took a deep breath, as if this were very hard for me to say. "You mean . . . you want me to get a tan? Oh, no. I really hate to say this, but I have to be honest. I burn like a lobster. Maybe you could . . . shoot everything in the shade?"

That afternoon, when the option came off my chart, I simulated a meltdown to my booker. "I'm just not sure I'm cut out for this," I said tearfully. "I should be getting better bookings by now." There wasn't much she could say to that.

After I left the agency, I stopped at a kiosk and bought some post-cards and a pack of cigarettes. *I'm coming home*, I scrawled across the cards to Mom, my father and Papa Dick, wondering if they would even care.

Four days later, I was on a plane to Calgary. I didn't have the slightest idea what I was going to do with my life now, but I figured anything that moved me into something more normal was a step in the right direction. I had enough money to last me a little while. My boyfriend was meeting me at the airport. I might even call Mom. I'd rent a small apartment, maybe get a waitressing job until I worked things out. A waitressing job. Yeah. Right about now, something that pedestrian sounded just like heaven.

"Table seven, food's up!"

"Waitress, we still haven't got our drinks. We've been here for half an hour!"

"Can we *please* get some service over here?"

Fuck. I hated waitressing, and what's more, I was horrible at it. I'd been working at Pasta Frenzy for two months, and there was nothing about it that didn't suck. During the day, it was so dead I had to fight off catatonia, and at night, it was so busy my head spun. I wanted to quit—though what I might do next seemed a great, unsolvable mystery.

I slung food to tables, appeased impatient diners, tapped orders into the Squirrel machine. Then I made my way over to another server's table to deliver their food.

"Sorry it took so long," I said breathlessly to the two men, setting their plates down. "It's just been a little crazy—" I stopped short when I saw the face before me. "Uh—George? Oh my god, how are you?" My face was burning red. George, of all people, the man who'd been responsible for starting my modelling career. I wanted to die.

"Cea," he said with a pleasant smile. "I'd heard you left Paris. What happened?"

"I . . ." I shrugged lamely, completely flustered. Not only was I serving my former agent in a restaurant, but I suddenly didn't have a clue what had made me think I should throw it all away. "I just . . . wasn't happy, that's all. Long story." I tried to smile.

"Well. It's a real shame, I have to say. Such wasted potential. You should really reconsider."

"I . . . I might. I just needed a break. Anyway . . ." I pulled the pepper grinder, which was as long as a bedpost, from under my arm. "Pepper?" I asked, holding it in position above his plate.

"Please."

I slid my hand up the grinder to grasp the top, and it slipped from my fingers, crashing to the table and shattering the glass top. Shards of glass flew onto the table, into the food, onto George's lap and his companion's. Nearby customers turned to stare.

"I am so sorry," I said. I grabbed the plates off the table. "Don't move. I'll get a broom and find you another table." I looked around wildly for an empty one, but it was Friday night. All the tables were taken. Naturally.

George stood up and lightly brushed his pants off with his hands. "Don't worry about it, Cea. Really. I mean it."

I looked into his eyes, afraid of seeing pity or disappointment, but I only saw empathy. My sense of embarrassment and failure were mine alone.

"You want to make it up to me? Go back to Paris. Or New York if you want, or Milan. Call me, I'll set it up. Just don't . . . don't sell yourself short. Okay?"

"Okay," I whispered back. I was going to cry. Instead I turned away and headed to the dish pit to get my emotions under control.

I stood over the stainless steel sink with my hands braced against the counter, inhaling the smell of chlorine and food scraps. What the hell was wrong with me? There were plenty of people in the world who weren't given even a single chance to escape their past, and here I was throwing mine away for a job waiting tables. After more than a decade of dreaming of a modelling career, was I really giving up this easily?

I stood up straight and squared my shoulders, turning away before my approaching manager could catch my eye. He had once told me, in a roundabout way, that he would walk over broken glass for the chance to sleep with me. *Well, there's your broken glass,* I thought to myself giddily. I was pretty sure his worship would not morph into sympathy if he knew I was planning to quit the next day.

The following morning, I picked up the phone and called Mom.
After I moved to Paris, she'd been forced to give up the duplex we'd lived in since I was eleven. When we first moved there, she'd made rent by bringing in a string of roommates, and later I'd helped out with my modelling income until I announced that I was moving to Paris and couldn't do it anymore. But the day before I left, plagued with guilt as I thought of her sitting in her cheap apartment with no furniture or vehicle, I'd had a change of heart. I drove my car over to let her use it while I was away.

I'd seen her only once since returning home, to get the car back. She'd driven it for eight months at that point, and she returned it to me filthy and with an empty gas tank. I pretended not to notice, but my eyes had filled with tears the moment I drove away. How many times could I tell myself I was done with her, only to give her another chance and end up, yet again, disappointed and heartbroken?

"Mom? It's me. I was thinking we could do lunch tomorrow. My treat," I added, forever feeling I needed to sweeten the pot to interest others in spending time with me.

"Sweetheart! Wow, that is far-out—I was just thinking about you! I had this dream last night. It was all about you as a little girl, and . . ."

I tuned her out, waiting for the line to fall silent. I could tell by the breathiness in her voice that she was stoned, though it was barely eleven o'clock in the morning.

"I'll pick you up at one," I said flatly when she finally finished. "Can you please be ready?"

"Of course, darling. I just haven't seen enough of you since you've been back!"

The next day, precisely at one o'clock, I pulled up to her apartment building and climbed the exterior stairs to her unit. The place was a hole. "Spruce Acres" looked like rundown welfare housing, complete with ancient cracked stucco, broken lawn furniture littering the green area and yellowed sheets covering the windows. I knocked on the door, and she answered it wearing a bathrobe.

"You're not ready," I said without preamble, pushing the door open and stepping inside. Unsurprisingly, the air smelled like pot smoke.

She put her hands to her head and made a helpless gesture. "I just . . . I got a bit of a late start. Here, come in for a minute. I've, um . . ."

I walked into the living room and stopped short. A bearded man was sitting on a tattered wicker sofa, reading Mom's astrology book.

". . . been wanting you to meet Darcy anyway," she finished.

"Greetings," he said to me, and I scowled at him darkly.

Never mind who he was and what he was doing in my mother's apartment; for some inexplicable reason, I'd always hated the name Darcy.

Mom walked across the room and sat down at his side. "Darcy just loves the outdoors," she said proudly, running her hands through his hair. "I've told him all about our years in the tipis. He's fascinated. And . . ." She leaned closer to him and gave his thigh a squeeze. "He's going to buy me a brand-new Swiss Army knife. Isn't that groovy?"

I looked from her to him and back to my mother again, speechless. Mom was not only now officially living like a white-trash pothead, she was using our years in the wilderness as some sort of weird currency. A new Swiss Army knife? Did she really think that was all she was worth? As usual, it was clear to me that she had made her choice of who was more important to her. Ever since I could remember, I had played the fading star to the shining sun of whatever man happened to be in her life, whether he'd entered it years before or just a few days ago.

I pulled my cardigan around me. "Well. I was going to tell you at lunch, but I guess there's no reason to wait. I'm going back to Paris. Or somewhere."

"Cea's a *model*," Mom said to her new boyfriend, and though I knew she was trying to pay me a compliment, the way she said it just made me feel cheap.

He lifted an eyebrow appraisingly as he scanned my makeup-free face, torn jeans and plain grey sweater. I ignored him.

"Anyway. Like I said, I'll be leaving in a couple weeks. I just have to find someone to take over my apartment."

"But . . . you just got here. Why are you leaving so soon?"

I shrugged. "I don't know. I guess . . . there's just nothing here for me." I turned away and then looked back at her. "Oh, and one more thing. I'll be selling my car. So, sorry, but no free wheels for you this time."

Two weeks later, I was on a plane headed to Hamburg. In Germany, I knew, I would be able to pursue a path of modelling that didn't involve starving myself or deflecting advances. My two months working at Pasta Frenzy had made me realize that returning home had had nothing to do with hating modelling. What I had wanted was the feeling that I belonged somewhere. But that hope was gone.

Chapter 15

2008
Vancouver

Let's have a talk," James said to me.

I nodded, trying to banish the anxiety that had erupted inside me. This was it, I thought, this was the end. I wanted it and needed it as much as James did, but I still felt like I was about to walk onto a high wire without a safety net.

Since returning from Mom's memorial, I'd prepared for this moment the best I could. I'd sent out emails to liquidators soliciting my swimwear stock, thankful that at least I had something to sell. It seemed that ever since I'd started CeaSwim, my timing had been off. As I struggled to sew perfect samples with my industrial machines, my factory would miss production deadlines, and I'd find myself receiving product half a season behind schedule. This meant most of my retailers would cancel their orders, and I'd then try to sell the line as the new one for the following season, but no one was buying between seasons. At this point, I didn't have enough money or credit to produce another collection, so the only option that made any sense was liquidation. A day after I sent my emails out, I got an offer from Overstock.com. I knew this was not the time to think about the three years of backbreaking hard work, huge financial investment and possibility of future income I was throwing away. Quite simply, I needed enough money to leave my husband.

Thirty minutes after James and I sat down together, our seven-year marriage and nine-year relationship was over. Marriages in their final death throes come down to a division of numbers, time and often blame and responsibility. James and I had managed to stick to the first two. We promised each other we'd stay amicable, knowing we still shared a future together through our child.

I stood up and left the room feeling relieved and absolutely terrified. I went upstairs, found Avery playing with his train set, and wrapped my arms around him for dear life.

After selling my swimwear stock, I had enough money to live on for a few months—about long enough for my book to sell, I figured. I emailed Arnold—*Just wondering if we're ready to send my manuscript into the world yet?* He wrote back that he planned to submit it to publishers the following week, and my pulse quickened nervously. My book was good enough—it had to be. I had not revealed all, but was that really necessary? Of course not.

One of the first people I told the news to was my old friend Carleigh, who'd been living in Vancouver since high school. All these many years later, we were still as close as ever, holy-roller camps and fabricated rapes all but forgotten.

"I found a place to live," I told her optimistically. "A duplex. Small but cute."

"That's great. But what are you going to do about a car?"

"I have no idea."

"I do. You can use our second vehicle. It's old, but it'll get you around."

"Seriously?" My eyes filled with tears. "Thank you. I really can't thank you enough."

I smiled a little as I hung up the phone. Carleigh had been with me through so much—we'd even been bridesmaids at each other's weddings to our first husbands, whom we'd both since divorced.

Kevin—I hadn't thought about him for a long time. Our relationship had been wrong in so many ways, but now I found myself reflecting on our separation almost nostalgically. Things had been so much simpler then, with no children to think of and enough money in the bank that I had no worry of supporting myself. At the time, I'd promised myself I would never go through another divorce. I'd seen my future as something that stretched before me with endless possibility, providing me with all the time and tools and experience I'd ever need to make the right choice next time. What I hadn't understood was that without an honest cataloguing of my mistakes and failings, I was destined to keep repeating them.

1990–1991
Hamburg & Calgary

Frau Bittner was an alcoholic. At least that's what I'd heard from the other models in Hamburg who had lived with her. For me, the word conjured up an image of someone emptying a bottle of gin and passing out on the floor every night. The idea of living with a bona fide alcoholic was a little unsettling, but I also knew that Frau Bittner was sixty-plus years old and lived in the best part of town, and that her room was the right price. So I didn't blink an eye when my agency placed me with her on my first trip to Hamburg. I was twenty years old, I'd just left my mother and her lame-ass boyfriend behind in Calgary, and I was focused on one thing: making money.

My new home was a long, dark apartment with walls lined in oil paintings of cats, flowers and young women in repose. The paintings were done by Frau Bittner herself, I learned a few weeks after moving in. I was making myself a salad in the kitchen, and she was sitting at the table drinking a glass of wine.

"I still paint a little. When the fancy strikes, you know."

"Well," I said. "They're really amazing."

I could feel her eyes on my back, and when I turned around, she was giving me an appraising look.

"You know, plenty of models have stayed here over the years. You're the first one who doesn't go out. All the other girls, they never buy groceries. Just go for dinner with lots of boys."

"Yeah, well, I guess I'm a bit more of a homebody," I replied with a smile, and, sensing impending questions, I left the room swiftly with my plate. I was determined to turn over a new leaf in Hamburg, one that didn't involve partying or dealing with men looking for a fair trade.

Each night I'd eat with Frau Bittner's big-boned cat purring at my feet, then read a book or write a letter to a friend back home, or sometimes attempt to write poetry in my doodle-covered notebook. Frau Bittner stayed in her bedroom at night, usually only emerging to refill her wineglass. For some reason, though, there were rarely any empty bottles in the recycle bin.

One evening Frau Bittner surprised me by knocking lightly on my door. I opened up, and she stood before me with a book in her hand.

"I noticed you enjoy writing," she said in her heavily accented English. I could smell booze on her breath, but she didn't seem unsteady. "I wrote a book of poetry once, many years ago. It is in German, of course, but I will translate if you ever wish to take a look."

"Wow. Thank you," I said with genuine admiration. I'd never known a published writer before, and my other dream, besides becoming a model, was to write. The cover of the book had a painting of a weeping angel on it, her wings wrapped around herself like a winter coat. "Is this one of your paintings? It's beautiful."

She nodded, adjusted her thick glasses and gestured at the notebook on my desk. "What are you writing about?"

"Me? Oh, just some poetry." I waved my hand dismissively. "It's dumb. I think I suck at it."

She shrugged. "Would you read me one?"

"A . . . a poem?"

"Yes. I am curious."

"Oh . . ." I could feel my cheeks burning. I'd never really shared my poetry with anyone other than Mrs. Bell, my high school English teacher. "Um . . . sure." I picked up my book and flipped through the pages, wondering which one was my least embarrassing. Clearing my throat, I began to read:

"The leaves changed early that year
fell from the trees and returned to the earth
   more beautiful dead than when alive.
One by one, I crunched them underfoot
Yellow for the warnings I didn't heed
Orange for the energy I spent pleasing you
Red for the love you didn't return

"I told myself that when spring came
With its buds of green
I would be healthy again
like I was before you came
Not envious as I am now, of her
   and the choice you made
With no regard for the hurt child inside

"I wish I could dive naked into freezing water
And emerge reborn, wiped of your memory
But my feet won't take me where I want them to go
Instead they just wander,
   crunching and crushing
Reminding me each day
Of the brightly coloured scar of you upon my soul."

"I was, um, writing in character," I added quickly, glancing up at Frau Bittner.

She was staring off into the distance with her head tilted to one side. "Very good," she said finally. "You have a natural talent, a . . . what do you say—instinct? You want to be a writer?"

"Yes . . . I mean no. I mean, I want to be a model—"

"You *are* a model," she pointed out. "So why not be a writer too?"

"Maybe in my next life. Next career, I mean."

She took a large sip from her wineglass and gazed at me directly. "You are an interesting girl. Not like the others who have stayed here. You have something to share, no? Something from your past. Difficulties, perhaps."

"Ahh . . ." I tapped a finger on my chin, wondering how much to say. "Not really," I replied finally.

Frau Bittner smiled and raised her glass to me ever so slightly. "Well, then. Maybe I am wrong. But everyone has a story. And I know that if I hadn't been able to express mine . . ."

I nodded and dropped my eyes. I wasn't sure if I wanted to hear Frau Bittner's story. Judging from the shadowy male figures in the background of some of her paintings, I was pretty sure her ex-husband, or perhaps her father, was a big part of it. She waved a hand in the air.

"Anyway, it is late. I will let you sleep." With that she walked into her own bedroom, closing the door behind her.

I lay awake for a long time, thinking about the poem I'd read. I knew that to Frau Bittner, it probably sounded like something I'd written about a lover who'd scorned me. What I could never tell her, or anyone, was that the poem was about Barry.

My weekdays were busy with work, but my weekends were dull. Since I didn't go out and only had sporadic friendships with other models who were always travelling, I'd spend hours reading, shopping, strolling the city and basically waiting for Monday to arrive again so I could get back to earning more money.

One Saturday I got a call from a friend back home, who reminded me that my ex-boyfriend Kevin was also living in Germany, after moving there to pursue his hockey career. Hearing Kevin's name brought back mixed feelings. He had been my high school boyfriend, my first real lover, and we'd stayed together for nearly two years until I'd moved on with Jason. Everything about Kevin had seemed right—he was handsome, hilarious, on the honour roll, a talented hockey player with a promising future, from a family that appeared as perfect and normal as I'd ever seen. And he clearly adored me, showering me with flowers and cards and date-night dinners. He always wanted me to choose the movie, the radio station, the restaurant. All I had to do was mention liking a pair of shoes or a book, and the items would materialize. He lived in my neighbourhood and had a car, so sometimes he'd drive over and knock on my bedroom window when I was sleeping. I'd let him in, giggling, and we'd cuddle in my single bed. We never had sex there, for the simple reason that my mother had told me I could feel free to.

But Kevin also had a dark side. When he drank too much, he got nasty. His behaviour was mysterious and unsettling—we would spend a wonderful Saturday together, and then he'd go drinking with his friends and come knock on my window. I'd open it, excited to see him, and he'd started spewing at me about how my best friend was a whore or how he'd caught me looking at some construction worker, which was totally untrue. It only happened a few times, but enough for me to give this side of him a name: Dark Kevin. Always the next day, though I doubt he even remembered what he'd said, he would be full of apologies. Flowers, poems, tears—whatever it took to make me forgive him. Many times I took him back, not only because I loved the real, daytime Kevin, but also because I didn't realize that the small amount of power I felt when he was begging for forgiveness was part of the cycle of the abused and abuser. So it was not Kevin's behaviour that ended our relationship but rather something I saw in him that I didn't want to face in myself.

One night Kevin came to my window drunk and said he wanted to tell me a secret from his past. As I listened, I felt my irritation grow—not because of what he was saying, but because he was crying about it. My heart felt like ice in my chest. *You poor baby*, I thought harshly. *You think that's trauma? Deal with your shit and leave me alone.* For the first time ever, I slammed my window shut and told him to go home.

The next day was a Saturday. I lay in bed, ignoring the ringing phone and thinking about Kevin's window visits. Then I called Jason, whom I'd met at a party the month before. He'd been badgering me for a date ever since, so he was pleased when I accepted one with him that night. We went to a movie, and when he dropped me off at home, I saw Kevin sitting in his car at the curb. I let Jason kiss me and then went into the house. Kevin chased after me, bawling and asking me *why why why*, as we stood on the porch. I just stared at him, wanting nothing more than to see the back of him. It was like I wasn't even in my own body. Only a couple of days ago, I had been madly in love with him, and now he just seemed pathetic. You didn't see me whining about my childhood or getting pregnant and smoking pot like Mom had at my age. No way. I was seventeen years old, and I'd dealt with my shit.

"I don't think Kevin ever got over you," my friend was saying over the phone. "I saw him last summer, and he was going on and on about you."

I smiled in spite of myself. It was kind of nice to think of someone carrying a torch for me after all these years, though I had to admit he'd barely crossed my mind. I'd recently broken up with Jason and had hardly given him a thought since either, though we'd been together for almost three years. Men bored me, I realized. As soon as the initial rush of attraction wore off, I found myself feeling restless and sticking around more for their sake than anything else. Was that normal? I wasn't sure. Some of my girlfriends had been with their boyfriends for years and still seemed perfectly content.

I ended the call with my friend and sat for a minute, staring at Kevin's number. *Why are you even thinking about it?* I asked myself, but of course I knew the answer. I picked up the phone again and dialled.

A week later, Kevin and I went on our first date. He took me to an Afghan restaurant, where we ate stuffed eggplant and flatbread sprinkled with sesame seeds. Kevin ordered a chicken dish, and when I mentioned I'd become a vegetarian, he sent it back to the kitchen. It was then I remembered his eagerness to please me.

We returned to my place afterward, letting ourselves into the darkened apartment well past midnight.

"Shh . . ." I said to him in an exaggerated whisper as we tumbled onto my bed. I'd had three glasses of wine at dinner and was feeling rather tipsy. "My landlady," I said, pointing at the wall that separated our bedrooms. "She's supposed to be an alcoholic, but I don't believe it. She's just an artist who drinks wine."

Kevin rolled on top of me, pinning my wrists down playfully. "I don't want to talk about your landlady. I want to talk about you. And us." He kissed me.

I waited to feel a rush of passion, but it didn't come. I pushed him away and sat up.

"Do you remember why we broke up?" I asked.

"Yes, but that's all in the past . . ."

He leaned forward to kiss me again, but I moved sideways to avoid his lips.

"No. Tell me why."

He looked surprised. "Because . . . you met someone else. You kissed him that night, in front of me."

I shook my head, feeling a little buzzed on power. I easily could have called this a night and never seen Kevin again, but I could tell he was already emotionally reattaching to me.

"No. That was just a result. You were an asshole to me. Do you remember those nights you used to come to my window when you were drunk?"

He nodded, shamefaced. "I don't know what was wrong with me, but I'm so much better now. I was dealing with some . . . things from the past."

"Right." Kevin was even more normal than he knew, I realized. Quite likely, these were the darkest skeletons he had in his closet, and they were nothing compared to mine. I leaned in to him and lowered my voice. "That stuff you told me about? Let's make a deal. Let's live in the present, not the past. You don't tell me your shit, and I won't burden you with mine. Okay?"

"Okay, okay," he replied, anxious to please.

I held his eyes for a minute so he'd know I was serious, and when he started to squirm, I placed my hand on his thigh.

"I always knew we'd find each other again," he said, reaching out to stroke my hair. "And this time, I'm not letting you go."

I smiled at him. This was so easy. Dark Kevin was gone, and his feelings for me were obvious. I was quite certain that if I just gave myself a little time, I could feel the same way about him.

"Surprise!"

I stared uncomprehendingly at my mother and Grandma Jeanne, who were both clapping their hands with excitement. We were standing at the entrance of Golden Acres Garden Centre in Calgary, and four of my friends had just materialized from behind a display of Christmas trees. It was December sixth, 1990, six days after my twenty-first birthday. I'd flown in from Germany a few days before, leaving Kevin behind to play his season games so I could go home for two weeks. Though I saw Mom and Grandma Jeanne during my visits, *home* really meant Kevin's parents' house. I always stayed with them when I came to Calgary, fitting cozily into their farmer's market runs and movie nights and Sunday dinners. I loved their predictability more than I could ever admit to anyone.

"What's going on?" I asked Mom.

"It's your birthday party!" she said, as if it were perfectly obvious.

"My birthday party? But . . . my birthday's already over," I replied with mounting panic. That was the least of my concerns, but I was too shocked to say much else. I glanced at my friends again, looking for a sign that this was a bad joke, but it seemed they had all taken a sudden interest in a display of Christmas ornaments.

"Yes, right here in the store!" Mom replied. "The staff said we could, wasn't that nice of them? Here . . ." She grasped my hand, pulling me through the Christmas trees.

I saw a folding table with eight chairs positioned around it. Grandma Jeanne was busy putting tin plates and plastic cups out, as curious shoppers looked on.

"Staff Christmas party?" a woman with a small child asked.

"No, we're having my daughter's twenty-first birthday here!" Mom responded enthusiastically. "Isn't that groovy?"

"Wow. How original."

I could feel my face reddening as she turned away.

"Well, let's sit down," Mom said, bustling me toward the table. "I've had each of your friends bring a dish."

Said friends stood around the table like soldiers awaiting orders. One of my old high school classmates held up a foil pan. "I brought lasagna. Your mom said it was your favourite."

I nodded, too embarrassed to fake a smile. I couldn't even cheer myself up by thinking what a funny story this would make to tell Kevin later. I hadn't told him many details about my past, but one only needed to spend a day or two around Mom to realize she lacked basic social skills and all sense of propriety. Though Kevin wouldn't have admitted it, I was pretty certain he wondered sometimes how he'd ended up with a girlfriend with such a nutty family. At least, thank god, it looked as though my mother hadn't invited Kevin's parents to the party.

Mom was rooting through a cardboard box from home that she'd apparently snuck in earlier. She lifted up her coffee maker triumphantly. "Excuse me," she said, accosting a passing employee. "Do you have an extension cord? I need to plug my coffee maker in."

He looked at her blankly. "Coffee maker?"

"Yes. For the birthday party?" she answered, as if he were slow. "The birthday girl is right over there. Isn't she beautiful?"

"Um, I guess so," the kid said awkwardly.

While he went off, presumably in search of the requested item, Mom continued unpacking. Out came paper napkins, utensils, salad tongs, a homemade cheesecake. "Oh, darn it, I forgot the knife," she muttered. "I wonder if . . ."

"They might have one here? I don't think so," I said sharply.

"It's probably in the car. I'll be right back," Mom said in a singsong voice, oblivious to my pain.

By this time, a crowd was forming, peering through the trees at where we were sitting. When Mom returned, she brought a whiff of pot smoke with her. I cringed.

"Mom," I hissed. "You're *stoned.*"

"Oh, honey, don't be so *proper.* I'm celebrating! It's your birthday, after all."

"Birthday *party,*" I corrected, once again at a loss for words. "My birthday was six days ago."

She put her arm around me and looked at the table happily. By this time, my friends had succumbed to the weirdness and were gamely loading up their plates with lasagna and wilted Caesar salad. I prayed for them to eat quickly.

"Isn't this wonderful? It's just like when you were a little kid."

"How so?" I asked, genuinely confused.

She gestured at the fake Christmas trees surrounding us, some of them nude and some fully decorated. "The trees, of course! It's like we're in the middle of the forest!"

I looked at her blankly, but she was busy pulling a bottle of wine from the paper bag in her purse. She unscrewed the cap and started pouring wine out for my friends.

"Mom!" I whispered furiously. "We can't have that here."

"Oh, bother," she responded, waving her hand dismissively. "I'm sure they won't mind."

I threw mine back in two gulps, and she refilled it. Right on cue, an employee came bustling over to us.

"I'm sorry, but there's no way we can allow you to have alcohol here, ma'am. I'll have to ask all of you to empty your glasses."

Chastened, we dutifully dumped our glasses into an empty plant pot, while our audience of shoppers exchanged knowing glances. And then, to my utter dismay, I saw a familiar face making its way through the crowd toward our table.

"Goodness me, sorry I'm so late. I think your mother sent me to the wrong garden centre across town . . . Never mind, I see the festivities are well under way. Happy birthday, dear."

I blanched. Dressed in trousers and a jaunty scarf, smiling broadly before me, was Kevin's mother.

All at once, my embarrassment was replaced by anger. It didn't matter how hard I tried to orchestrate my life to look normal, because my mother would always ruin it for me. Every time her world collided with that of anyone else in my life, disaster struck. Memories ticked through my mind: Mom coming to the door to greet a kindergarten friend, topless with a joint in her hand. Mom pressing a note into my hand that asked my father, whom I was going to meet in California for the first time in my memory, to send me home with a form of birth control that wasn't available in Canada. Mom offering a fourteen-year-old friend of mine vodka at our house party, then telling her it was high time she lost her virginity. Mom landing on my doorstep in the middle of dinner with Jason's parents, crying over a fight with Sam. And then the worst—a Christmas Day in high school. After spending the morning with Mom, I'd gone over to celebrate with Jason's family. As we were eating dinner, the doorbell rang, and there stood my mother. I cringed at her showing up uninvited, but Jason's parents graciously invited her in. She then proceeded to give each family member stoned descriptions of each of their astrological signs, and then, horror of horrors, asked my boyfriend's sister if she was into pot. "I just wanted to connect with you," she said to me, when I exploded at her later.

I pulled out a chair for Kevin's mother and sat down beside her. "Thank you for coming. My mother . . . she has some very creative ideas when it comes to parties. You should have seen my sixth birthday," I added with forced cheer.

She smiled back at me. "Indeed. Well, good for her. The world needs more creative types."

Mom bustled over. "I'm so glad you made it!" she said, giving Kevin's mother a hug. I prayed she didn't know what pot smoke smelled like. "Isn't this just the best party—?"

"Mom," I interrupted, eager to separate them. "Maybe we could do the cake now?"

"Oh, yes, the cake . . ."

She flitted off to find some matches, and then there was the "Happy Birthday to You" song to be gotten through and the candles to be blown out. My friends provided scattered applause. I wolfed down my cake, thankful this would soon be over.

"Well, this has been nice," I said when I had finished, standing. "But we should really—"

"Honey, I have one last surprise for you," Mom said excitedly, and I tried not to cry. "I'm just going to have to blindfold you for a minute."

There was no point in resisting. I let her tie a scarf around my eyes and take my hand.

"You're going to *love* this," she promised, leading me through the store to god knows where.

I could picture Kevin's mother and my friends trailing behind me, a store full of shoppers exchanging confused glances.

"Here," she said finally, stopping. "Are you ready?"

"Mm."

My hand was placed on something warm and furry. *What the hell?* Mom whipped off my blindfold just as her camera flashed in my face. I stared. Before me was a nativity set-up, complete with hay bales, fake wise men and a plastic baby Jesus in the cradle. The difference was that this one had several live animals, including the goat who was currently nuzzling his nose into my crotch. A Christmas-themed petting zoo.

"Isn't it wonderful?" Mom said, clapping her hands gleefully. "Real animals. Just like when you were little. Remember, sweetie? How you used to love chasing the rabbits and deer?"

As I looked at her hopeful face, my humiliation morphed once again into a crawling guilt. Why couldn't I just accept my mother for who she was? She truly thought she was connecting with me by trying to bring me back to my childhood. She didn't have a decent home to hold a party in, even if she'd wanted to—she still lived at Spruce Acres, a.k.a. hard-luck central for crackheads and former wilderness dwellers. In two weeks, I would return to my life in Europe, and god only knew when we'd even see each other again.

Kevin's mother moved to my side and placed her hand on my arm. "Isn't this lovely," she said quietly. "What a wonderful idea, Michelle."

I patted her hand gratefully. At least I had her and all her normalcy. And Kevin, of course. They were both willing to accept my crazy mother, and neither of them pried into my past. Kevin was talking a lot about marriage lately. He was a sensible choice for me, I knew, a *healthy* choice. He reminded me a bit of Mike the bachelor—a good, decent man. And though I wasn't exactly sure if Kevin was right for me, I couldn't think of a single reason he was wrong for me.

Chapter 16

2008
Vancouver

On my first night in my new home, I sat on the sofa with boxes piled around me, feeling nothing less than ecstatic. The constant suffocation, the urge to hide my truth and the certainty that I was failing at everything I tried to do was lifting, just as surely as fog being burned off by the sun. For the first time in nearly a decade, I felt happiness was no longer an impossibility. I reflected on how complex leaving an unhealthy relationship was, with its many reverberations and expected losses, and yet how it also resulted in such relief. The only issues to deal with now were my own—which, admittedly, were still plenty.

I gazed at Avery sleeping peacefully in the new bed I'd bought him at IKEA. I couldn't afford it, of course, but I was certain my ship would come in soon. Yesterday Arnold had sent my manuscript out to twelve editors. I'd scanned down his email to the list of publishers to which he'd submitted: Random House, Doubleday, HarperCollins, Penguin, Scribner—my dream list. At least one of them would love it. All I had to do was stretch my money to last until the book was bought and the first book advance payment came in. I figured if I was careful, I should be able to make ends meet, but just for insurance, I let my local modelling agency know I was open to taking bookings. There wasn't much work in Vancouver for a more "mature" model of thirty-eight, but it wouldn't hurt to try.

I spent the next few weeks distracting myself by setting up my new home and touring playgrounds with Avery. My days were an almost bipolar roller-coaster ride of his toddler emotions, forcing me to keep my own mood even. I thought about Mom, who'd never had the chance to be anything but a single parent. That wasn't me; Avery's father was involved in his life, so my child would never go hungry. Rather, I was a solo mother, caught in the in-between of going it alone and being relieved of my duties for half of every week. I never cried when I thought about Mom. Crying was my doorway into a black hole of fear, so instead I chose resentment. She hadn't been the mother I needed, and then she had left me when I needed her most. It was so typical of her.

Each morning I opened my email with renewed hope, and day after day, I heard nothing from Arnold. I could have contacted him any time for an update, but I was afraid to. As I went to bed each night with no news, the flower of hope I'd harvested wilted a little more. I knew my chances of finding a publisher for my book were slipping away. A lump of fear took up residence in my stomach; it was so massive that I couldn't smile, couldn't eat, couldn't sleep. I lost weight, obsessively checked the balance of my dwindling bank account and spent my nights tossing and turning.

And then, five weeks after Arnold had submitted my manuscript, I finally got an email from him. I could find a summary of his submission report attached, he wrote. He'd heard back from everyone, and they'd all passed. He was sorry it hadn't worked out and wished me all the best in my future endeavours.

Terror swept through me. My rent was due in a week, and after I paid it, I would have less than six hundred dollars to my name.

One morning when I was nine years old and living in the Yukon with my grandparents, Papa Dick and I set out for town. It was so cold that my grandfather had decided even the sled dogs should stay inside the tipi. But we were desperate for supplies, and the weather hadn't broken for days, so off we went. Dressed in five layers of clothing, I was so cold and my legs were so stiff I could barely walk across the frozen lake. About a quarter of the way across the lake, it started to snow. As it swirled around us in a thickening cloud, Papa Dick took my hand and began to lead me back home. My grandfather could handle anything, so if we were turning back, I knew it was serious. The snow was falling so heavily and the wind blowing so hard that I couldn't see the shore anymore. And then Papa Dick's hand slipped from mine. In an instant, he was swallowed by the whiteness. I called for him, but the howling wind whipped the words from my mouth. I walked forward and stopped, looking down at my footprints. They filled in immediately with snow. I stood still, uncertain which way to turn and as cold from fear as from the weather. The way I felt then was exactly the way I felt now. The difference was that then, I was almost certain of rescue.

And yet it all made sense to me. I'd always known this moment was coming, and in a strange way, it was almost a relief that it was finally here, because now I could stop worrying about it. My mind drifted back thirteen years, to a time in my life when my behaviour and morals had been at their lowest point. *Karma will get me. Someday I will pay for this*, I used to think.

Now that all seemed like a distant dream. I was as far from the person who'd acted that way as I was from the child of the wilderness I'd once been. All the same, it seemed that today, my payback had arrived.

1995
Cannes & Florence

Where am I? Here. I am here, right here.

I opened my eyes and stared at the ceiling, trying to orient myself. A hotel room, small but high-end; blue toile wallpaper; my clothing tossed across a desk at the end of the bed. An empty bottle of champagne sitting upright on the floor. And Kevin, my husband of two years, sleeping beside me.

Shit. I was in Cannes, France, for a modelling job. Kevin had flown in from Germany to join me last night, one of a series of desperate attempts he'd made over the past six months to save our marriage. What he didn't know was that he'd already been replaced by someone else and tucked into my brain file of *really annoying things I have to deal with soon.* There was nothing about Kevin I didn't loathe. That he brought me flowers and wrote me loving postcards just made me want to run farther away from him, though six months had passed, and I'd failed to do that.

I glanced at the clock beside my bed. It was five thirty, and my call time was six o'clock. I showered, shaved my legs and blow-dried my hair upside down. Flipping my head back, I admired my jutting hip bones in the mirror. The stress of leading a double life was good for my figure. A year ago, I'd had clients calling my bookers to complain about my hefty-ish thighs, and now I could barely eat enough to keep myself in a size two. One more day on this job, and then I was off to Cape Town for another catalogue, and then Paris. I'd never been busier.

The bathroom door was pushed open, and Kevin stood in front of me in a pair of boxer shorts. I automatically pulled the towel around myself.

"Hi," I said, forcing a smile. "I have to get going. You going to do the tourist thing today? I should be done around four."

"Sure." His voice sounded funny.

"What's up?" I asked, rubbing moisturizer on my face.

"Nothing. Hey, someone called while you were in the shower."

"Oh. Someone from the photo team?"

"No."

Nausea washed over me. No, it couldn't be. Chris didn't even know where I was right now. I'd lied and told him I had a job in some nondescript German burg, so he wouldn't ask to join me here. And when it came to Kevin, I'd been excruciatingly careful to never reveal my affair. It simply wasn't possible he'd found out.

"Well, who was it?"

"He said his name was Chris."

"Chris?" I replied breezily. "That's weird. I don't know anyone named Chris."

"Really?"

"Yeah, really. Unless—oh, hey, it must have been my booker in Zurich. He probably has a job for me. Listen, I have to fly." I pecked Kevin on the cheek and darted out of the bathroom to get dressed.

The morning was torture. Makeup, hair, two locations, four outfit changes. The famous view of Promenade de la Croisette stretched behind me as I slipped into my lifestyle-modelling persona: casually strolling down the street, checking something in my purse, glancing back over my shoulder at an unseen friend. Same standard-issue stuff I'd been doing for more than a decade.

The second I could get away, I slipped into a phone booth and inserted my phone card. A minute later, I hung up the phone with shaking hands. Chris from my agency in Zurich had not called me. That meant that if *my* Chris actually *had* tracked me down, my secret was out to both him and Kevin. I felt almost giddy with nerves. Was this it? After half a year, was my double life about to come crashing down on me?

I lit a cigarette with shaking hands and dialled Chris's number. The first six men I'd cheated on Kevin with had been flings, mostly drunken one-nighters. I'd justified them by telling myself that leaving Kevin would break his heart, that I wasn't emotionally attached to these other men, that Kevin had brought it on himself. But then Chris came along; I met him at an Oktoberfest party and fell hard. I knew I had to leave Kevin, but I also knew that giving up the security and normalcy he represented to me would be like letting go of a life raft in a stormy sea. So instead I did the worst thing possible, playing both men as if they were my one and only.

"Yes?" Chris said into the phone, jerking me back to the present.

"Hey, it's me."

"Baby!" he said happily, and I knew I was off the hook.

"You didn't call me this morning, did you? At my hotel?"

"Me? No, why?"

"No reason. Just . . . missing you."

Ten minutes later, I hung up the phone. I was relieved, but the question niggled at me: How had Kevin found out Chris's name?

Even though Kevin had messed up, I had to admit that he hadn't been the one to break our deal—I had. On the day he proposed to me, he'd taken me on a picnic near a remote lake and told me he'd brought me there in honour of my childhood. He wanted me to know I could trust him, that if I ever wanted to talk about it, he was there for me. I accepted his proposal and his custom-made engagement ring. The next day, the watch he'd given me a few months before stopped working. I took it off my wrist and shook it in frustration, knowing the timing was just a little too serendipitous. But that didn't stop me from pushing stubbornly forward.

On a night several months later, after I'd had a few drinks, I started telling Kevin about my wilderness days. Hunting with Papa Dick when I was a kid, the day Apache was shot, the crazy road trip with Mom and Karl. Kevin was a great audience—interested and empathetic. The next thing I knew, I was telling him about Barry: his quiet approaches to my bed, my mother sleeping an arm's-length away, and finally, my hand landing atop hers as it rested on his penis. I didn't spare details about my encounters with him, even revealing the deepest part of my shame—that Barry hadn't actually touched me but rather had made me touch him.

Kevin said all the right things. How it hadn't been my fault, how my mother should have stopped it, how he wished he could get his hands on that bastard right now. Meanwhile I kept drinking, and then

I decided to tell him a story I'd never told anyone. The time I had never even allowed myself to think about.

It had been a typical day in the half-finished house, meaning not typical at all. We'd all come home from a shopping trip in the middle of the day. After we unpacked groceries, I was sitting on my bed engrossed in *The Call of the Wild* when I heard the all-too-familiar noises that I dreaded coming from their bed a few feet away. Puzzled—because although they had no problem doing it in front of me, they usually didn't do it in the middle of the day—I glanced up. Barry's naked body was on top of my mother's. I jumped up in disgust and made a dash for the front door. The problem was that I had to pass the foot end of their bed.

As I scurried by, Barry called out my name. I froze, involuntarily glancing his way.

"What are you looking at?" he asked with a laugh.

Beneath him, Mom was quietly murmuring to him to leave me alone. My head was spinning.

"Well, what are you looking at?" he asked me again.

"Nothing," I replied. The room felt like it was squeezing the breath out of me. I had to get out, out, *out*—

"Nothing, my ass. Here, why don't you take a better look? Stay awhile. Maybe you can learn a thing or two."

I turned and fled, but not soon enough to miss seeing him shift position to give me a better view.

"You like it, don't you?" he said, laughing again, as I bolted out the front door.

I ran as far away from the house as I could, until my lungs felt like they would burst. I didn't know who I hated more: Mom, for being too weak to make him stop—or better yet, not let it happen at all—or Barry, because just a couple months ago, it had been me he wanted instead of Mom.

After I told Kevin that story, I felt like I'd had handfuls of mud smeared all over my body and shoved down my throat. I ran to the toilet, gagging. Kevin followed me.

"I don't know how you forgive something like that," he said, as he sat on the floor beside me, and I said nothing.

I knew he was trying to be supportive, but what Kevin didn't understand—what no one who hadn't experienced the ambivalence of a parent who was neglectful and selfish and weak but also loving and encouraging and even sacrificing at times could understand—was that his comment just made me feel worse. Almost accusatory, like I was devoid of a backbone for continuing to allow my mother to be in my life. But at the time, she was all I had. I couldn't explain to him that when you're eight years old and have nowhere else to turn, you do your best to ensure that the one person who hasn't abandoned you never will. That you do that by pretending the horrible thing is no big deal, so she doesn't have a reason to leave you. That as you grow older, you may still remember the horrible thing, but it happened decades ago, and by then it's mixed up with so many kindnesses and moments of closeness between the two of you that you feel you have no right to strike her down. That degrading events like those, especially when combined with others, can affect every single choice you make later as an adult. And that even though you know that you sold your childhood soul to hold on to a bit of security, the last thing you want is for someone, however well-intentioned, to point that out to you.

The next day, as I lay in bed hungover and regretful, Kevin took my hand and spoke to me in a voice that was almost painfully earnest.

"I love you. You don't have to be afraid. I want to know everything." I shook my head as the gravity of what I'd revealed to him hit me full force. Would he see me differently now, picture a childish image of me touching a grown man's penis? Did he think about me watching them? But despite my fears, I had to admit to myself that releasing my pain to someone had made me feel a little freer and a little less ashamed. For a short time after that, I felt closer to Kevin. And then Halloween night came.

The Germans didn't really celebrate Halloween, but the Irish did, at least at their pubs. I dug through my closet and pulled together a cat costume, and Kevin went as a lumberjack. Drinks flowed, music blared, tables were danced on. Friends snapped photos of Kevin and me kissing and laughing. We finally stumbled home, giggling, Kevin's arm slung low around my waist. Kevin was the type to stay up and watch TV after a party, but I fell into bed. Much later, I awoke briefly when I felt him lie down beside me. He smelled like way too much gin, so I rolled away from him. As I was drifting off to sleep again, I heard him mumbling.

"Hmm?" I asked, only half interested. He let out a long, drunk-sounding laugh. I pulled the pillow over my head. "What are you laughing at?" I asked irritably.

"You."

I peeled the pillow off my ear. "Me? What did I do?"

"You, and that . . ." He was slurring, hard to understand, but one thing was clear: Dark Kevin was back.

I sat up straight, suddenly wide awake.

"What are you talking about?"

He grinned in the dim glow of the streetlight. "You liked it. I think you liked it."

"Liked . . . what?"

"Watching them," he said softly.

I couldn't be certain. My gut told me all I needed to know, but Kevin denied and claimed forgetfulness and too much to drink, and then, just for good measure, he bought me a new outfit and tickets to see Soundgarden. And I couldn't accuse him of something I wasn't a hundred percent sure of. Right?

Our jobs kept us apart. During the week, I lived in an apartment in Munich, where I did many of my bookings, and Kevin lived a four-hour drive north in a small town where he trained all week and played tournament games on the weekends. If we wanted to see each other, it was up to me to visit him—and I did, making the drive nearly every weekend for three years. But after Halloween, I started taking more bookings away. It wasn't a conscious decision but a progression that felt almost natural to me. I told him I had to work on the weekends and went out instead, dancing in a boozy blur at the clubs until morning. Coke had always been available in my world, and for the first time ever, I stopped saying no. But mostly, I drank. I drank until I felt infallible and a little bit wild and until the thought of leaving my husband didn't fill me with fear, and then I drank some more. When I awoke the next morning, I was once again certain I'd never have the strength to follow through and sever myself from the one constant in my life.

Sometimes he and my mother became mixed up in my dreams—I'd be kissing him, he'd turn into Mom, I'd pull away, she'd ask me where I was going, I'd tell her I didn't need her anymore, that I was going to divorce her. But even then, I didn't put their parallel roles in my life together.

Instead I'd dress in my tightest clothes and put pretty waves in my hair and finally go to visit him, and when he tried to kiss me, I'd roll away from him.

"You're just not touching me right," I would say, not caring if my words hurt.

Shortly after that, I cheated on him for the first time.

The obvious course of action would have been to leave him. But Kevin represented two things that I desperately needed: a piece of normal in a world I sensed would spin completely out of control without his grounding presence, and a person I could punish—justifiably, in my mind—for the pain of my past. And so I stayed, and he pretended not to know what was clearly true: that I was having an affair with Chris. It became the great white elephant in our relationship.

"I've got secrets too, you know," he said to me one night, and I wondered if he was sleeping with someone else.

"Tell me what they are," I drunkenly implored him a few weeks later, but he laughed at me and promised he never would.

I knew our relationship was becoming increasingly depraved, but it wasn't enough to make either of us leave. I kept working and lying and visiting Kevin and lying some more and sleeping with Chris and wondering how long we could all go on like this.

Friends who knew my situation suggested I talk to someone about it, specifically my mother. It was pointless to explain to them that Mom, who was now living with Sam after a reconciliation, wasn't exactly someone I could turn to for advice. But if one thing was certain, it was that my mother was the one person who wouldn't—and couldn't—judge me. One night, I poured myself some wine and dialled her number.

"Cea!" she said. "How lovely to hear from you, darling. I've been missing you."

"I miss you too," I replied, suddenly realizing it was true. There was something about Mom's unfailing optimism that I'd never found in another living human being. It was one of the few things I deeply admired about her, especially when I thought about our shared past. Men had left her. She'd lost track of her parents. For years on end, she hadn't had a penny to her name. But again and again, she had picked herself up and found a way for us, without ever complaining or victimizing herself.

"How's work?" she asked.

"Great, really great. I'm pretty much fully booked for the next few months."

"That's wonderful, sweetheart. I'm so proud of you. You know that, right?"

My voice caught in my throat. "Of course." I did know it. And maybe we could have a chance, I thought, if we tried our relationship on different ground. I hesitated and then blurted it out. "Hey, Mom, I was thinking. Do you want to come and visit me? I could send you a ticket."

"Wellll . . ." she said slowly. "That would be kind of tough. I'd have to check with—"

"Yeah, right," I interrupted before she could say his name. Just the sound of it on her tongue was enough to make my skin crawl. I took a deep breath, trying to control myself. "Mom, listen. Do you want to be a part of my life, or what?"

"Cea, what a silly question. Of course I do. Having you was the best thing I ever did, I've always told you that."

"Yes. But you say that, and you don't show it. Time and again, all you show me is that your boyfriends are more important than me."

"Cea, don't be that way. It's not true—"

"But do you see why I might feel this way? Does it even make any sense to you?"

"I had you. I kept you. Doesn't that tell you everything?"

"Yeah," I said softly, as tears filled my eyes. "Your duties to me are over now."

I hung up the phone and reached for a cigarette. I wanted to feel angry, but all I felt was sadness, which was always worse. Every time I talked to her, she went on about how strong and independent I was, as if that let her off the hook for not being there for me. And whenever I tried to reveal the truth—that the picture wasn't quite as pretty as it seemed—she hid behind the shield of her boyfriend. But maybe it wasn't fair of me to expect so much from the person who had at least stuck around to raise me. I did have two parents, after all.

I took a swig from my wineglass, gathering my courage. I would call my father. As I dialled his number, I rehearsed in my head the person I wanted to be: collected, together, happy. Not needy. *I know, it's been much too long [light laugh]. Things are really great! Did I mention in my last letter that I'm going to Africa for a job? So listen, I was wondering if you might ever have a reason to come this far across the globe. No? Well, I was thinking, we haven't had much chance to spend time together, and I'm kind of travelling all over the place, so if you ever wanted to come my way it would be really great. I could take some time off . . .*

I got his answering machine. I hung up, gulped more wine and then dug out my stationery set. *It would be great to see you,* I wrote to him. *Let me know if you'd ever like to visit.* As was my habit, I carried my empty wine bottle directly out to the recycle bin, so my roommate wouldn't question how much I was drinking, and then I opened another bottle. *I need you, Mom,* I thought. *I really need you.*

But I didn't have Mom. I had Kevin.

Two months later, Kevin and I went on another Band-Aid trip, this time to Italy. We spent the weekend in Venice, trying to stroll romantically by the canals and pose for smiling, coupley photos on the gondolas. My heart wasn't in it, but Kevin was determinedly happy, cracking jokes and springing for pricey wines and announcing to anyone who would listen that he had the most beautiful wife in the world. I smiled tightly, embarrassed and guilty for feeling like I wanted to run away.

The next morning, we headed for Florence. I was driving, winding through the countryside on roads slicked with a light rain.

Halfway there, Kevin turned to me. "Well, I guess this is it."

"What do you mean?"

"I mean . . . let's stop pretending. You're in love with someone else."

I was just going into a curve in the road. I hit the brakes too hard, and our rented BMW fishtailed. The next thing I knew, the back of the car was careening into the cement divider. The vehicle spun around once and came to rest at the side of the road, facing the wrong way.

We were in the middle of nowhere. Kevin and I got out of the car and inspected the damage, and a passing motorist offered to call us a tow truck on his mobile phone.

"It will be here . . . one hour," he said in broken English.

We thanked him and sat down on the gravelly shoulder to wait. No cars passed, and the silence settled over us. I lit a cigarette with shaking hands, wishing that a truck might run over me, or that at least that motorist had remained with us. Anything was better than facing this horrible moment of reckoning.

"How did you know his name?" I asked finally.

He laughed dryly. "You talk in your sleep. Always have."

I nodded, humiliated. Who knew what else I'd been babbling at night? Maybe we're even now, I thought. My infidelities for his betrayal of my trust.

As if reading my mind, Kevin turned to look at me. "We could see this differently. As a new start, you know? All the cards on the table. Hey, I've got my stuff too—maybe we should talk about it. I mean, even after everything, I still love you."

I shook my head. Whether Kevin had mocked me that night or not made little difference, because his knowing my shame now was enough.

"It'll never work," I said softly, looking down the road away from him so I couldn't see his face. One day, I thought, this would all just feel like a sad and distant dream.

Chapter 17

February 2015
Galiano Island, British Columbia

Nerves jangling, smile in place. My first literary festival. Stepping through the doors of the Galiano Inn, I glanced around for a familiar face. None were to be found, which just made me smile harder. These were the times I called on Tough Cea, because if there was one thing that still felt less than natural to me since my book came out, it was promotion. I'd never been one to talk about myself much, which was, of course, ridiculous considering I'd written a memoir. It *was* getting easier—dealing with the jumble of gratitude, wariness and even pride that came each time someone said to me, "I read your book." What had started out as appreciation that *anyone* had read it had morphed into a slight guardedness when I was pressed for more details, and now, with practice, I'd become more open to people's curiosity. But the face-to-face encounters were different from the emails, tweets and Facebook messages; I could read and respond to those at my leisure, giving thought to the written responses.

The festival coordinator waved at me from across the room. Relieved, I was walking her way, when a woman of about sixty-five stepped toward me.

"Do you know me?" she asked in a friendly tone.

Long white hair, and the telltale flowing clothing of a lifetime hippie. She wasn't familiar. "No, I'm sorry. Have we met?"

The woman nodded. "Long, long ago. I knew your grandparents. And you too, when you were a child. My husband, John, and I visited you several times when you lived in the tipis. John Bristow."

An image flashed through my mind of a red-haired, bearded man grinning at me, mountains in the distance behind him. "Adrienne?"

"Yes! You remember me?"

"Of course!"

We hugged and then gazed at each other for a moment. Adrienne looked nothing like the young mother I remembered from four decades ago, holding her son's and my hands as we tripped through meadows and streams.

"When I heard you were going to be here, I just had to come," she continued, gesturing to the scene around us. People milled about, on their way to readings or workshops. "I have some pictures. Can I show them to you?"

"I'd love that," I responded.

She drew a worn photo-developer envelope from her purse. "Your book, it just brought me right back to the wilderness, like I was reliving it. What a time that was!"

"Yes. It certainly was," I said, flipping through old photos of my grandmother making bread, holding a small child in her lap. Me, I realized.

"Your family would have been proud. Dick might have been a little pissed off, but he'd have gotten over it."

I laughed. "I don't know. We saw things pretty differently, he and I."

Adrienne leaned in and touched my shoulder. "After reading your book, I have to tell you that I questioned everything. My convictions, the lifestyle I led back then. I mean, I couldn't help but wonder what I could have done differently. To rescue you, I mean."

"Rescue me?" I repeated, taken aback. "Hey, um . . . don't think twice about it." I gave her a huge smile, as if proving how absolutely fine I was. I'd never thought of myself as a child who should have been rescued—that was for kids who were beaten, neglected, sexually abused. My childhood had only been brushed by those atrocities, and I'd always been loved—my mother had told me that I was, every single day, even if she hadn't always shown me. And if the people who'd known me in the past had questioned my safety, I certainly didn't see it as their responsibility to do anything about it.

But Adrienne's face remained serious. "No. I mean—I *know* how crazy your family was, Cea. I was there. And I don't mean just wacky-crazy, you know? I mean stark-raving mentally ill crazy. I think it's a miracle you survived at all."

I shifted my weight uncomfortably. What Adrienne said was true—I'd been the only real voice of sanity within my family, torn between accepting their choices and trying desperately to make them see how their world looked through my eyes. As a result, I'd endured near-drownings, fires, encounters with wild animals, getting lost in the forest, Mom's crazy boyfriends and a deranged uncle with whom my family left me, unsupervised, even after he had *kidnapped and sexually assaulted me as a baby.* It really was unbelievable when I looked at it in such black-and-white terms—the same way people looked at it as they read my book.

Though Adrienne's words offered validation of what I'd long believed about my family, they also pained me. I thought about Papa Dick, who had always told me there was nothing to fear in the wilderness as long as you kept your wits about you and knew your survival skills; as an adult, those teachings had saved me on several occasions. Despite the madness of my early years, there was no doubt that I'd learned some unique and valuable lessons. And if I were to acknowledge that my family had put me in danger because they were too selfish or lazy or crazy to care, it seemed even more important to me that I find the positive in those experiences. So maybe it all evened out. Maybe in some weird way, all the hardships had set me up to be the pattern-breaker of dysfunction in my family. Because I knew that those who continued their family's patterns of destruction not only hurt themselves but also admitted defeat to those who had damaged them, intentionally or not.

From the corner of my eye, I saw the festival coordinator waving me over from across the room. I turned toward Adrienne, reluctant to say goodbye.

"Listen, Adrienne, I have to run. It's been so great seeing you."

"You too. And whatever you've been doing . . . keep doing it. You're a survivor, if I've ever met one."

I smiled as I made my way to the Gallery Room for my reading. If there was one thing I'd learned today, it was that I'd wasted too much time doubting myself. How many times in my life had I questioned whether an experience was normal, weird, unacceptable or downright terrifying, when all along the answer had been right here inside me?

1998
Tunisia

My plane was late—not just a little bit, but several hours late. I cupped my hands around my eyes and gazed out the window as we taxied into the gate, but all I saw was blackness. I sighed and sat back in my seat, praying there was a taxi service at this airport. I could never be certain—I would land at my photo shoot destinations at all hours of the day and night, and if it was a location I hadn't been to before, I had to be prepared for anything. Usually there were taxis available, and sometimes the client would send a car, but if not, it would be up to me to figure out the public transportation system. Once, I'd stepped off a train in the Austrian countryside. I waited for half an hour for a taxi or bus to pass by, and then I just started walking to town.

One way I'd grown since leaving Kevin three years ago was that I was more courageous now. I'd discovered my physical and emotional independence and realized that I was absolutely fine without a man. But there was a flip side to this coin: I'd been right about my ex's grounding effect. Since our split, I had spent way too much time partying, and my only real criteria for the men that passed through my life was physical attraction. At least my career was thriving—there was little more important to me than that.

I disembarked from the plane and strode purposefully through the airport, surreptitiously scanning the overhead signs. I saw one with a picture of a taxi, and, breathing a sigh of relief, I made my way in that direction. Two cars with lighted domes sat waiting at the curb. I climbed into the first one and gave the driver the name of my hotel.

Tunisia? Be careful there, my friend Suzana had warned me when I told her where I was going, but I had waved off her concerns. My job didn't exactly take me to destinations worthy of CNN news bites. Most of the time, my biggest worry was whether I had packed enough sunscreen to avoid having to pay the prices levied by the hotel shops in Mauritius, Cape Town or Guadalupe. But I certainly wasn't naive about such things. As always in these circumstances, I splayed my keys between my fingers and kept my fist hidden in my lap in case I needed a weapon. Though most people imagined dangers in modelling to be horny photographers, drug-pushing industry insiders and agents who put their girls on a diet of rice cakes and water, the real threats were less glamorous. They lay in situations such as this—travels to foreign cities where languages and cultures were unknown, or the apartment on the seedy side of town she was expected to inhabit, or the hurried walks home after dark when a photo shoot ended late at night. Sixteen-year-old girls from Brazil or the Ukraine without a dime to their name lived at the mercy of their agency's willingness to keep them sheltered and fed. I'd known three models who committed suicide over lost jobs and waning prestige. Though I'd seen enough to be realistic, I also felt just this side of untouchable because I'd almost always managed to avoid the ugliest side of my industry.

Eventually the driver pulled into a palm-tree-lined driveway that ended at the entrance of a gorgeous resort hotel. I smiled. Any potential danger was behind me—from now on, I'd be under the protection of my photo team, whom I already knew well.

"Welcome to Tunisia," the receptionist said when I approached her desk. "Your name, please?"

"I'm here with the Marika party, for the photo shoot," I said, already digging through my purse for a cigarette. It was close to midnight, but I would smoke just one before bed.

The receptionist was still tapping at her computer.

"I'm so sorry," she said. "But your party has all checked in, and I'm afraid there are no more rooms available. I am obliged to send you to the hotel next door for the night. Please don't worry. Before the Hotel Riu was built, it was the best in the area."

"Oh," I responded, annoyed. "Can you call me another taxi then, please?"

"There is no taxi necessary—it is the next hotel over from us. The fastest way there is to proceed through these doors to the beach and walk fifty metres. You will see the gated entrance directly to your right."

"Okay, then," I said with a comfort I didn't feel. I was tired and hungry, and I had to be up in less than five hours. I just wanted a bed.

I picked up my bag and went out the door. When it closed behind me, deafening the sound of the late-night partiers in the bar, I could hear waves crashing on the shore just a few feet away. The moon shone in the night air. I made my way down the pathway until my feet hit sand and then turned right. The beach was completely deserted, which initially relieved me but then quickly set me on edge. I could see the lights of the other hotel beckoning, though they looked much less inviting than those I had just left. Cheap and too bright, they revealed a building in a serious state of disrepair. *Who cares?* I thought. *It's only for one night. I can survive anything for a night.*

There was someone behind me. I heard footsteps and turned to see a bearded man strolling along the beach. I felt a pang of unease.

He was huge, so huge in fact, that I wondered if he might be one of those gargantuan people like Andre the Giant. He was at least seven feet tall and two-fifty, with hands like baseball mitts. Though he was walking nonchalantly, looking out at the crashing waves, I quickened my pace. My carry-on bag, which I was used to rolling on wheels, suddenly felt very heavy. I swung it up into both arms to lighten my load. It was then I realized that with my suitcase in both hands, I couldn't access my makeshift key weapon.

Behind me, I heard soft thuds on the wet sand breaking into a run. Without looking back, I made a dash for the hotel gate and grabbed at the handle. It was locked.

Fuck. I turned to face my enemy, who stood not three feet away from me. Then I dropped my bag, knowing at this point I would happily give it up if it meant saving my ass, and crossed my arms over my chest in a way that I hoped looked aggressive.

"What do you want?" I asked furiously.

He said something unintelligible. I narrowed my eyes at him. "Sexy lady," he said, stepping toward me.

I was terrified, but there was something else. Something familiar about the way he was standing and the words he had just said. I realized I had three choices. One was to run—but where to? The second was to pound desperately on the gate's intercom button, praying for them to let me in before he overcame me. The last was to confront him.

I threw my arms out at my sides in an effort to look menacing. Quick as a flash, I saw myself doing the same thing as a child when faced with a wild animal. The man grinned back at me as I searched my brain desperately for something I could say that would disarm him. I came up blank. *Humans are different from animals*, I thought. *Challenge him.*

I locked my eyes on his and stepped closer to him. He looked triumphant for a few seconds, and then something changed. I squinted at him with a confidence I didn't feel. *Don't fuck with me,* I repeated over and over in my head, as if he could read my mind.

Don't fuck with me—don't fuck with me, or you'll regret it. His gaze dropped. We were still three feet apart, but I knew I was winning.

I bent down, snatched up my bag and walked back to the gate. Jab jab jab on the button. Static crackled sharply over the intercom.

"Let me in, please," I said with simulated calm. "I'm a hotel guest."

The gate clicked open. I stepped inside and slammed it quickly behind me. *Thank god, thank god*, I thought to myself, finally breaking into a run. *The nightmare is over.*

But I was wrong.

The hotel room was disgusting. Mouldy smelling, cockroach-ridden, with hair on the bathroom floor and a sagging mattress at centre stage. But none of these were conditions I hadn't withstood in the past. The thing that worried me was that there was no dead-bolt on the door; the only lock was a flimsy safety button on the doorknob.

I could go back to the front desk and complain, but remembering the looks I'd received from the male receptionists didn't make me want to draw attention to the fact that I was alone in a poorly secured room. My only other option was to push the dresser against the door. I did so, then went to bed fully clothed, so I wouldn't have to touch the sheets, and tried to sleep.

Instead I lay wide awake for a long time, thinking about the man on the beach. My adrenalin was still pumping, but there was more to it. What was it about him that had niggled at me? I couldn't figure it out, and I was exhausted. Eventually I drifted into a fitful sleep.

Bang bang bang!

Someone was pounding on my door. I shot upright in bed, my heart thundering out of my chest.

More banging.

For just a moment, my mind flashed back to another time. I was six years old, living in a cottage we weren't supposed to be in. My mother was out, so I was hidden in a closet. I heard hammering on the outside door and was terrified, but I covered my ears until it stopped.

This time it wasn't stopping.

What the fuck? Was it the guy from the beach, or someone else? What the hell was wrong with this place? I picked up the phone and dialled Reception. After eleven unanswered rings, I hung up.

I stole silently out of bed, looking around in the dark for anything that could be used as a weapon. The clock radio was the only thing I could find. I snatched it up and yanked the cord out of the wall. On shaking legs, I moved toward the door and stood with the clock poised over my head.

"What do you want?" I said loudly.

The banging stopped.

"Listen," I continued with a bravado I didn't feel. "Get the fuck away from me. I swear to god, I will kill you if you come near me. You picked the *wrong fucking girl*!" The pitch of my voice on the last three words shocked even me. I wasn't just scared, I realized. I was furious. As terrifying as my circumstances were, there was more to it. The events of the night had triggered an unwelcome hailstorm of old memories and emotions.

I listened with my ear to the door. I could hear someone breathing, and then a few minutes later, footsteps shuffled away. I sagged against the floor and finally allowed myself to cry.

On the plane back to Munich, I reflected on how thankful I was to feel safe again—strapped into my seat, fashion magazines in my lap, an apartment to return to in one of the lowest-crime cities in the world. The morning after the scare, I'd told the photo team what happened, and they were suitably horrified. But no one said anything about calling the police or even registering a complaint. And as so often happened to me after a stressful or traumatic event, I found myself questioning my judgment. Was it really that frightening? Or was I just tired and stressed out and overreacting? This was a running theme in my life: I'd experience something that I thought was a big deal, and then dismiss myself as being dramatic after it was resolved. It was the same way when I thought about my childhood. I knew it was different, but I honestly didn't think it was any more traumatic than anyone else's. It occurred to me that maybe I had no idea what the normal realm of experience looked like.

I picked up my magazine and tried to focus on the words on the cover, but my thoughts wouldn't stop circling. Every time I thought about the man on the beach, it wasn't his face I saw—it was another that I recognized from my past but couldn't for the life of me put a name to. And whoever it was, he left me with a lingering sense of dread.

Chapter 18

2008
Vancouver

I **dipped my roller into the tray and slapped paint onto** the wall, working furiously. Paint splattered into the air, showering my face with speckles of white. I glanced at my watch and ran a hand across my forehead, wiping the sweat from my brow. Shit. If I didn't get out of here in the next fifteen minutes, I'd miss closing time. I increased my pace, thankful this carpet was going to be ripped up and I didn't have to worry about the paint splatter. I finished the wall and then ran to the kitchen sink to clean my rollers and brushes. Yanking my headscarf off, I hurried to my car—*Carleigh's* car—and hit the gas.

Twenty minutes later, still in my painting clothes, I parked at the curb and ducked into the shop. Damn it. The same man I'd dealt with last time was behind the counter. Only this time, a boy of about six sat on a stool beside him, playing a game on an iPhone. The man looked at me placidly as I handed over my wedding ring set. Not that I minded parting with it, but I did mind that this was the last item I owned of any real monetary value. He peered at the diamond through his glass.

"You understand, everyone want to sell it, but no one want the used engagement rings," he said in heavily accented English. I

251

nodded. "Eighty bucks. Best I can do." He dropped the rings back on the counter with a clatter. The boy looked up from his game and stared at me.

I kept my eyes steady, but I could feel my cheeks burning. I wondered how much this child understood about his father's business, if he knew that people who visited this shop were in the throes of desperation. I wondered if my own son would ever understand how near we were to the edge. When I was a child, I always knew how close my mother and I were to having the bottom fall out of our world, and it terrified me.

Eighty dollars for a set that I knew had cost thirty times that. In my head, I spent the cash—twenty for gas, fifteen for the utility bill, the rest for food. That would get me through to the next week, until I got paid for my painting job. Then my rent cheque would clean out my account again, and Avery's birthday was coming up—but I would worry about that later.

"That's fine," I said to the man, forcing a smile. "Thank you."

As I watched him slip the jewellery into his glass case, I thought about the day I'd come across James buying the rings at the mall. I'd been wealthy then compared to now, but I'd valued myself about as much as this man in front of me valued my rings. Maybe that was something I'd learned, at least—that my self-esteem had little to do with materialism and everything to do with perception.

If there was a way to earn a dollar without compromising my morals, I was doing it. My weeks were divided into two separate realities—the challenge to be a present and nurturing mother to Avery for three and a half days a week, and the scramble to do anything I could to make money for the other three and half days. I painted, cleaned houses, did the odd modelling job and built websites for friends. Which was another problem, because my Mac had nearly called it a day—every five minutes or so the screen would black out, forcing me to reboot it and pray that it would hold out just long enough to finish the job. Like a person lost in the desert, I kept putting one foot in front of the other in the hope that water would eventually materialize. I sold furniture, clothing, anything I could bear to part with. I scraped together change to buy gas. I lived on beans and pasta and went grocery shopping with a calculator running through my head. In my darkest moments, it occurred to me that history was repeating itself—that this was exactly how my mother and I used to live.

Though my bank account was poverty-stricken, and I was finding ways to survive that many would have found unthinkable, my careful persona still exuded middle-class. None of my friends knew how bad it was. When they asked me to meet them for lunch or go out for a drink, I cited other obligations. It wasn't that I was embarrassed or afraid they would lose respect for me; it was that telling them the truth would open up the fear in me that I was trying so hard to hold at bay. I could feel the darkness of depression trying to take over, and I worried that if it did while I was in such a vulnerable state, I might never be able to shake myself from its grip.

Each morning I gazed up at my ceiling and told myself that I had no choice but to remain optimistic—no easy feat considering I had no career prospects, no education, no great business ideas and no capital to start one even if I had. I thought of getting a job at Starbucks and trying to work my way up to manager, but after a quick calculation of what I would need to spend on child care for Avery versus income, I realized that what I made wouldn't even cover my monthly rent. So what did I have, I wondered, besides a willingness to work hard? My answer was immediate: I had my story. Yes. I had my story, and despite what every editor in New York may have had to say about it, I still believed it was publishable.

One evening I put Avery in front of some cartoons and sat down beside him to scan my manuscript. Sometimes when I'd been writing about my child self, I'd made myself cringe. *Wake up*, I'd felt like yelling at that little girl. *Stop being so eager and trusting.* I could see now that instead of honouring my true personality through my writing, I'd shifted it slightly. It was still me, but the cooler version of myself that I wished I'd been, more like a sitcom character than one from a movie. Tough rather than strong, lacking vulnerability and a natural curiosity about my world. I realized that the success of my story lay partly in my willingness to reveal the true Cea, but the thought of that made me downright squeamish. I didn't want to feel the wounds of that young child again.

"We can't give up," Avery said softly beside me, and I whipped my head around to look at his face. He smiled shyly at me. He'd just repeated a character's line from *My Little Pony*, I realized.

I grinned back at him and ruffled his hair. Refusing to give up wasn't a one-time promise; it was something to which you renewed your commitment every single day. And I was *not* a victim; in fact, I was rather lucky, because my life had prepared me for this.

As I adjusted to my new normal, I thought about the things I could keep within my control. I sat down and made a list of what I could offer others in exchange for money, and another of seemingly impossible-to-obtain wishes for myself. Predictably my second list dwarfed the first. *Stability. A man I can finally be truthful with. A marriage that won't fail. A writing career. A house and a car to call my own. Another child?*

After I'd made my lists, I called a friend who'd used a surrogate to carry her first baby. This was how I would make enough money to support Avery and myself. Though the idea would have sounded outlandish and unthinkable to many, to me it made perfect sense. It was something I could easily offer a family while allowing me to stay home with Avery and continue writing. I called the number of the surrogate centre and asked them to send me the paperwork to get started. Then I got on my laptop and went on the Plenty of Fish website. I'd never thought about internet dating before, but given my financial and child-care situation, there wasn't really any other way for me to meet someone. I liked that I could type my wish list for a man right into my profile. For the first time in weeks, I had a genuine laugh when I imagined myself sitting in a café waiting for my date, trying to figure out how I was going to explain away my pregnant state before he could run in the other direction.

My perspective was changing. Despite—or perhaps because of— my nomadic past, I realized I'd been trying to create permanency in my life just like everyone else. Letting go of that expectation gave me a calm and strength I hadn't felt before. Tough Cea may have been long buried, but she was not dead.

1998
Milan & Munich

"Man, you look like crap," Suzana said, when I entered our shared train compartment.

I smiled ruefully. I loved my best friend's honesty, and what she said was true. I was dreadfully ill with the flu. I'd just come off a four- day shoot in the Canary Islands with an unforgiving schedule that had forced me to model outfit after outfit instead of resting. The makeup artist had covered my red nose with pancake makeup and Visine'd my watery eyes, and I'd lived through it, trying not to faint from weakness. All I wanted now was to go home to bed, but I had another job to go to.

"I'll survive," I replied weakly. "Just have to get through this next one. I couldn't exactly cancel."

"Yeah, I know," Suzana said sympathetically, and we grinned at each other knowingly.

As a fellow model who'd started nearly as young as I had, Suzana knew all too well the ins and outs of our volatile business. We were neither top girls nor bottom girls. We were mid girls, the ones who worked steadily but were easily replaced if we cancelled a booking or dared voice a complaint. I'd worked in minus-twenty degrees for full days with no place to warm up, and I'd posed in swimsuits, being bitten by sand fleas for hours and later counting more than five hundred bites on my body. I'd taken trains with dodgy-looking passengers through the night to reach remote destinations, worn clothes so ugly I wanted to cry when I looked in the mirror, and worked through entire days without being offered a bite of food. I never complained. I knew my place, my value and my limitations.

I sat down across from Suzana in our compartment. We were doing a shoot in Italy the next morning, and because of the job's location in a small town, it was more practical to take the train than to fly. As always when I travelled, I stuffed my passport under my shirt and placed my wallet under my coat beside me. I was slightly nervous, because the Canary Islands client had paid me partly in cash, and I hadn't even had time to go to the bank before catching my train.

"Hey," I said. "I heard from James. He sent me a letter last week. He seems really nice."

"Really? That's awesome! I seriously think you guys would be a great match."

"Mm. Well, we'll see."

"Okay, bedtime for me," Suzana said with a yawn, glancing at her watch. "Remember, no sleeping at the same time. Wake me up in two hours."

"Of course."

As I gazed out the window at the passing landscape—green fields punctuated by tiny storybook towns—my thoughts drifted to James. *A great match.* I barely knew him yet, but I already agreed with my friend's statement.

The moment I opened my eyes, I sensed something was wrong. My head hurt, and my eyes ached. The train, bearing down on Milan Central Station, rocked beneath me. Passengers clomped down the aisle outside the curtained window, chattering in Italian and German. Across from me, Suzana sat up and rubbed her eyes.

"We were supposed to take turns." I groaned. "How did we both fall asleep?"

"I don't know. Did you wake me up?"

"I—I can't remember." I brought my hand to my temple. I could vaguely recall the conductor coming in to check our tickets and passports, passengers opening our door to look for empty seats and then moving on, but it all seemed like a fuzzy dream. "My head is pounding. Something feels weird."

"Holy shit," Suzana said, catching sight of my face. "Look at your eyes!"

I turned to the small mirror behind my seat. My green eyes were swollen into narrow, red slits. "What the hell?" I reached for my handbag and grabbed my wallet, but I already knew what I would find. It was unzipped, revealing an empty space that last night had held more than three thousand Deutschmarks in cash. "The gas sprayers," I said furiously. "They got me. I can't fucking believe it."

The sleeping-gas sprayers were notorious on the night train that ran from Munich to Milan. It was rumoured that conductors were paid off to allow them to go about their nasty business, and I didn't doubt it. Train compartments weren't lockable, and all the perp needed to do was slip a hose through a crack in the door, release the gas, wait for the victims to fall asleep and then rob them. And as if that weren't enough, I'd also had an apparent bad reaction to the gas. I was due to start my modelling job in an hour, and I knew exactly what would happen when they saw my eyes: they'd send me straight back home.

Home. Whatever that meant.

When I returned to my apartment in Munich, there was a large yellow envelope on the floor beneath the mail slot. I picked it up and looked at the return address. Papa Dick? It had been years since I'd heard from him. I still wrote him the occasional postcard from my more exotic shoot destinations, but he rarely replied.

The envelope was thick. What could he be sending me? Years' worth of correspondence that had been returned to him, perhaps? I ripped the envelope open at the kitchen table.

It was a magazine. Staring at me from the cover was my grandfather's face, with his familiar blue eyes and long greying hair. He was dressed in his usual bush garb of wool shirt and suspenders. A yellow sticky-note affixed to the cover said, *Dear Cea, I thought you'd like to see this. There's a big feature on me on page 62. Love, Papa.*

I dropped the magazine in disgust. *The self-centred prick* was my first thought, but then I realized that maybe this wasn't so different from the postcards I sent him—a way of saying *Look how well I'm doing! And I'm doing it all without you!* Maybe this was just a stupid contest to see who had the better life. It wasn't a thought that made me feel any better about him, or myself.

I lit a cigarette and grabbed my purse. I'd had a shitty week, and I knew a couple of ways to make it better. I walked the few blocks to Leopoldstrasse, Schwabing's main shopping street, and started at my favourite clothing store. Two hours later, over a thousand dollars lighter and many shopping bags heavier, I let myself back into my apartment and opened a bottle of wine. I had a party to get ready for.

By the time I sauntered into my favourite bar, Cosmo's, to meet up with my friends, I'd finished off a bottle and a half. They all gathered around and hugged me. My friends were my salvation. We came from everywhere—Australia, Sweden, America, Brazil, Canada—and landed here with two things in common: we were models, and we were outsiders. This lifestyle made my carefully constructed persona so easy to uphold. No one knew where I came from, and questions were easy to deflect—because really, people were way more interested in talking about themselves than hearing about anyone else. *I'm from Calgary. My mom was a hippie and had me young. We don't talk much now.* In a world of models striving to stand out as being unique and special, my story was plausible and not very interesting.

But tonight was different. I kept drinking, and each drink made me a little surer of myself. I felt popular, invincible, powerful. I enthralled everyone with my story of the train fiasco, and since that went so well, I decided to keep going. "Guess what?" I slurred, placing my empty wineglass down on the table too hard. "You guys will never believe this. I used to live in a *tipi* when I was little!"

My friends looked at me blankly for moment, then they all drunkenly cracked up. "You mean, like, a wigwam?" someone said.

"Totally! We hunted for our own food and everything. My favourite was bear meat!"

Before long, I was running through my craziest stories: the pot bust, stealing from cottages, starting school while we were squatting in one, the tree fort my mother used as a babysitter while she went off to meet her lover, falling through the ice and almost dying. They all stared at me in shock, laughed hysterically, asked for more. I'd never felt more accepted and loved.

After the bar closed, we took the party back to my house. I stood barefoot in the kitchen, swaying in place, while my friends chatted drunkenly around me. I was beginning to feel ill. I leaned forward, lost my balance and fell against a free-standing cabinet. Something landed hard on my head. Liquid poured down my face as the bottle crashed to the ground and shattered. I looked down at it, stunned, and then began laughing maniacally. My current favourite song was blaring from the CD player: "Seether" by Veruca Salt. Without another thought, I jumped barefoot into the red puddle of wine and broken glass and started to dance.

The next morning dawned harsh. My body was racked with pain, but that was nothing compared to the pain of my emotions. I couldn't remember a lot, but I knew I'd said way too much. Remorse and guilt replaced my bravado of the night before. The self-loathing I felt was pushing out reason. My carefully constructed mask had finally crumbled.

My feet were screaming at me. Slowly I lifted the covers to inspect them. The soles were bloody and raw, with glass shards sticking out. My face and hair were soaked with booze, and beside my bed was Papa Dick's magazine. Black marker was scribbled all over his face. I dropped the magazine on my bed and gingerly lay back on my pillow. Papa Dick. Sure, he had disappointed me by not being the person I'd thought he was—by being a narcissistic egomaniac, rather than the hero of my childhood. But did that really warrant *this* much resentment toward him? I glanced down at the cover again and, in that moment, heard a name in my head that was not my grandfather's. Before I could stop myself, I picked up the phone and dialled Mom's number.

"Are you okay?" she asked when she heard the hangover in my voice.

"No," I said, rushing on before she could ask more questions. "Listen, I have to ask you something. A while ago I was doing a job in Tunisia, and a man—well, I was pretty sure he was going to attack me—"

"Oh, Cea, I'm sorry—"

"It's fine," I said abruptly. "I dealt with it. The point is, ever since then, I've had this face in my head. And now there's a name. Like that guy triggered a memory, only I can't remember what it is. I don't even know if the name and face belong to the same person." I paused. "Who's Darcy? Every time I think of that name, I feel like throwing up. Who is he?"

"Darcy? You mean . . . the guy I dated for a while? Before Sam and I got back—"

"*No*, obviously."

She was quiet for a moment. "Well, I don't know, then," she said finally. "I have no idea."

I closed my eyes against my throbbing head. Mom was an easy read, and I knew she was telling the truth.

The darkness knocked me back onto my bed like a physical force. My past was the boogeyman coming to get me, and I was pretty sure I couldn't outrun it anymore.

Chapter 19

2008
Vancouver

I leaned across the restaurant table toward Remy and touched his hand. "So I'm standing there with my little kindergarten friend, and here comes my mom to the door all, like, 'Hi, girls, did you have fun at the birthday party?' And not only is she topless, she's *smoking a joint*!"

Remy threw his head back and laughed. It was one of the many things I loved about him—his emotions were always close to the surface, and there was something about him that made me sure I could trust him. We'd been together for two months, and I'd already told him more stories about my crazy past than I'd told James in nine years.

"Hey," Remy said suddenly. "Do you get Avery back tomorrow? I was thinking we could take him to the water park."

I smiled so hard I felt my face might split in two. Against every odd, it seemed I had met my perfect match on my very first internet date. Right from the beginning, I'd felt something different with Remy. Unless you counted that he seemed too perfect to be true, there were no red flags. Unlike me, he came without baggage—at forty-two years old, he'd never so much as lived with a woman. He had no kids, no exes to speak of, was financially secure, handsome, romantic, attentive, and best of all, hilariously funny. His family wasn't perfect, but

262

they weren't horribly dysfunctional either. We'd even both lived in Europe and lost our mothers to breast cancer. He insisted that he loved kids and wanted his own and had just been waiting for the right person to come along. And so far, though I'd told him about my two divorces, wild family and current financial situation, that person appeared to be me.

Needless to say, after telling Remy about my surrogacy plan and having a good chuckle about it, I'd thrown it out the window. Lately I'd landed a few modelling jobs, which was keeping me in groceries and allowing me to continue work on my memoir. Even my being an aspiring writer who planned to reveal her crazy life story to the world hadn't scared Remy off.

"So," he said, taking my hand. "When do I get to read this book of yours? I'm dying to know every little thing about you."

"Soon," I promised. "Soon." Not surprisingly, my old go-to fear about revealing my past had not died. But in that moment, I realized one of the reasons Remy was so different from the men in my past: rather than making me feel like damaged goods, he made me feel like some sort of treasure.

I thought about the wish list I'd made when my world had bottomed out just a few months ago. Of the bad karma I always knew I'd pay off someday when I was cheating on Kevin. Of Guthrie the astrologer, predicting that my time of trouble was finally nearing an end. Of our dead mothers, plotting our meeting somewhere in the ether. And I felt a tipping toward a truth that I'd long suspected—one that, just as my beginnings had dictated, defied the passivity of hope and affirmed the power of action.

I sat beside Remy, nervously tapping my foot on the floor. A glance at the wall clock informed me that exactly one minute had passed since I'd last checked it. I tried to distract myself by looking around the room. It was small and drab, with a few posters of puppies and kittens. It looked more like a waiting room in a children's hospital than a genetic counsellor's office.

I placed my hand on my belly, feeling for movement beneath my T-shirt. My second baby was an active one, an endless source of entertainment as Remy and I watched its *Alien*-like antics.

"I don't know why I'm so nervous," I remarked, and Remy squeezed my leg reassuringly.

"Because this is important to you."

I smiled back at him and then glanced down at my eternity engagement ring. We planned to get married in December, before our baby boy was due to come along. Just as I'd predicted when we first met, Remy was not only a man to be trusted but the right one for me. We'd barely been together a year when I got pregnant, and he had been ecstatic about it.

At long last, the door opened to admit our counsellor. "I'm Alice," she said, all perky smiles and professional pantsuit.

I instantly felt at ease.

"Sorry about the wait—it's nuts around here today. Now. What concern has brought you in?"

Remy gave me an encouraging look, and I cleared my throat. "It's . . . my family. My family of origin, I mean. This is hard for me to explain, but . . . mental illness runs deep. My mother had three siblings, and they were all affected. One was bipolar and schizophrenic. One was born mentally challenged. My uncle was the worst—he was a severely paranoid schizophrenic."

Alice nodded. "And your mother?"

"Yes. Not those things, but . . . something. She was slow. Terrible memory. Couldn't do basic math. I mean, she smoked a lot of pot, but it was more than that . . ." I let my voice trail off, frustrated as always by my inability to explain my family's indefinable strangeness to others, and even to myself.

"Hmm. All four children—that *is* certainly unusual. And your grandparents?"

"I think my grandmother was okay—depression, but that's about it. My grandfather, though—he was very narcissistic. Wasn't really interested in talking about anything that didn't involve himself. Maybe . . . I've sometimes thought he had a narcissistic personality disorder? He did some really crazy things in his life."

"And how about you? Any health concerns?"

I glanced quickly at Remy. He knew about my history with depression, but it was still one of those things I found uncomfortable talking about around someone who'd never experienced it. I imagined that he pictured me lying in bed with the blinds drawn for days, wringing my hands and weeping. The reality was that one could pass a whole lifetime being depressed without another person ever knowing it.

"Depression," I said. "Years of Celexa."

"Okay. And your concern is that your baby could be affected by any number of these mental illnesses?"

"Yes. My first son is fine, but—yes, I worry." I'd actually felt like I was rolling the dice when I got pregnant with Avery, but my strong desire for a baby combined with my apprehension to discuss my fears with James had prevented me from doing anything about it. There wasn't a day that passed that I wasn't grateful my son was healthy.

Alice and I got down to details. She wanted everything—physical descriptions, speech patterns, medical histories, body shapes, unusual habits, estimated intelligence. She nodded thoughtfully while I spoke, revealing details I hadn't thought about in years. To my surprise, I began to feel emotional.

"It's just . . ." I leaned toward her. "I've had a long road with my family. And I just don't think . . . I don't know if I can handle any more mental health issues. I've spent my whole life wondering what the hell is wrong with my family. I want answers that I'll probably never get."

Alice flipped open a massive medical book. "To me, it sounds possible that your family was suffering from this genetic condition— Fragile X. It results in intellectual disability and some of the physical features you described, like long faces. Now, is it possible to obtain a genetic sample from any of them?"

"You mean like hair or spit or something? No. My mother and grandparents have passed away, and I don't know where my aunts or uncle even are anymore."

"Ah. That's unfortunate. The best I can do, then, is offer the tests to you. It's possible that you are a carrier of the gene without being affected. If the tests come back positive, you will have your answer. But if they're negative, it doesn't mean we can rule it out—it means only that you aren't a carrier. This doesn't mean that your family doesn't have it, necessarily, only that it wasn't passed to you. In other words, without testing one of them directly, we'll never know for certain."

"And if it's positive . . . can I pass it to my own child?"

"No. You or your husband would need to be a full premutation carrier, meaning you display the symptoms, and that's not the case."

I exhaled with relief. No matter what, my unborn child was safe from the Person curse of craziness. That should have been enough for me, but I realized it was only half of the answer I was seeking.

A few days later, I went to the clinic to have blood drawn.

"How long until I get the results?" I asked the receptionist.

She pulled out a folding chart that flopped open onto her desk and ran a finger down it. "Let's see . . . Can't say I've ever seen this particular test run before . . . Here it is. Looks like about eight weeks."

Eight weeks. As my belly grew, so did my impatience. Not a single day went by without me thinking about it, wondering if I was finally going to get my answer. I hoped upon hope for a positive result. One moment I'd think that a concrete answer would mean everything to me, and the next, I would think, *Would it really? What would it change?* But that question was too easy. I'd spent my entire life feeling like an outsider looking in, and having this confirmed would justify those feelings. The pain and the unfairness I felt over ending up with a completely insane family. Yes, I was nearly forty years old. Sure, I prided myself on how I had moved on and beyond. But in my darker moments, I still recognized the truth: that those negative emotions lingered, even if as a shadow of their former versions. I was still pissed off. Maybe if there was a genetic component that I could point to, I could really and truly forgive.

I waited. And when the call finally came, I glanced down at my cell-phone screen and just held the phone for a moment while it rang, prolonging the inevitable. I took a deep breath and picked up.

"Cea. It's Alice from BC Genetics. I have your test results."

"Yes?"

"It's good news. Your test came back negative." Alice was a smart woman. My two beats of silence conveyed my feelings. When she spoke again, her voice was softer. "You're disappointed."

"It's so stupid, but . . . yes. A little."

"You wanted concrete answers. I'm sorry it wasn't to be."

I pressed my palm into my forehead. This, for me, was the end of the road. "I was just . . . hoping, that's all. For an answer. I mean . . ." I shook my head, wishing I could sum up the craziness of my family in one perfectly significant event. "My mother gave me a birthday party in a *garden centre*, for god's sake!"

Alice laughed. "Well, that's certainly original. But don't forget, this doesn't conclude anything. There still may be a genetic component. If you want my personal opinion, your mother and her siblings were predisposed to mental illness, and the heavy drug use in their teens pushed them over the edge."

"Yes, that makes sense. Just . . ."

"Yes?"

"My grandfather. What about him?"

"Cea. From everything you've described, it's clear to me that he had a disorder. For you to have come through it all as you have, and for your children to, is nothing short of incredible. Forget the genetic component for a minute. What you went through being raised by these people is miraculous. I think that's all the answer you need."

"You're right. Thank you so much."

I hung up the phone, reflecting for a moment. Alice was right. This was the answer I needed to settle for. It had to be enough. I must let go now, focus on building the next generation of the Person family. So why was I left feeling like I had been handed the fruit of healing, only to bite into it and find it rotten?

2012
Vancouver

I sat on the sofa with my laptop across my legs, typing as fast as my fingers would allow. Any minute now the front door would open, letting the chilly spring air into the house along with my husband and three children, signalling an end to my writing time for the week.

Finishing the chapter and closing my laptop, I felt the familiar mix of satisfaction and self-doubt settle in. I was almost done with what had to be the twentieth draft of my memoir. In a few weeks, I would query agents again, and the fate of my life story would once more be in someone else's hands. *Am I a fool to continue like this? How many hours of work have I put in now? I have so much good in my life. Why can't I just give this stupid idea up and move on?*

I made a frustrated sound and jumped up to start the laundry. Once more, my world had been radically transformed. *Recreated,* I reminded myself. *You made this happen. Be proud of yourself.* I sighed, annoyed at the constant dialogue that ran through my head. I *did* have so much—Remy, my amazing and supportive husband of three years; Avery, now a well-adjusted seven-year-old with two loving households; two-year-old Emerson, my adorable second son; Ayla, my beautiful newborn baby girl; a house in the suburbs; a fantastic relationship with my father; wonderful friends; and even a minivan, for god's sake. What more could I possibly desire?

Peace with your past. Forgiveness toward your family. The ability to make sense of all the pain.

Despite having rewritten my manuscript countless times, a sense of closure still eluded me. When I read the words back to myself, all I felt was a strange detachment, as if the story had everything to do with a protagonist named Cea and nothing to do with me. The puzzle pieces of my life still didn't fit.

I thought about my mother's memorial, almost five years ago now. My aunt Jan had waited until we had a private moment, and then she told me something I thought I'd never hear—that my mother had sent a message to me that she was sorry about what happened with Barry. As I sat listening to my aunt's words, I realized it had been thirty years almost to the day that he had molested me by forcing me to touch him. Though I wished the words had come directly from my mother, that acknowledgment of her mistake had helped me move forward. But really, it was only a small piece in the maddeningly complex jigsaw of my life.

I had come to think that having a publisher believe in my story would validate how insane my life had been and help to heal me in a way that nothing else had. But what if this never happened? How would I muddle through my existence without ever knowing where I stood on the scale of crazy, dysfunctional, distinctive childhoods?

Ayla cried out, signalling the end of her afternoon nap. I walked to the bedroom and scooped her out of the crib, smiling at her warm red cheeks. She put her arms around my neck and laid her face against mine.

"Should we get dinner started? Daddy will be home soon," I said, placing her in her Bumbo seat. She waved her arms excitedly at her brothers, who were sitting at the kitchen island drawing.

"Look, Mommy," Avery said, holding up his picture. "It's all of us!"

"Honey, it's beautiful," I said, and it was. There weren't many things more special than these moments when everyone was happy, and my children were creating things that proved their sense of contentment and belonging within our family. My kids' lives were more stable than I could have dreamed of as a child. *There, see? You're a success. Nothing like your mother.*

I put water on to boil for the pasta and grabbed my phone to check my email. When I saw the message, I froze. Quickly, before I could read a single word, I clicked the phone off and put it down. I wasn't ready for this, and I didn't know exactly when I would be.

Two months ago, I had sent my third round of query letters out to agents. I'd had a few bites, but only one agent had wanted to read beyond the first fifty pages. I'd sent her my entire manuscript several weeks ago, and now her answer was sitting in my inbox. If she said no, it would all be over—again.

I couldn't take it any longer. I picked up my phone, held my breath and opened the email, scanning it quickly.

Dear Ms. Person . . . read the entire manuscript . . . you're an excellent writer . . . but I'll never find a home for this . . . not very interesting . . . sad and upsetting . . . good luck.

The air whooshed out of my lungs. In the background, I could hear Remy opening the front door, shouting hello, the boys running to him, Ayla babbling happily. I felt faint. *How many hours? Not just of my own life, but of Remy's, of my children's?*

"Hey," Remy said as he entered the kitchen. He gave me a kiss and then studied my face. "Are you okay?"

"Yeah," I replied with a nod. "I'm fine." It was all I could get out. Remy and my children had seen me cry before, but with the shedding of these tears, they would also be witnessing the death of my dream.

"Scat!" said my father triumphantly, laying his cards on the table. "That would be *my* seventy-five cents right here, thank you very much." He scooped the change into his palm, and I rolled my eyes.

"About time you won." I reached for the bowl of chips and eyed the clock. "Remy should be home from work soon. I guess I should get the kids off the TV."

Dad smiled at me. Our visits were regular but too far between, and they were forever run by three children clamouring for their grandfather's attention. When a rare silence fell, it was always an easy one. I gave a little laugh.

"What's funny?" Dad asked.

"Nothing. I was just thinking of that time I went to visit you when I was eight. How scared I was to be alone with you. Terrified, really."

"Yes. That was pretty horrible for me." He gave me a sideways look. "Have you ever thought about why you reacted that way?"

"Thought about it? Of course, a ton. I always figured it was because of what was going on with Barry at the time, but now I think it was something different."

"Really? Like what?"

"I'm still trying to figure that out. I was hoping it would all come out when I started writing about my past, but . . ." I shrugged. "I guess it wasn't meant to be."

"Are you really going to quit? Even that horrible agent said you were an excellent writer."

I grinned. It was true that in all my disappointment over her rejection letter, I had overlooked her one compliment. But she had indeed succeeded in killing my dream, because eight months had passed since I'd received that letter, and I hadn't written a word since.

"Okay, great. So first I had a good story and terrible writing, then I had good writing and a terrible story. I don't know. What's the point? I mean, I had two goals going into this—to get published and to work out my past. But neither of those things has happened."

"And why did you want to get published?"

"For the money, mostly. To try to save myself from that awful financial hole I was in."

"And now you don't need to be saved anymore. So don't you think this is a wonderful opportunity? To be able to just write freely with no pressure to be published?"

I hadn't thought of it like that before. Even after I met Remy, I'd always written my book as if it were my lifeline, proof to myself that I could support myself financially if he left me. Some might call that a practical tactic, but I recognized that it meant I wasn't quite ready to believe in us yet. In a way, though he'd never given me any reason not to trust him completely, I'd been preparing for him to leave me.

"What I really wanted to write this book for was to help others. To reach out to people like myself who felt like outsiders. But I was in such a desperate financial situation that writing it for that reason seemed like a luxury I couldn't afford."

"Maybe that's why you weren't able to get it right," Dad said carefully. "Maybe purpose has everything to do with it. Finding your purpose, and making sense of it."

I nodded slowly. What my father said made so much sense that I couldn't believe I hadn't seen it myself, but the thought of delving as deep as I needed to in order to make sense of things was terrifying. Dad reached across the table and took my hand. "You did not come through so much in your life for nothing. You have a message to deliver. Don't miss this opportunity."

I smiled at his insight. Though my father had been absent from my childhood, when he did show up for me, he showed up big. He'd given me the money to start my modelling career when I was thirteen, and he'd been there for me when I hit rock-bottom after leaving James. In the years I'd gotten to know him, I was continually shocked by our similarities—we had the same habits, temperament and values. It made me believe all the more strongly that we simply were who we were at birth, and that environment had little to do with the person we ultimately become. Maybe the reason I'd endured so much as a child had less to do with creating my personality than creating my life's purpose.

So, yes, I would write my story. Only this time, I would write it not as if my life depended on it, but as if someone else's did.

1998
Munich

—*PTSD.*
—*What's that?*
—*Post-traumatic stress disorder.*
—*Oh. Right. What about it?*
—*I believe you had it. Classic symptoms, from what you've described.*
—*What? That's impossible. My life was never that—*
—*Traumatic? Cea. Do you even listen to yourself when you speak to me?*
—*Of course.*
—*So, then. Can you please just reflect a little here, and accept that your childhood was difficult? Too much, maybe, for a little girl to handle on her own?*
—*I guess so, but—*
—*But what?*
—*But it wasn't that bad. I was never, like, tortured or raped or anything.*
—*And you think that people who experience that are the only ones who experience trauma?*
—*I don't know. I mean, at least I had a mother who loved me. That's a lot more than a lot of other kids had.*
—*A mother who loved you, yes. And so, you had no right to anything more than that? Not a real childhood, not stability? Not protection?*
—*That's right. It could have been a million times worse.*
—*Yes, it could have been. But let me explain something to you. Your fear of war, when you first moved to the city. Your anxiety and panic—*

—What about them?

—Let's review a little bit. Age five and six, you endure a life on the run with your mom's boyfriend. You're constantly terrified of being discovered by the people he's stealing from, of the cops coming after you and of losing your mother. You watch your beloved dog get shot in front of you. You survive a fire, getting lost in the forest and squatting in other people's homes. Then you move in with Karl's mother, who treats you like you're so much dirt. Your mother repeatedly leaves you alone so she can meet up with her lover. You watch her have a miscarriage—

—Didn't watch her. Just heard her through the door.

—Clarification noted. Let's move on to age seven. One of your only friends, Art, breaks your trust by molesting you. You know you can't tell your mother about it, because she'll chastise you for being, according to her, prudish. When you're eight, her boyfriend Barry molests you for several months. You find out your mother knows about it and does nothing to stop it. Barry tries to coerce you into watching the two of them have sex. When you and your mother finally leave him, you're frightened out of your mind by a man who picks you up while you're hitchhiking. Then, after finally beginning to integrate into society and feel a little normal, you're sent back into the wilderness to live with your grandparents. Your mother, the only constant throughout your life, leaves you behind for a year. Then you almost drown when you fall through the ice. Shortly after that you move to the city, where not only are you navigating a completely new environment, you discover your mother is once again living with Barry. Is that all accurate?

—Uh-huh.

—So, would you consider any of these things, on their own, to be traumatizing events?

—Traumatizing events? I don't know if I'd go that far. But I'll play along.

—Cea?

—*Yeah?*

—*When we first started our sessions, you brought something up, and we haven't talked about it since. Something that happened just a little while after you'd returned to live in the wilderness with your grandparents. When you were eight.*

—*Eight, right. The year it all went down.*

—*I think we need to explore it.*

—*Explore? I don't think so. I mean, like I told you before, all I have is these little memory fragments.*

—*Yes. But let's go a little further than that and see if we can put them together. So—you were living in the Yukon. Your mother had gone to Calgary, leaving you behind with your grandparents.*

—*Okay, yeah. And I was babysitting for some friends of theirs. In Whitehorse. They wanted to go to some folk festival or something, so they left me in charge of their kids. I looked after them a few times.*

—*Yes?*

—*And . . .*

—*It's okay, Cea. This is a safe place for you to talk. Tell me what happened.*

—*It's hard to remember. I know there's more to it, but I keep seeing this one thing happening, but every time I think about it I feel so disgusting. Like I really really hate myself. But it's still there. Not going away. Like it will never go away.*

—*It's okay. I want you to just close your eyes. Take me back there. Tell me where you are, what it looks like, what you can see.*

—*Do we have to do this? I really don't think it's going to change anything.*

—*Of course we don't have to. But think of it this way: you say you feel like it will never go away, so what do you have to lose? Maybe this will help. Maybe you just need to confront it.*

—*All right. Okay, I guess. Well, it's a living room. There's an old brown couch, one of those velvet poster things everyone had in the seventies on the wall, and a small TV on an oak table.*

—Where are the kids?

—In bed. I finally got them to sleep.

—Good. What do you hear?

—A clock. The clock ticking. Some cars going by on the street.

—Tell me what you're touching. You're sitting on the couch—what does it feel like?

—The cushions are too soft, like they're all old and sunken in. The arm I'm leaning on is cold and hard. They have those plastic protective thingies on the arms.

—Great. That's great, Cea. And what do you smell?

—. . . Smell?

—Yes. Do you smell anything?

—

—Cea?

—

—Cea? Are you all right?

1978
Whitehorse

I awoke with a start and sat up in the bed, glancing around the darkened room. On either side of me, the babies slept. *Finally*, I thought as I slipped carefully off the mattress. I closed the door quietly behind me and crept down the hallway to the kitchen. I'd been wanting to do this all night, but the kids had needed snacks, new diapers, toys, more snacks, pyjamas and stories. I'd finally passed out between them in their parents' bed as they squirmed and kicked.

I hadn't wanted to babysit again, but Papa Dick had insisted that I'd be just fine, because I did such a good job last time. I looked up at the clock on the kitchen wall: just after nine o'clock. Papa Dick and

Grandma Jeanne had gone to a concert with the parents, and I was pretty sure it would be hours before they got home. Last time I'd gotten through an entire bag of Doritos and two chocolate bars before they came through the door, breathy-voiced and shiny-eyed from smoking pot all night. As I'd watched them leave earlier, I'd comforted myself with the knowledge of what was in the kitchen.

I opened the cupboard and looked inside. Yellow boxes of macaroni and cheese, tins of soup, a stack of candy, two half-eaten bags of chips. Perfect. I took a bag down and crammed half its contents into my mouth. The chips were a little stale, but I didn't care. I folded the bag loosely, so it didn't look empty, and put it back on the shelf. Then I pulled out a bag of Nibs, tore it open and emptied the little black candies into my hand. How would I explain if they discovered them missing? Papa Dick would kill me if he found out I'd eaten junk food. No, not kill me, just give me that disappointed look that always withered me. They wouldn't notice, I decided. Not in the state they came home in. I popped the candies into my mouth one by one. They tasted like the rough, barky sticks Grandma Jeanne sometime gave me to chew on after supper, but much sweeter.

As I was reaching for a chocolate bar, I heard a noise at the front door. A key turning in the lock. Afraid of discovery, I shoved everything back in the cupboard and slammed it closed.

"Hey," said a voice behind me, and I whipped around.

A tall boy of about fifteen was standing in the doorway. He had a bit of black fuzz on his top lip. I stared at him, petrified.

"Who—who are you?" My voice was shaking.

"Um, I *live* here? Didn't they tell you?"

"Uh—no."

"Figures. I'm Kate's kid. Not Jeff's, though." He looked at me more closely. "And what are *you* doing here?"

"Babysitting."

"Oh yeah? How old are you?"

"Eight."

"Mm. Well, eight-year-old, you've got something on your face."

I wiped my sleeve across my mouth, and it came away with a black smear.

"You like licorice, huh?"

I shrugged, praying he wouldn't tell my grandparents. He was looking at me kind of funny. Something stirred in my body. I dropped my eyes.

"Kate say when they'd be home?"

I shook my head.

He tossed his keys on the table and took the stairs down to the basement. Junk-food binge interrupted, I went into the living room and opened my book.

Something was behind me, curled around my back. I opened my eyes and turned over on the couch.

"I like you," he whispered into my ear. "Do you like me?"

The room was pretty dark, only a little light coming through the window from a streetlamp. I could hear a clock ticking, a car whooshing by outside. His hair brushed the side of my face. He smelled like cigarettes and soap. His hand was down there, on me.

"I like you. Do you like me?"

My compass spun. Out of control, righting itself briefly, and then off again. Did I like him? He was good-looking. He was nice. He gave me that funny feeling in my belly that I got when David and I had our first kiss. He only knew me as the babysitter, not some freaky girl from the wilderness.

"Yes," I said.

"Prove it."

"Prove it?"

"Yeah. What do you do if you like a guy?"

"I can't do *that*. I'm only eight."

"There are other things you can do, sexy girl."

I could hear the blood rushing through my ears. I was scared, nervous, but also excited. A guy liked me and had even called me *sexy*. A guy who wasn't Art, the old pervert, or Barry, who had belonged to my mother. I felt suddenly as if I were the one in control. For the first time, I understood why Mom had always told me there was nothing more important in life than this.

He unzipped his fly. It sprung out toward my face, bigger than I'd expected. So close I could even smell it. It smelled kind of funny, different from the rest of him. I held my breath and opened my mouth.

It was over in a minute. My jaw was sore from opening too far, and there was slimy stuff in my mouth that I spat out into my hand. He tucked it back into his underwear and zipped up his fly. He was standing above me now, so I sat up a little bit taller. I didn't want him to remember that I was just a kid. He smiled at me.

"Did you like that?"

I looked up at him, but I couldn't see his face with the light behind him. He was a dark silhouette looming over me. I nodded.

He gave a little laugh. "Figures," he said. Then he turned away and walked down the stairs.

The power I'd felt slid away, replaced by a fiery ball of regret a hundred times bigger. I went into the kitchen and drank a glass of warm water, hoping it would stop the nausea that had suddenly come on. I thought about Mom, hundreds of miles away in Calgary. What would she say if she knew what I'd just done? I had a pretty good idea. Very possibly, she was doing the exact same thing with some guy right now.

I went back to the couch and stayed there until my grandparents got home, hating myself for wanting him to come back to me again.

I stopped typing and stared at the words on my screen. Three memories—babies, junk food and him. Until that therapy session in Munich, the rest had always been connect-the-dots. Over the years since, Darcy's face sometimes came to me as I was drifting off to sleep.

Instead of letting myself think about him, I would just repeat his name again and again in my head until it sounded warped and ridiculous. It joined the other words I avoided in the English language, like *stoned* and *pussy* and *lovemaking*—words that grated on my nerves because my mother used to use them all the time, years before I should have known what they meant.

This story I had promised myself I would take to the grave. But even sitting here with my memories released onto digital paper, I felt a slight loosening of my shame. Darcy. He was fifteen, sixteen years old, and I had let him do it, because that's what I thought you were supposed to do. Now I saw the truth. That it wasn't really about Darcy—sure, he'd done something unconscionable—it was about me, how I hated myself forever afterward because I *let* him. Because I'd behaved like my mother, the one person in the world I never wanted to be like. How long had I carried this around like a black tumour, festering and growing? Every time I tried to be happy, it would remind me of how worthless I was.

This was the last scene I would write for *North of Normal*, I thought. I'd revealed all that I comfortably could elsewhere in my manuscript and knew that what I'd written was the best work I'd ever done.

I sipped from my coffee cup, sighed and put it down. *No.* The Darcy story still hurt too much. Barry had been enough—the decades I'd argued with myself against being his victim, because rather than touching me, he had made me touch *him* and thereby become his accomplice. And then Darcy, straight on Barry's heels, again not forcing me but guiding me to fulfill his desires, proving once again that I was unable to say no. How deeply and pathetically I had craved approval of any kind. I copied the entire chapter and pasted it into a deleted-pages document. There it would live, I decided, recorded but safe from the public eye. The world would know my story, at least most of it, but there were some things I needed to keep for myself.

I closed my laptop. I was ready.

Epilogue

December 2015
Vancouver

I **sit in my home office, surrounded by pieces of my** past and present. On the wall are four pen and pencil sketches done by my father in 1969, the year Mom was pregnant with me: young versions of Papa Dick, Grandma Jeanne, Mom and Dad himself. Faces straight and expressionless, breasts exposed. Los Gatos, California: these are the memories I wasn't there for but almost feel I was, because the stories are so detailed in my mind. I like the idea that my family members touched these sheets of paper, possibly shuffling them among themselves while they got high and discussed health food, rock 'n' roll, the state of the nation. How I would have loved to see the inner workings of the Person family during that time. Things were simpler then, before I came along.

Beside the sketches is a photo of Remy and me celebrating our fifth wedding anniversary, happier and closer than ever. On my desk are photos of my three children, frozen in time in a world completely different from the one in which I was raised. Well-adjusted, expected to be nothing other than kids, by turns needy and vulnerable and independent and rebellious in their journey to self-discovery. A few days ago, Avery, who's ten now, asked me if I'd be writing a third

281

book about my life. "Not unless something really crazy and exciting happens in the future," I replied, and his face lit up.

"We're going to Hawaii for spring break. *That's* crazy and exciting!" he said, and it made me ridiculously happy that such an event was the height of insanity in his young world.

Being Avery's mother has given me a new perspective. He was eight when *North of Normal* came out, which seems kind of perfect, because I was eight myself when I endured some of the worst moments of my childhood. When I look at his absolute innocence, it's hard to believe I ever thought I was responsible for Barry's or Darcy's actions. I try to imagine Avery coming to me concerned about nude photos of children, or seeing him as competition for my lover's sexual attention, as my mother did when I was his age. Then I imagine Emerson, who is five, squatting in summer cottages and fearing the cops will take me away from him. Shivering under a sleeping bag while we camp in a truck by the side of the road, and then watching his beloved dog get shot. I think about my three-year-old, Ayla, confused and afraid as night after night, she witnesses her mother having sex beside her with an array of strangers. And in these moments, my anger rises to the surface, and I feel like maybe I really do despise my mother after all and have not forgiven her and never will. But then time allows me to take a step back, and I remember how much better equipped I am to make good choices than she was, and how I believe that we are put on earth to learn lessons that often take a lifetime to figure out. And how I was wrong about something—that while my mother wasn't really able to learn from her mistakes, I was.

Many but not all of those mistakes are catalogued in one of the products of my own life's purpose. Here in my office, positioned next to my children's photos and held up by a paperweight presented to me by a book club, is *North of Normal*. That I can even hold it in my hands still feels surreal sometimes—that six years of writing and rejection resulted in this, a best-selling book. The whirlwind when it all finally happened—offers from five agents within a week, landing my dream agent, and then her selling my book with multiple offers—just proves to me that my reason for writing it meant everything.

Do you feel normal now? is the question I get most often from my readers.

Almost, I say. Nearly normal.

Over the past year and a half, I've marvelled at how the power of truth and story can break down preconceptions. My readers have given me the strength and confidence to tell the rest of my story, even the smaller moments I thought no one would care about. It had never crossed my mind to tell the story of Art the pervert. He only touched me that once, I thought; it hadn't affected me. So many have experienced much worse. But I came to realize that it wasn't so much what he had done as how my mother reacted to it: no big deal, your body is beautiful, stop being such a prude. Laying the groundwork for me to accept Barry's and Darcy's abuse.

After my book came out, something I'd always suspected was confirmed for me—that my gauge for what was normal, interesting and acceptable was not to be trusted. My readers fixed that gauge for me. I think about the story of the fake bear chasing me. While I'd once dismissed it as boring, it actually held valuable insight into my grandfather, myself, and the power struggle between us. Our lives have so much meaning if we just look a little deeper.

Once, in a moment of self-pity, I moaned to Remy that my family had set me up for a life of failure by not modelling healthy behaviour and relationships. No, he responded, they'd just given me blind spots. He was right, and I still have them—insecurity when it comes to setting boundaries, resolving conflict, parenting, managing finances, trusting my judgment. But I've learned to check my blind spots carefully before I take action, just the way I do before changing lanes in a car. Which isn't to say that I don't still crash now and then. After all, my longtime friend and enemy, impatience, is also my fire. It bubbles inside me like a mini-volcano, reminding me what must be done— the house bought, the renovation handled, the business started, the wedding planned, the baby planted in my womb, the book written. But I've learned to temper it.

I've almost finished writing my second book, but I have a few things to add. I open the file labelled *North of Normal—Deleted Scenes* and read through the Darcy chapter. These pages tell a truth I've always held about myself—that I'm tainted, worthless, a product of my family's values despite my best efforts not to be. I realize now that my outrage toward Papa Dick is about more than his abandoning me as an adult—it's about his leaving me in charge that night, never considering that I was far too young for such a responsibility. Darcy isn't the only memory I told myself I'd never reveal but then did here. My fight with Mom in the food court, her offering my bedroom to a friend for sex, the story about baby Grace and the fact I'd never tried to find her again—these chapters disclose a harsh truth about my feelings for my family members that I didn't want to admit to. And then there were the events that were simply too raw for me to write about in my first memoir: the stories of Shyla and Apache, my PTSD when I moved to the city, overhearing Papa Dick on the phone, my feelings about Sam, and mostly, Halloween night with Kevin.

Kevin is dead now, taken by pancreatic cancer just five weeks after he was diagnosed at the age of forty-seven. We barely talked after our divorce, but his death still hit me hard. I think about the secrets we kept from each other in our twisted struggle for power. They say you don't take anything with you, but that's not necessarily so. You take your secrets with you, leaving empty holes in the pages of your life and, sometimes, the hearts of your loved ones. I still wonder what my mother and grandparents took with them.

I've passed more judgment on myself than anyone else possibly could. By including these stories in my second memoir, I'm making a statement to everyone—but mostly, to myself—that I will no longer live in shame.

I think about my meeting with Adrienne at the literary festival, nearly a year ago now. I tried to find her after my reading, but she'd disappeared. I wanted to thank her again for reaching out to me, talk to her more about the things she remembered better than me or knew that I didn't, but that she was gone seemed fitting. Since my first book came out, I've learned plenty of new things about myself, but, with the exception of what came out of conversations with Fred, very little about my family. I can live with that. Sometimes the search for truth is more important than the truth itself.

Among the lessons and pain and love they gave me, my grandparents and aunts and uncle still sit in my heart like a giant question mark. And within that is a special place just for Mom. How my love for her endured through all of our trials is something I still ponder. I know I could attribute my feelings for her to the low self-esteem I suffered for most of my life, or the obligation I felt toward her for sticking with me when she could have ditched me. But it's more than that. I believe that she truly didn't know she was harming me. She didn't have the intelligence or insight to question the way she had been raised, so she didn't see that she was repeating many of her parents' mistakes. Certainly she put her own desires first—I think about the time Barry asked me to stay and watch them—but I believe she also thought that with little else to offer, she was ensuring our survival by keeping her men happy.

I remember a conversation Mom and I once had, about two years before she died. She called to tell me that as part of her cancer treatment, she was working with a therapist to try to come to terms with her diagnosis and her life's journey thus far. I was harried, making dinner with Avery attached to my breast, stressed about tasks for CeaSwim that had gone undone that day, only half listening. Then she said something that took me by surprise.

"You turned out so well, and I don't think it was because of me." When I didn't say anything, she continued. "I mean it. You're so, I don't know, *with it*, and me, well . . . I'm mentally deficient. I know it. You know it. And I know it's been frustrating having me for a mother. Really, I had no business raising a child. But I'm so glad I did."

"So am I, Mom, so am I," I responded, and there was nothing else I could think of to say. She had finally put into words herself what I'd long known to be true—but did that change anything? Not really. My moments of connection and revelation with her had always been and always would be interwoven with anger and resentment, a cocktail that made it impossible for me to completely accept or reject her.

"I have to go. Goodbye, Mom," I said, and hung up the phone. I found myself smiling just a little as I did, reflecting that really, only two things about Mom were inarguable: that she was a godawful mother, and that she loved me.

I still miss her terribly.

Author's Note

This is the story of my life. Most of the memories depicted here are my own, but I have also drawn on the memories of my mother, grandparents, aunts, father and various family friends. My early life was a complicated jumble of events that was difficult to put into order, even for my family, but I have done my best. Timelines may not be exact, and dialogue and settings have obviously been recreated in the interest of storytelling. I have also omitted certain events in my life that were not significant to this memoir. Some names, distinguishing features and locations have been changed.

Acknowledgments

My net of gratitude cannot possibly capture all the people I have to thank or the appreciation I have for them. But here's trying.

First and foremost, to all the readers of *North of Normal* who received my book so positively and provided me with much of the inspiration I needed to write *Nearly Normal*. It's been such a pleasure communicating with those who have reached out to me. Please know that without you, there would be no second memoir.

I am forever indebted to my wonderful agent, Jackie Kaiser, for her steadfast belief in my story, her guidance and her friendship. Likewise to my amazing editor at HarperCollins, Iris Tupholme, who I suspect knows me even better than I know myself. Her eye for detail and insight into the complex workings of my family helped me produce a second memoir that far surpasses anything I could have written without her perspective. Thank you to my copy editor, Allyson Latta, who once again polished my words to perfection. To Jake Babad at Westwood Creative Artists, and to Laura Dosky, Kelly Hope, Doug Richmond and Natalie Meditsky at HarperCollins for their valuable input into my project. Also the wonderful sales, marketing and publicity team at HarperCollins, which does such a fantastic job of championing my work: Michael Guy-Haddock, Cory Beatty, Sandra Leef, Leo MacDonald, Julia Barrett and Sabrina Groomes. To Greg Tabor for creating my beautiful cover. To the many booksellers who believed in and promoted my book to their readers, in particular Deb McVittie and her staff at 32 Books, the staff at Indigo Marine Drive, Indigo Park Royal, Book Warehouse on Main, Black Bond Books in Ladner and Albany Books in Delta. To Kyle Mann, for believing in my dream.

To all my early-draft readers, including Gwen Floyd, Isabel Bleim, Janie Fitzpatrick, Michelle Clay, Susan Arntsen and Sylvia Shury—thank you so much for your time and invaluable feedback. To Bob Robinson, Bob Massad, Carleen Amos, Dawn Macdonald, Diane Peacock, Fred Norgard, Jason Goldsmith, Phil Chatterton, Scott Aver, Tom Godber and Vicky Robertson for opening up your stories of my family to me, and to Adrienne, who entered my life long enough to give me Chapter 17 but not long enough for me to get her last name.

The telling of a life story warrants gratitude to those who share it. I could never find the words to thank my family enough—Remy, the most awesome husband on earth; my beautiful children, Avery, Emerson and Ayla, who give my life more meaning and joy than I can even deal with sometimes; my father and his wife, who I only wish I could have more time with; my sister Megan, for her beautifully creative soul; and my late great relatives—my mother, Michelle, grandparents Dick and Jeanne, and grandparents Ed and Bee. Without you all, I'm certain my story would be a lot less interesting.

I am grateful to the many friends who have supported me both personally and in my writing process, in particular Amanda Tapping, Carleigh Kage, Cori Creed, Dianne Wood, Fiona Claire Geoghegan, Heather Greaves, Jenn Park, Karen Zen, Melissa Raynier, Nicole Oliver, Shannon Nering, Stephanie and John Lecomte, Susan Scarlett, Suzana Rummery, Traci Crivici, Tracy Comessotti and Wendy McDevitt—your friendship over the years has meant so much to me. Also Bernadette Burns, Bill Crow, Brook Davison, Chris Ainscough, Cintia Martins, Craig Cameron, Cynthia Merriman, Debbie Salzman, Heather Hood and the rest of the LB gang, Janet Allan, Jenny Drake, Joanne and Mark Falvai, John Elliott, Josh Moody, Lisa Rose Snow,

Marlene Bailey, Martin and Giovanna Seiz, Martin Wood, Michelle Morgan, Nikki Lund, Romy Kozak, Sabrina and Phil Chatterton, Saleema Noon, Stephen and Tessa Geoghegan, Teresa Wood and Alfie Zeilburger, Tiffany Haziza and Tracey Rossignol—thank you for everything. To my book club babes Andrea Zenko, Ann Hickey, Brigit Forsyth, Joanna Clark, Joanne McKinney, Lonnie Macmillan, Melissa Raynier, Sharon Ferriss, Terri Green, Tiffany Fraser and Wendy O'Neill, you ladies make life a lot more fun.

I carry all of you with me; you are part of my story.